OXFORD LEGAL PHILOSOPHY
Series Editors: Timothy Endicott, John Gardner, and Leslie Green

Conscience and Conviction

OXFORD LEGAL PHILOSOPHY

Series Editors: Timothy Endicott, John Gardner, and Leslie Green

Oxford Legal Philosophy publishes the best new work in philosophically-oriented legal theory. It commissions and solicits monographs in all branches of the subject, including works on philosophical issues in all areas of public and private law, and in the national, transnational, and international realms; studies of the nature of law, legal institutions, and legal reasoning; treatments of problems in political morality as they bear on law; and explorations in the nature and development of legal philosophy itself. The series represents diverse traditions of thought but always with an emphasis on rigour and originality. It sets the standard in contemporary jurisprudence.

ALSO AVAILABLE IN THE SERIES

The Ends of Harm
The Moral Foundations of Criminal Law
Victor Tadros

Corrective Justice
Ernest J. Weinrib

The Nature of Legislative Intent
Richard Ekins

Conscience and Conviction

The Case for Civil Disobedience

Kimberley Brownlee

UNIVERSITY PRESS

Great Clarendon Street, Oxford, OX2 6DP,
United Kingdom

Oxford University Press is a department of the University of Oxford.
It furthers the University's objective of excellence in research, scholarship,
and education by publishing worldwide. Oxford is a registered trade mark of
Oxford University Press in the UK and in certain other countries

© K. Brownlee 2012

The moral rights of the author have been asserted

First Edition published in 2012

Impression: 1

All rights reserved. No part of this publication may be reproduced, stored in
a retrieval system, or transmitted, in any form or by any means, without the
prior permission in writing of Oxford University Press, or as expressly permitted
by law, by licence or under terms agreed with the appropriate reprographics
rights organization. Enquiries concerning reproduction outside the scope of the
above should be sent to the Rights Department, Oxford University Press, at the
address above

You must not circulate this work in any other form
and you must impose this same condition on any acquirer

Crown copyright material is reproduced under Class Licence
Number C01P0000148 with the permission of OPSI
and the Queen's Printer for Scotland

British Library Cataloguing in Publication Data

Data available

Library of Congress Cataloging in Publication Data

Data available

ISBN 978–0–19–959294–4

Printed in Great Britain by
CPI Group (UK) Ltd, Croydon, CR0 4YY

Links to third party websites are provided by Oxford in good faith and
for information only. Oxford disclaims any responsibility for the materials
contained in any third party website referenced in this work.

Series Editors' Preface

Principled law-breaking has been a central issue for legal philosophy since the time of Socrates. Among modern liberal writers, conscientious refusal has generally been treated more generously than has civil disobedience, which is not private but public and which aims not only at avoiding complicity with immoral laws but at changing them. Civil disobedience may sometimes be the right thing to do, many argue, but it is not something to which we have a right. In this volume, Kimberley Brownlee upends that consensus. Exploring fundamental issues in the morality of conviction and conscience, she argues that it is actually civil disobedience that has the stronger claim to the protections that liberal moralists favour. She makes a case for legal defences based on the demands of moral conviction and on necessity, contending that, here too, civil disobedience merits special immunity. Civil disobedience is thus not merely a kind of law-breaking whose motivation and consequences warrant mitigation, it is part of a valuable dialogue between citizen and state, a form of political communication to which we do have moral rights, and which should be protected by legal rights. Lucid in argument and bold in vision, Kimberley Brownlee's book will force liberals reconsider much of what they take for granted about law and disobedience. Anyone concerned with the authority of law and the justifications for punishment will find familiar problems recast here in a new and illuminating way. *Oxford Legal Philosophy* is delighted to present this challenging work from one of the most interesting new voices in the subject.

Timothy Endicott
John Gardner
Leslie Green
September 2012

Acknowledgments

I wrote this book between 2008 and 2011. My first expression of gratitude goes to my DPhil supervisors John Tasioulas and Joseph Raz for their counsel, patience, and support. It was under their guidance that the seeds for the book first began to sprout.

An equally deep expression of gratitude goes to the members of the Manchester Centre for Political Theory (MANCEPT) for being a wonderful academic family for me for six years. I am profoundly grateful to Hillel Steiner, who has not only given me the benefit of his philosophical acumen, but also provided me, as he has provided many others, with a home away from home during my time at Manchester. The intellectual heart of the Manchester political philosophy scene is at his kitchen table. I wish to thank Alan Hamlin for being an exemplary mentor and a fount of unfailingly good advice. I also thank Stephen de Wijze, Jonathan Quong, Thomas Porter, Mark Reiff, Zsuzsanna Chappell, and Zofia Stemplowska for being the best colleagues anyone could hope to have.

Much of the armchair thinking for the book was done during a period of research leave from Manchester. In the fall of 2008, I spent a semester in the Philosophy Department at Vanderbilt University on a Canada-US Fulbright Visiting Research Fellowship. I am grateful to Jeffrey Tlumak, Chair of the Department, for being such a caring host, right down to closing my US bank account for me. I also thank Robert Talisse, Jonathan Neufeld, Florence Faucher-King, Joel Harrington, and Melissa Smith for making the visit so enjoyable. In the spring of 2009, I spent a term in the Centre for Ethics and Philosophy of Law at University College, Oxford, as an HLA Hart Visiting Research Fellow.

I thank John Gardner for a very kind welcome to the college and the University of Manchester for a sabbatical. Finally, in the fall of 2009, I spent a semester at the Centre for Ethics, Philosophy, and Public Affairs in the Philosophy Department at St Andrews University. I am grateful to John Haldane for being such a gracious host. I also thank Elizabeth Ashford, Sarah Broadie, James Harris, Tim Mulgan, John Skorupski, Katherine Hawley, Jens Timmermann, and Lucas Thorpe for many stimulating lunch discussions and reading group meetings. I thank the AHRC for a Research Leave grant.

I am grateful to Daniel Weinstock and the Centre de Recherche en Éthique de l'Université de Montréal, and to Carolyn McLeod and the Conscientious Refusal in Healthcare Research Group at the University of Western Ontario, supported by the CIHR, for hosting a one-day workshop on the manuscript in April 2011. I thank Chloë FitzGerald, Adina Preda, and Carolyn for their commentaries on the book and the participants at the workshop for highly useful feedback.

As a farewell gift, the members of MANCEPT kindly made the manuscript for this book the focus of their reading group in the fall of 2011. For eight weeks' worth of pressing comments, I thank Mark Reiff, Brian Carey, Zsuzsanna Chappell, Stephen Cooke, Eve Garrard, Joseph Horton, Sara Kallock, Christopher Mills, James Pattison, Jon Quong, Tom Porter, Hillel Steiner, and Steve de Wijze. Thank you also to my informal female mentors at Manchester—Rosaleen Duffy, Angie Wilson, Veronique Pin-Fat, and Maja Zehfuss—for their guidance and support, and to the students in my final-year undergraduate module *Protest and Punishment*, who offered acute criticisms on many parts of the book.

For comments on individual chapters and sections, I would like to thank Anna-Karin Andersson, Christopher Bennett, Rafael Cejudo Córdoba, Emanuela Ceva, Adam Cureton, Antony Duff, John Gardner, Claire Grant, Alan Hamlin, Lisa Herzog, Matt Humphreys, Matthew Kramer, Michelle Madden Dempsey, Christoph Ortner, David Lefkowitz, José Luis Martí, Larry May, Jeff McMahan, David Miller, James Morauta, Zofia Stemplowska, Malcolm Thorburn, Victor Tadros, and Laura Valentini. For their support of the project, I thank Matt Matravers and Mark Philp. I wish to thank Adam Slavny for his efficient assistance with proofreading and compiling the bibliography and index. I am grateful to two OUP referees for valuable feedback on the proposal. And, I am particularly grateful to the OUP reader who provided 19 pages of wonderfully helpful comments on the book.

The chapters were presented in various talks between 2008–11. I thank audiences at the Universities of Brighton, Keele, Leeds, Manchester, North Carolina (Chapel Hill), Oxford, Pompeu Fabra, Santa Clara, Sheffield, St Andrews, Stirling, Vanderbilt, Warwick, and York (Toronto). I wish to thank Luca Malatesti, the Croatian Society for Analytic Philosophy, and the Faculty of Arts, University of Rijeka, for inviting me to give a public lecture and hosting a half-day workshop on civil disobedience in September 2010. I am grateful to Luca, Elvio Baccarini, Boran Berčić, Snježana Prijic-Samaržija, and Nebojša Zelić for thought-provoking discussions.

Three published papers were substantially revised for inclusion in the book. They are: 'Responsibilities of Criminal Justice Officials' in *The Journal of Applied Philosophy* 27: 2 (2010), 123–39; 'Penalizing Public Disobedience' in *Ethics* 118: 4 (2008), 711–16; and 'The Offender's Part in the Dialogue' in *Crime, Punishment, & Responsibility: The Jurisprudence of Antony Duff*. R. Cruft, M. Kramer, & M. Reiff (eds.) (Oxford University Press, 2011), 54–67. A fourth article was drawn upon for a section of Chapter 2: 'Moral Aspirations and Ideals' in *Utilitas* 22: 3 (2010), 241–57. I thank Wiley, Cambridge University Press, University of Chicago Press, and Oxford University Press for permission to include revised versions of these papers. I thank the Norman Rockwell Foundation for permission to reproduce *The Jury* (1959) on the cover of this book. I thank the Warwick Law School for covering the cost of the permission fees.

For their support for the project, I am very grateful to the series editors: John Gardner, Leslie Green, and Timothy Endicott. For their editorial work, I thank Alex Flach, Natasha Flemming and Emma Brady at OUP.

Finally, to my parents, my sister, my nephews, and my partner, for whom it is easiest to feel gratitude and hardest often to express it, I am lucky to say I owe everything. This book is dedicated to my parents, Dave and Jill Brownlee, and to my partner, Christoph Ortner.

Kimberley Brownlee
March 2012

Contents

Introduction   1
  1. Conviction and Conscience   3
  2. The Conviction Argument   5
  3. The Conscience Argument   10

Part I. Morality

1. Conviction   15
  1. Communicative Disobedience   17
  2. Non-communicative Disobedience   27
  3. The Communicative Principle of Conscientiousness   29
  4. Ambiguities   47
  Conclusion   49

2. Conscience   51
  1. Common Conceptions of *Conscience*   55
  2. Conscience and Moral Pluralism   62
  3. An Ideal of Conscience   72
  4. Conscience and Virtue   79
  Conclusion   83

3. Responsibilities   85
  1. Formal Expectations and Moral Responsibilities   88
  2. The Forms and Purposes of Non-conformity   104
  3. Objections and Replies   107
  Conclusion   117

4. Rights   119
  1. Moral Rights versus Legal Rights   120
  2. A Moral Right of Conscience   126
  3. A Moral Right to Inner Control and Free Thought   128
  4. A Moral Right of Conscientious Action   140
  Conclusion   151

Part II. Law

5. Demands-of-Conviction Defence   155

1. Justifications and Excuses	161
2. The Demands-of-Conviction Defence	167
3. The Strategic Action Problem	172
4. The Democracy Problem	174
Conclusion	178
6. Necessity Defence	179
1. The Nature of Necessity	181
2. The Competition of Values Problem	192
3. The Proportionality Problem	197
4. Avoidance of Punishment and Slippery Slopes	204
Conclusion	206
7. Dialogue	209
1. The Scripting Problem	215
2. Conditions for Moral Dialogue	217
3. The Generic-Script Problem	222
4. The Status Change Problem	227
5. A Pluralistic Theory of Punishment	234
Conclusion	236
8. Punishment	239
1. The Right to Civil Disobedience	240
2. Symbolic Punishment	248
3. Some Ways Forward	250
Conclusion	253
Bibliography	255
Index	263

Introduction

The painting on the cover of this book is Norman Rockwell's *The Jury* (1959). It captures a charged scene of a jury of 11 men and one woman who are long into their deliberations. We do not know the facts of the case or what verdict they are debating. All we know is that the woman sits in a rickety chair with her back straight and her arms folded while 10 of the men stand or sit around her, leaning over her in united opposition. One man dozes to the side. In this smoke-filled, wood-panelled room echoing of a men's club where jackets have been shed and tempers are running high, she is entirely alone. She is exposed. And, she might be wrong about what she thinks of the case. She seems to be aware of this since she is listening attentively to the men around her. But, she is also unflinching. In her folded arms, straight back, and attentive expression lie the kernels of the conception of *conscientious conviction* that I defend in these pages.

It is a largely descriptive conception that emphasizes non-evasion and dialogic effort as well as consistency and universal moral judgement. A person who has a conscientious moral conviction has a sincere and serious, though possibly mistaken, moral commitment that she is willing both to articulate to others and to bear the costs for holding. She contrasts with the person who engages in purely private acts or evasive acts that raise a doubt about the sincerity of the conviction. The man dozing to the side in the jury scene might have the same view as the woman, but he is unwilling to articulate it and bear the costs of dissent. She also contrasts with the person who seeks not so much to articulate his view to others as to impose it upon them by force. The four features of consistency, universal judgement, non-evasion, and dialogic effort comprise together what I call the communicative principle of conscientiousness. This communicative principle has important implications for what it means to respect persons' moral convictions as part of their dignity and agency. Respecting dignity and agency requires respecting, as well as possible, the fact that genuine moral conviction has a communicative element, which can include constrained, communicative disobedience of law.

The other core concept of this book is *conscience*. Suppose that the woman in the jury room is not wrong in how she sees the case. Suppose she is morally justified in how she sees it. Since this is a Norman Rockwell painting it is likely that she is morally justified and that, as a modest but impressive embodiment of courage, she will prevail. Suppose also, perhaps, that if the jury adopts her view they will be disregarding the judge's instructions. By holding reflectively to her morally justified commitment, she shows herself to be genuinely morally responsive. She privileges the role-related moral responsibilities that underpin the office of juror above both the judge's directives and her fellow jurors' pressure to conform. She is animated by conscience. As this suggests, *conscience* is a rich set of practical moral skills that stem from a deep understanding of the nature of our hearts and minds. In my hands, conscience requires both sensitivity to the complex, pluralistic nature of morality and an awareness of the actual moral quality of our own and others' conduct. Such understanding and the processes through which it is cultivated are not morally neutral. They require the cultivation of practical wisdom, generosity, attention, thoughtfulness, and compassion. Conscience enhances both our appreciation of our special moral responsibilities and our willingness to privilege them before formal expectations when necessary.

As these comments indicate, my purposes in this book are, first, to distinguish *conscientious conviction* from *conscience*; second, to defend the moral and legal merits of both conscientious disobedience and conscience-driven disobedience; and third, to show that the disobedience that best falls under either of these two headings is non-evasive and communicative rather than private or evasive. In short, I show that it is civil disobedience and not 'conscientious objection' that has the best claims to the protections we give to conscientious conviction and conscience.

This Introduction is divided into three sections. The first fleshes out the conceptual distinction between *conscientious conviction* and *conscience*. The second outlines my argument for civil disobedience based upon conscientious conviction. The third outlines my argument for civil disobedience based upon conscience. In both this Introduction and the book, I proceed at a certain level of abstraction partly because I cannot hope to settle longstanding debates about the morality of concrete cases where conscience and conscientiousness come into play such as reproductive services for women, parental responsibility, and war. When I do come down to earth to give examples to elucidate my views, I do so knowing that my examples will be intuitive only to those who share my intuitions.

1. Conviction and Conscience

Conscientious moral conviction is necessary but insufficient for conscience. *Conscientious conviction* is a descriptive property. *Conscience* is a moral property. Both are comparatively neglected concepts in contemporary moral and legal theory even though they are fascinating in themselves and key to some hotly contested practical debates such as the ethics of war, the ethics of healthcare, political participation, parental discretion, personal attire, and official duty. When *conscientious conviction* and *conscience* are appealed to in those debates, they tend to be run together and invoked unreflectively to claim that some conduct is evaluatively distinct from other seemingly similar conduct that is ordinarily deemed objectionable. One example is the religious parent who refuses on grounds of 'conscientious belief' to take her sick child to the doctor because she believes that healing should be done through prayer alone, a refusal that would otherwise be seen as child neglect.

The distinction I draw in Chapters 1 and 2 between *conscientious conviction* and *conscience* tracks certain linguistic intuitions and common-sense uses of the terms 'conscientiousness' and 'conscience'. Typically, we use the term 'conscientiousness' descriptively to refer to fastidious, assiduous, sincere, and serious, if not pedantic, conduct. Think of the secretary who conscientiously completes every form by hand even though typing them would be more efficient. The moral valence of such conduct is not fixed by its being conscientious. The valence depends on its moral character and consequences.

Likewise, typically, we use the term 'conscience' evaluatively to pick out the limits of what we should reasonably bring ourselves to accept. We speak of acting on 'grounds of conscience', and of 'answering to conscience'. We speak of having a 'clear conscience', and of responding to 'demands of conscience'. In Shakespeare's *Much Ado about Nothing*, Benedict says to Claudio and Don Pedro in mild warning, '... ere you flout old ends any further, examine your conscience'.[1] In *Hamlet*, our eponymous hero says, plotting to himself, 'the play's the thing wherein I'll catch the conscience of the king'.[2] The term 'conscience' connotes the angel on the shoulder. It connotes an intuitive moral awareness that may not be wholly accessible to us, but which we'd better not ignore. These are lofty connotations that we must be careful not to attribute to mere conviction.

Admittedly, my distinction between *conscientious conviction* and *conscience* seems to depart from other linguistic intuitions and commonsense uses of the terms. One problem is that 'conscientiousness' and 'conscience' are cognate terms. Therefore, my effort to distinguish the concepts to which they refer must push against the linguistic inclination to see them in the same light. This is not an insurmountable problem. The same linguistic inclination haunts the terms 'right' and 'rights', but liberal philosophers have successfully prised those two concepts apart.

A second possible problem is that the term 'conscience' is sometimes used descriptively, such as in international human rights agreements like the Universal Declaration of Human Rights (UDHR) to refer to our freedoms of thought, conscience, and religion (Article 18), which I would call our freedoms of thought, *conviction*, and religion. But, this descriptive use of 'conscience' does not undermine the commonsense credentials of my evaluative use of it because the UDHR equivocates in its usage. In contrast with Article 18, the Preamble to the UDHR states that '... disregard and contempt for human rights have resulted in barbarous acts which *have outraged the conscience of mankind*...'.[3] And, Article 1 continues in this spirit that, 'All human beings are born free and equal in dignity and rights. *They are endowed with reason and conscience* and should act towards one another in a spirit of brotherhood'.[4] These evaluative uses align with my conception of *conscience*.

A third possible problem is that the term 'conscientiousness' is often given a positive connotation when we are talking about war. The term 'conscientious objection' connotes a morally sensitive refusal to

---

[1] Shakespeare, William, *Much Ado about Nothing*, Act I, Scene I.
[2] Shakespeare, William, *Hamlet*, Act II, Scene II.
[3] Italics added.   [4] Italics added.

participate in the barbarities of war. But, this does not weaken the commonsense credentials of my descriptive use of 'conscientiousness' because, once we stop talking about war, 'conscientious objection' has a descriptive gloss. The label is applied somewhat indiscriminately to the doctor who objects to performing an abortion, the nurse who refuses to shut off a patient's life support, the employee who refuses to cover or uncover her hair, the grocery store clerk who refuses to process the sale of alcohol, and the registrar who refuses to conduct same-sex partnership ceremonies. Not all of these people are conscientious. I simply note for now that many of our commonsense uses of 'conscientiousness' have the descriptive character that I attribute to the concept.

The distinction between *conscientious conviction* and *conscience* sets the stage for the two core evaluative aims of this book, which centre on defending the moral and legal merits of civil disobedience. The first is the conviction argument. The second is the conscience argument. The book is not structured to follow first one argument and then the other. It is structured instead to highlight key issues for each of these arguments. Part I looks at moral issues. Part II looks at legal issues. The key issues of the book can be spotted in its chapter titles: 1. Conviction, 2. Conscience, 3. Responsibilities, 4. Rights, 5. Demands, 6. Necessity, 7. Dialogue, and 8. Punishment. Chapters 1, 4, 5, 7, and 8 advance the conviction argument. Chapters 2, 3, 4, and 6 advance the conscience argument.

2. The Conviction Argument

The first evaluative aim of this book is to challenge the idea that private, non-communicative acts of so-called 'conscientious objection' are more conscientious than suitably constrained *communicative* acts of disobedience such as civil disobedience. Standard liberal views see private 'conscientious' objection as a modest, unassuming act of deep personal conviction, and civil disobedience as a strategic, political act that eschews ordinary participation channels in favour of riskier, but potentially more effective, undemocratic channels.[5] Standard liberal

---

[5] For criticism of civil disobedience as a political, strategic, and anti-democratic act, see Horder, Jeremy (2004) *Excusing Crime*. Oxford: Oxford University Press, ch 5; and Raz, Joseph (1979) *The Authority of Law*. Oxford: Oxford University Press, ch 14. See also the judgments cited in Chapter 5 of this book. The risks associated with civil disobedience are: 1) its divisiveness in society; 2) its ability, as a practice usually designed to attract public attention,

views see the costs of civil disobedience as being sometimes worth bearing, but not generally so.[6] Moreover, standard liberal views say that, if there were a general moral *right* to engage in disobedience on grounds of conscientious conviction, only private, non-communicative acts of what I'll call 'personal disobedience' could be protected under such a right.[7] The standard views have traction in practice. There is a growing set of legal exemptions for non-communicative refusals of performance. In Illinois, for example, the law not only gives broad protection to healthcare professionals to refuse to participate in services that offend their conscientious beliefs, it also does not explicitly prohibit refusals of service that are based on invidious discrimination against patients' colour, ethnicity, sex, religion, or sexual orientation.[8] By contrast, there is, at best, a mixed reception from the law and society for constrained *communicative* disobedience. In many judges' eyes, civil disobedience is indistinguishable from ordinary offending; and in many other judges' eyes, it is more serious than ordinary offending. One Texas judge, whose cases I discuss in this book, took a strikingly anti-civil disobedience stance by ordering an anti-fur trade

---

to lead others to think of breaking the law to achieve whatever changes in policy they espouse (see Raz (1979), 262); and 3) its ability to encourage a general disrespect for the law, particularly when the law is seen as being lenient towards certain kinds of offences. For a discussion of some of the risks, see Greenawalt, Kent (1987) *Conflicts of Law and Morality*. Oxford: Oxford University Press, ch 10. For a defence of three stringent conditions for justifiable civil disobedience—that it must be undertaken 1) as a last resort, 2) in defence of justice, and 3) in coordination with other minority groups—see Rawls, John (1971) *A Theory of Justice*. Cambridge, Mass: Harvard University Press, 375.

[6] Joseph Raz, for one, says that civil disobedience is sometimes justified and even obligatory, but it is not a general moral right. Raz (1979), 272–3.

[7] John Rawls argues for both a right to conscientious objection and a right to civil disobedience, but applies the latter to only a very limited subset of civilly disobedient acts. He argues that only when civil disobedience satisfies his three conditions for justifiability (see n. 5) may it be supposed that, in his ideal society, there is a right to engage in it. Rawls has been criticized, rightly, for not properly distinguishing his account of justified civil disobedience from his account of the disobedience we have a right to take, and for giving no indication of how his account is to be extrapolated to non-ideal societies. Raz does not restrict the acts of civil disobedience that could be protected by a right. Instead, he rejects the idea that this right exists in all societies. He argues that only in an illiberal regime is there a right to civil disobedience and this right is reserved for those citizens whose rights to political participation are violated. They have a right to reclaim that portion of their political participation rights that are not recognized in law. In a liberal regime, there is no right to civil disobedience, Raz says, since, by hypothesis, the law adequately protects citizens' rights to political participation. Raz says that a stronger case can be made for the right to private conscientious objection than for civil disobedience (1979), ch 15.

[8] Ill Rev Stat c 745, 70/2 (1998). Cited in Wicclair, Mark (2011) *Conscientious Objection in Health Care: An Ethical Analysis*. Cambridge: Cambridge University Press, 210.

activist to stay away from animal rights protests and ordering anti-abortion activists to stay away from abortion clinics (cf. Chapters 5, 7).

I reverse the standard liberal picture and show that civil disobedience is more conscientious than personal disobedience in virtue of its constrained, communicative, and non-evasive properties. As such, first, it has a better claim to any rights-based protection that is appropriate for conscientious action (Chapter 4). Second, it has a better claim to any putative legal excuse that can be given for conscientious breach of law (Chapter 5). Both the moral right and the legal excuse are rooted in a humanistic principle of respect for our agency and dignity as persons. This respect turns on appreciating that our deepest commitments come with non-evasive, dialogic efforts. Society and the law place undue pressure on us when they require us always to privilege the law before our deeply held moral convictions. And they place undue pressure on us when they tolerate only our non-communicative, private disobedience in support of our convictions. This principle of humanism says, first, that society has a duty to honour the fact that we are reasoning and feeling beings capable of forming deep moral commitments, and second, that genuine moral conviction is essentially non-evasive and communicative. Let me flesh out the moral rights and legal excuse a bit more fully.

Moral rights: Conscientious moral conviction gives rise to two moral rights. One of these is a limited moral right of conscientious action as our expression of our conscientious convictions. It follows from the principle of humanism that this right includes a moral right to civil disobedience. This means the animal rights activist, the anti-abortion activist, the neo-Nazi, the environmentalist, and the anti-war protester each has a moral right to engage in certain *constrained*, communicative breaches of law in defence of her cause.

The other moral right flowing from conscientious moral conviction protects the pre-conditions for moral conviction as such. It is the right to have a certain control over our own mind including a right to free thought. I show that our rights of the mind are more limited than we might suppose. We have no general right to control our attention, no general right against manipulation, and, in various contexts, no right to think as we like. Nevertheless, the right to inner control and free thought is a fundamentally important one for personal agency, dignity, and morality. Indeed, although standard liberal views in the spirit of John Stuart Mill tend to run freedom of thought together with freedom of expression on the ground that there is no free thought worth the name without free expression, in fact the right to free thought is valuable independently of any right to free expression. The right to free expression, however, is not valuable independently of the right to free thought (Chapter 4).

The moral right to conscientious action including civil disobedience protects a sphere of conduct with which, in general, others may not justifiably interfere. As such, this right includes a defeasible moral right against state punishment for civil disobedience. It protects against both concretely burdensome punishments and symbolic punishments. Any punishment wrongs the civil disobedient by breaching her moral right to act without interference. But, since this moral right against punishment is defeasible, in principle, it can be justifiably overridden by competing moral considerations.

That said, there are good reasons to maintain respect for the moral right of conscientious action and, hence, to favour non-punitive restorative responses to civil disobedience even when punitive ones would be justifiable (Chapter 8).

As this implies, I reject the pre-theoretical idea that to be civilly disobedient at all we *have* to be punished for our breaches of law. In my view, it is neither conceptually necessary nor evaluatively necessary for civil disobedients to be punished for their acts. To *be* civilly disobedient, we must accept only the *risk* of being punished. The willingness to accept that risk flows from the non-evasive and communicative qualities of our conscientious conviction. And, to be *justified* in civilly disobeying, we must have a good cause, a good set of motivations, and a suitably constrained set of practices with modest consequences, but we need not be willing to accept punishment by turning ourselves in or embracing punishment as a legitimate response (Chapters 1, 7, 8).

Legal excuse: Any legal excuse grounded in conscientious conviction applies more readily to *communicative* disobedience than to personal disobedience in light of the communicative principle of conscientiousness. By recognizing such a demands-of-conviction defence, society would honour the links between autonomy, psychological integrity, and conscientiousness. It would do this by not requiring us either always to give priority to the law over our deep commitments or always to remain surreptitious and self-censoring in our efforts to dissociate from laws we oppose (Chapter 5).

My view of conscientiousness has significant practical implications. Liberal society could take a harsher stance than it tends to do towards evasive 'conscientious objectors'. And, it should take a far less harsh stance than it tends to do towards suitably constrained civil disobedients. Put in concrete terms, society should take a dimmer view of the civil registrar who tries quietly to swap assignments with colleagues so that she can avoid officiating at same-sex partnership ceremonies without bearing personal costs for it than of the registrar who openly gives her reasons for refusing to officiate at such ceremonies and braves the costs of refusing.

Dialogue: My communicative account of conscientiousness brings out another core idea in the book, which is dialogue. A dialogue is a progress-oriented, verbal exchange marked by mutual respect and reciprocity. For us to intend sincerely to engage in a dialogue, we cannot immunize ourselves from the communicative efforts of our would-be dialogue partners. We must be open to hearing them. We must try to understand what they say. We must also be willing to adjust what we say to ensure that successful communication is likely to occur. The *conscientious* dissenter appreciates that process-related constraints apply to anyone who has a sincere intention to engage in a dialogue. Therefore, irrespective of her cause, she engages in highly constrained breaches of law that are compatible with a dialogic effort to persuade others of the value of her view (Chapters 1, 4, 7).

The notion of *dialogue* is appealed to by many communicative theorists of punishment, such as Antony Duff who argues that punishment is a liberal state's effort to engage an offender in a moral dialogue about the wrongness of her act to lead her to repent and reform her conduct. But, as I show, a *monistic* communicative theory that justifies punishment strictly in backward-looking, retributive terms cannot claim to have dialogic ambitions because it disregards the communicative efforts of the offender. My criticism not only has general implications for the monistic communicative theory of punishment, but also has particular relevance for civil disobedience. This is because a civil disobedient seeks to engage society in a dialogue about the justness of laws or policies. As a well-intentioned party seeking a dialogue, she has good reason not to want to recite the imposed, generic script of the unrepentant offender who needs to go through the apology ritual of punishment to appreciate the wrongness of her conduct.

In contrast with the monistic communicative theory, there is a pluralistic communicative theory of punishment. According to this theory, morally justified punishment is informed not only by desert, but also by a concern for the offender's well-being. As such, it can have dialogic aims because, in principle, it can be responsive to offenders' communicative efforts. In particular, it can recognize that a civil disobedient's conscientious moral commitments make it onerous for her not to dissociate herself communicatively from laws that offend those commitments. It's onerous to ask of Rosa Parks that she wait for a better season to challenge segregation laws. And it's onerous to ask of staunch anti-abortion activists that they never step outside the law to oppose what they think is the killing of innocent lives (Chapter 7). The pluralistic theory can consider the impact of this onerous burden upon a disobedient's well-being when determining what legal response is morally justifiable.

These are the key elements of the conviction argument. It does not focus upon the value or disvalue of disobedients' commitments, and hence it applies to bigots and xenophobes as well as to noble campaigners. The argument focuses upon the *process*-related constraints of true conscientiousness as well as the links between humanism, agency, dignity, and dialogue.

3. The Conscience Argument

The second evaluative aim of this book is to defend conscience-driven disobedience. This argument begins by exploring the nature of *conscience* as genuine moral responsiveness, and by situating it within a pluralistic moral framework. Given conditions of moral pluralism, the function of conscience is not to give objectively right answers to moral questions. Rather, its functions are to make us sensitive to the complexity of the moral decisions we make, and to help us to privilege certain values over others in light of our personal moral situation. My account of *conscience* can, despite the pluralism of morality, make sense of commonsense notions such as a 'clear conscience' and a 'demand of conscience'. Moreover, unlike other accounts, it can recognize the celebratory potential of conscience to rejoice in our cultivation of moral integrity.[9] Indeed, in its richest form, conscience is a genuinely valuable, non-optional moral ideal (Chapter 2).

---

[9] Most accounts, particularly objective accounts such as that advanced by Immanuel Kant, see *conscience* in backward-looking, juridical terms as an inner critic or judge before which our thoughts accuse or excuse each other. See Kant, Immanuel (1889 [1788]) *Critique of Practical Reason and Other Works on the Theory of Ethics,* trans. Thomas Kingsmill Abbott (4th revised edn). London: Kongmans, Green and Co., 321.

Once we cultivate a sufficient degree of conscience, we become sensitive to the special moral responsibilities that we have in virtue of our circumstances, skills, and moral roles. Our sensitivity to our special moral responsibilities enables us to settle most contests between competing moral demands (Chapters 2 and 3). It also makes us willing, when necessary, to privilege our special moral responsibilities above formal expectations even when this means breaking laws that originate from normatively valid sources within a reasonably good society (Chapter 3).

In defending these claims, I use the following argumentative tools: 1) the *gap thesis* that, even in a reasonably good society, there is an ineliminable gap between the expectations of normatively valid formal offices and the moral responsibilities that underpin and legitimate those offices; 2) the *moral roles thesis* that we are morally obligated *ceteris paribus* to privilege our special moral responsibilities before formal expectations when the two diverge non-trivially; in the Rockwell jury scene, the woman does this if she has a well-founded view of the case that leads her to disregard the judge's instructions; 3) the *minimum moral burdens principle* that society must ensure as well as possible that the offices it sets up to address important concerns do not place undue moral burdens upon any would-be occupants of those offices; and 4) the *priority of special responsibility principle* that, except in extreme moral emergencies, we act in morally acceptable ways when we adhere to our special moral responsibilities instead of doing what we have most reason to do all things considered.

These arguments lay the foundation for, first, a duty-based moral right of conscience that protects us in honouring our moral responsibilities (Chapter 4), and second, a limited legal justification for conscience-driven civil disobedience rooted in a needs-based notion of *necessity* (Chapter 6). On the latter, I argue that we can claim necessity when our civil disobedience is animated by a legitimate concern for people's non-contingent basic needs and rights. These needs include not only brute survival needs, but also the equally fundamental humanistic needs of basic political recognition, social inclusion, and respect. For example, we could legitimately plead necessity for civil disobedience undertaken in defence of the basic needs and rights of prisoners not to be subjected to extremely degrading, cruel, or inhumane conditions.

In the course of articulating this defence for civil disobedience, I advocate a thoroughgoing pluralistic approach to necessity defences framed by non-contingent basic needs. This approach contrasts with a narrower, less humanistic approach that frames necessity simply in terms of emergencies and conflicts where a danger of death or serious injury is present.[10]

Like the demands-of-conviction defence, the necessity defence applies more readily, I argue, to civil disobedience than to personal disobedience. But, unlike the demands-of-conviction defence, the necessity defence is not available to all who engage in civil disobedience. It is not available to bigots, xenophobes, and misguided do-gooders. It is also not available to all disobedients who could appeal to moral arguments such as the priority of special responsibility principle. What the legal defence of necessity can protect is more limited than what the moral case for conscience shows to be morally justifiable. The legal defence is limited to civil disobedience taken in defence of non-contingent basic needs.

Two objections to such a legal justification are what I call the competition of values problem and the proportionality problem. The first says that the law cannot tolerate competition from other values, which it would have to tolerate if it acknowledged necessity as a justification for needs-responsive, conscience-driven civil disobedience. The second says that civil disobedience is never the only reasonable means to respond to necessity. My replies to these objections turn on, first, a proper understanding of *reasonableness* and *parsimony*; second, the constraints imposed by the communicative principle of conscientiousness; and third, the under-acknowledged capacity of democratic law to recognize the importance of values other than conformity with law (Chapter 6).

These are the core elements of the conscience argument. It focuses on the nature, value, and direction of disobedients' commitments. It defends the moral merits of conscience-driven civil disobedience as well as the legal merits of civil disobedience that is, additionally, responsive to non-contingent basic needs. If the jurors in the Norman Rockwell painting were considering such a case of civil disobedience, they would, I hope, move for acquittal.

---

[10] See Dennis, Ian Howard (2009) 'On Necessity as a Defence to Crime: Possibilities, Problems and the Limits of Justification and Excuse' in *Criminal Law and Philosophy* 3, 29–49.

PART I

Morality

1

Conviction

In Robert Bolt's play *A Man for All Seasons*, Sir Thomas More is presented as an impressive figure, gentle-hearted, yet wholly committed to his Catholic faith. In the scene where he resigns his office as Lord Chancellor because he cannot support the Act of Supremacy that would make Henry VIII Head of the Church of England, he has the following exchange with the Duke of Norfolk:

The duke says: 'Does this make sense? You'll forfeit all you've got – which includes the respect of your country – for a theory?'
   More replies hotly: 'The Apostolic Succession of the Pope is . . . [he stops: interested] . . . Why, it's a theory, yes; you can't see it, can't touch it, it's a theory. But what matters to me is not whether it's true or not, but that I believe it to be true, or rather not that I *believe* it, but that *I* believe it . . . I trust I make myself obscure?'
   Norfolk retorts: 'Perfectly.'[1]

Thomas More may not have persuaded his friend, but he has sought through dialogue to explain why he is resigning. He has also not sought to evade the costs of his beliefs, which include costs for his family once he is charged with treason. His consistency, non-evasion, and communicative effort are three hallmarks of conscientious moral conviction. *Conviction* is the first of the two core concepts in this book. *Conscience* is the second. Pinning down these two concepts is a necessary first step in determining what space should be made for either of them within a

---

[1] Bolt, Robert (1960) *A Man for All Seasons* (various edns).

reasonably good society, since our understanding of them shapes our view not only of the moral quality of the conduct they animate, but also of how important they are to have or to respect.

The first purpose of this chapter is to outline a conception of *conscientious moral conviction* as a descriptive property of sincere and serious, though possibly erroneous, moral commitment. I develop this conception by looking at the features of two practices that are generally taken to be conscientious, namely, civil disobedience and conscientious objection (Sections 1 and 2). I take issue with some oft-noted features, such as the supposed modesty of non-communicative conscientious objection, and appeal to other features, such as the non-evasion and communicativeness of civil disobedience, to build up a general principle of sincere moral conviction, which I call the communicative principle of conscientiousness (Section 3). This principle has four core elements: 1) consistency, 2) universality of judgement, 3) non-evasion, and 4) dialogic effort. Although I look to the familiar practices of civil disobedience and conscientious objection to flesh out my conception of *conscientiousness*, my conception is nevertheless a general, linguistically intuitive one that stands independently of any particular practice. In the course of fleshing out my conception of *conscientiousness*, I also specify further the nature of the dissenting practices considered in this book, the principal one being civil disobedience, and the others being personal disobedience (ie what is often called 'conscientious objection'), assistive disobedience, and radical protest.

The second purpose of this chapter is to begin to disambiguate *conscientiousness* from *conscience* (Section 4). In brief, conscientiousness is a necessary but insufficient condition for conscience. The staunch anti-abortion activist may be sincere and serious in her moral conviction, but that does not mean her conviction is animated by conscience. By *conscience*, I mean, as I argue in Chapter 2, a good inward knowledge of, and responsiveness to, the inner workings of our own mind and heart. I hold that such knowledge and responsiveness only develop through the cultivation of practical wisdom, virtue, and objective moral integrity. Conscience is a moral property. It means not just that we take morality seriously (conscientiousness), but also that we are genuinely, self-consciously morally responsive and aware of the actual moral quality of our own and others' conduct.[2] These are

---

[2] In taking this view of conscience and conscientiousness, I depart from my previous writings, which characterized conscience in descriptive terms. See Brownlee, Kimberley

empirical claims about how our minds and bodies work, but they are ones for which there is growing scientific support.[3] My account of conscience is distinctive in that I situate it within a pluralistic moral framework.

The current chapter—on conscientious conviction—outlines the conceptual foundation for the first strand of argument in defence of civil disobedience. This conviction argument is animated by respect for persons as reasoning and feeling beings who are capable of forming deep, persistent moral commitments. This chapter and the conviction argument it supports are not about the value or disvalue of those commitments.

1. Communicative Disobedience

In ordinary usage, the word 'conscientiousness' is associated with earnestness, care, diligence, assiduity, fastidiousness, scrupulousness, commitment, and self-conscious consistency, the moral quality of which depends on our actions, intentions, and objectives. The committed parent and committed friend contrast with the committed grass-counter, and the three of them contrast with the committed art forger, such as Han van Meegeren, or the committed killer, such as the fictional perfume connoisseur Jean-Baptiste Grenouille.[4] Each takes

---

(2004) 'Features of a Paradigm Case of Civil Disobedience' in *Res Publica* 10: 4, 337–51; Brownlee, Kimberley (2007) 'The Communicative Aspects of Civil Disobedience and Lawful Punishment' in *Criminal Law and Philosophy* 1: 2, 179–92. In those writings, I maintained that conscientiousness is characterized by an obedience or loyalty to conscience. I believe that *conscientiousness* is indeed properly understood in descriptive terms as sincerity and seriousness of commitment or belief. But, this is not true for *conscience*. I argue here that a richer, evaluative notion of *conscience* as moral responsiveness is most plausible. A possible ally for my effort to divorce *conscience* from *conscientiousness* is Michael Hickson, who examines refusals of performance in healthcare and argues that it is wrong to assume that we must determine the nature and value of conscience in order to assess the moral status of an assertion of conscientious refusal. See Hickson, Michael W. (2010) 'Conscientious Refusals without Conscience: Why Not?' in *Philo* 13: 2, 167–84.

[3] For an overview of current scientific research on the interdependence between the cultivation of wholesome states such as compassion, kindness, and generosity, on the one hand, and improved memory, attention, awareness, inner and outer perception, and accurate assessment of our own and others' emotions, on the other, see Hanson, Rick with Mendius, Richard (2009) *Buddha's Brain: The Practical Neuroscience of Happiness, Love, and Wisdom*. Oakland: New Harbinger Publications.

[4] Süskind, Patrick (1985) *Parfum: A Story of a Murderer*. London: Penguin. Grenouille killed young girls in the hope of capturing an illusive object: the perfect scent.

his or her own commitment seriously, but commonsensically van Meegeren, Grenouille, and the grass-counter are mistaken to think their projects valuable ones worth approaching with sincerity and assiduity. Yet, despite their mistake, we may still ask whether their (apparent) conscientiousness makes a positive difference to how we ought to treat them, a question that I answer affirmatively in the ensuing chapters.[5]

In debates about disobedience of law, *conscientiousness* is an important notion that identifies a motivational difference between ordinary offending, on the one hand, and practices such as civil disobedience and personal disobedience, on the other. Whereas ordinary offenders are not conscientiously motivated in any deep sense, people who engage in civil disobedience or personal disobedience typically are or think they are.[6] They tend to regard their disobedience as a matter of self-respect and moral consistency. I shall argue that self-conception is credible in the case of civil disobedients, but not entirely so, and sometimes not at all, in the case of personal disobedients.

1.1 Civil disobedience

Civil disobedience is one variety of communicative disobedience. I do not offer necessary and sufficient conditions for *civil disobedience* since such a definitional effort invites nothing but counter-examples and tends to anticipate the evaluation of the practice.[7] Rather, I highlight several necessary features of civil disobedience. It must include a deliberate breach of law taken on the basis of steadfast personal commitment in order to communicate our condemnation of a law or policy to a relevantly placed audience. That audience is usually our society or the government. Typically, when we civilly disobey, we have both forward-looking and backward-looking communicative aims. Our backward-looking aims are to communicate our disavowal of, and dissociation from, the protested law or policy as well as the reasons for our disavowal. Our forward-looking aims are to draw attention to the reasons for the protest so as to persuade the relevant audience to accept our position and, thereby, to instigate a lasting change in law or policy. Classic examples are Rosa Parks' 1955 bus-ride defiance

---

[5] I appreciate that we can use the language of conscientiousness in relation to non-moral commitments, but I shall reserve its use here for sincere and serious moral convictions.

[6] Cf Brownlee (2004).

[7] This is one objection to John Rawls' very narrow conception of *civil disobedience*, which I discuss later.

and the ensuing Montgomery bus boycott, the Woolworth's lunch counter sit-ins in Greensboro, North Carolina, in the early 1960s, and the marches led by Martin Luther King Jr in Birmingham, Alabama, in 1963. Of course, such conscientious communicativeness also distinguishes many anti-Vietnam war protesters, anti-Iraq war protesters, animal rights defenders, and anti-abortion activists.

A parallel may be drawn between the communicative aims of civil disobedience and the communicative aims of lawful punishment by the state. In a liberal society, lawful punishment is associated with a backward-looking aim to communicate condemnation of a person's conduct and a forward-looking aim to bring about a lasting change in her conduct. However, as I shall argue in Chapter 7, the communicative parallel between civil disobedience and lawful punishment has its limits because, although both practices have dialogic ambitions, it is much easier for civil disobedients to claim that they seek to engage their audience in a genuine dialogue about a perceived injustice than it is for courts, law enforcers, and the state to claim that they seek through punishment to engage offenders in a dialogue about their offences.

Within the category of civil disobedience, there are two sub-categories: direct and indirect disobedience. Direct disobedience is a breach of the very law that we oppose, such as Parks' refusal to give up her bus seat. The act is done both to dissociate directly from that law and to communicate condemnation and a desire for change. By contrast, indirect civil disobedience is a breach of a law other than the law we oppose, such as anti-Iraq war protesters holding sit-ins in government buildings. It is done in order to communicate condemnation and a desire for change, and, indirectly, to dissociate ourselves from the law or policy we oppose.[8]

There are notable implications of the conscientious, communicative aims of civil disobedience. Paradigmatically, if we engage in civil disobedience, we are wholly sincere and serious in our desire to

---

[8] On some accounts, *civil disobedience* does not include breaches of law that protest against decisions by non-governmental or private agencies such as trade unions, banks, and private universities. See Raz, Joseph (1979) *The Authority of Law*. Oxford: Oxford University Press, 264. This exclusion is arbitrary because the policies and practices of non-governmental or private institutions—such as the University of Mississippi's initial refusal to admit African American student James Meredith—are matters of law as the lawfully accepted practices of legally recognized institutions. In condemning such policies and practices, civil disobedients challenge, amongst other things, the legal framework that accepts these policies and practices as lawful.

bring about a lasting positive change in law or policy, and, in consequence, we appreciate the reasons we have not to be overly radical in our communication. In other words, we appreciate the reasons to seek rationally to persuade others of the merits of our view rather than to force them to make changes. These reasons are that, first, the appeal of our communication may be lost if it is drowned out by more forceful tactics. Second, our appeal rests in part on treating our audience as interlocutors with whom we can engage in a rational and moral discussion. Third, we realize that we may be mistaken in our views and therefore we select constrained acts that show that we bear this in mind.[9] Such implications of conscientious communicativeness narrow the parameters of civil disobedience, but not in the ways one might think.

For example, one might think that thwarting or sabotaging a practice in the way that anti-abortion activists block abortion clinics and anti-war protesters chain themselves to military property, cannot be civilly disobedient because such interference could not be done so as to communicate at the level of reason since it is likely to have a polarizing, dialogue-stifling effect.

However, to be conscientious, we need not take as our audience all the people who might be observing us. We need not take as our audience the people who are most hostile and unreceptive to us, though we do need to appeal to at least some people who do not share our outlook. Moreover, our appeals can take different forms and reach audiences in different ways. Therefore, in principle, thwarting and sabotage can be civilly disobedient since appeals to reason can be long-term, nuanced, and indirect.

The trickiest cases of thwarting and sabotage (and violence, as I discus shortly) are those that target one party in order to communicate to another party. Could acts that treat the targeted party as a means to our communicative ends satisfy the process-related constraints of conscientious communicativeness? The answer depends on whether our targeting 1) drowns out the moral appeal of our effort, 2) fails to respect the targeted person as an end in herself, and 3) is inconsistent with our acknowledging that we may be mistaken. It seems likely that at least some acts of targeted sabotage will pass these tests. Suppose I hold a

---

[9] The third implication flows from appreciating that there are other considerations that can bear on a case. This kind of appreciation is a necessary condition for intending sincerely to engage in a dialogue since a dialogue is a reciprocal exchange aimed at deliberative progress and understanding. See Chapter 7.

peaceful sit-in in a government building to protest against our military's activities in another country, and by doing so, I prevent you temporarily from carrying out your job as a civil servant. I have used you as a means to highlight my cause, but the impact on you is modest and my usage does not deny you your status as an end.

Turning to violence, one might think that acts of violence cannot be civilly disobedient because such acts also could not credibly be undertaken to communicate with others at the level of reason.[10] Certainly, this is the view taken by John Rawls who defines *civil disobedience* very narrowly as a public, non-violent, conscientious yet political breach of law typically done with the aim of bringing about a change in laws or government policies.[11] For Rawls, the non-violence of civil disobedience is one mark of its civility. Rawls says that violent acts likely to injure are incompatible with civil disobedience as a mode of address: 'any interference with the civil liberties of others tends to obscure the civilly disobedient quality of one's act.' Two other marks of civility, in Rawls' view, are disobedients' publicity and their willingness to accept the legal consequences of their act including punishment. The *public* nature of civil disobedience takes a distinctive *ex ante* form in Rawls' account. Civil disobedience is never done covertly or secretively. It is only ever done openly in public with advance notice to legal authorities. To Rawls' mind, these features together show that, unlike revolutionary actors or militant protesters, civil disobedients have a fidelity to law at the outer edge thereof and are willing to deal fairly with authorities. Their disobedience is a political act, but it is a conscientious one that invokes the commonly shared conception of *justice* that underlies the political order, which in Rawls' just society is a conception centered on his two principles of justice.

The presumed incivility of violence is problematic for several reasons. First, a commonsense conception of *violence*—as the likelihood or actuality of a person or group causing injury to someone or damage to something—includes not only a range of acts and events, major and minor, intended and unintended, that *cause* damage or injury, but also a range of acts and events that *risk* but do not necessarily cause damage or injury, such as catapulting stuffed animals at the police or shooting into

---

[10] The next four paragraphs closely follow and elaborate some ideas in Brownlee, Kimberley (2012a) 'Conscientious Objection and Civil Disobedience' in *The Routledge Companion to the Philosophy of Law*. Andrei Marmor (ed.), London: Routledge, 529–30.

[11] Rawls, John (1971) *A Theory of Justice*. Cambridge: Harvard University Press, 364ff.

the sky.[12] Given that such a range of elements can reasonably be counted as violence, it is implausible to hold that every instance of violence in the course of disobedience, however modest or non-injurious it may be, is, by definition, uncivil.

Second, focusing attention on violence draws attention away from the presumptively more salient issue of harm. As Joseph Raz argues, many non-violent acts and many legal acts can cause more harm to other persons than do violent breaches of law.[13] His example is that of a legal strike by ambulance workers, which will in all likelihood do far greater harm than, say, a minor act of vandalism. Moreover, he notes, sometimes the wrong or harm done by a law or policy is so iniquitous that it may be legitimate to use violence to root it out; such violence may be necessary to preserve or to re-establish the rights and civil liberties that coercive practices seek to suspend. Such observations about harm and violence are consistent, Raz points out, with the view that non-violent dissent is generally preferable because it does not encourage violence in other situations where violence would be wrong, something that an otherwise legitimate use of violence may do. Moreover, as a matter of prudence, non-violence does not carry the same risk of antagonizing potential allies or cementing opponents' antipathy, or distracting the public's attention, or providing authorities with an excuse to use harsh countermeasures against disobedients.

Third, conceptually, *civility* contrasts with *depravity*, *barbarity*, *disrespect*, and *rudeness*, not with *violence*. To see that civility and violence are not necessarily in tension, consider the sport of fencing. It is a highly civil yet violent form of engagement governed by strict norms of fair play. It is bad form to strike your opponent if she trips. It is bad form to try to win by hunting for loopholes in the rules. Fencing is *civil* in being highly rule-governed in ways that are respectful of the opponent as worthy. When thinking about dissent and disobedience, there seems to be a worry that, as soon as we step outside the law, we abandon all

---

[12] Some might question whether catapulting teddy bears at police or shooting into the sky are indeed acts of violence. I maintain that they are. In the case of shooting into the sky, there may be no intention to harm, but there is considerable risk of harm. In the case of catapulting stuffed animals, there is only a small risk of harm, but there is probably an intention to harm since the toys are not thrown up in the air. Neither the intention to harm nor the causing of harm is necessary for something to be violent, but each can be sufficient in combination with other things. I thank Chris Mills for prompting me to think about this issue more fully.

[13] Raz (1979), 267.

respect for norms and rules. But that is not the case. The law is only the most blunt manifestation of the social rules and moral norms that govern a reasonably good society, and the law is not the final arbiter on the content and force of those rules and norms. The thought that the rules have gone out of the window when we resort to disobedience is exactly what does not happen in cases of civil disobedience. (I pursue this further in Chapter 3.)

Also, as an aside, Rawls' other two tests for civility, which are publicity and a willingness to accept punishment, are equally strange. First, publicity can detract from or undermine the effort to communicate at all because announcing an intention to break the law gives political opponents and authorities an opportunity to abort it, which does no favours to the dissenter's cause even though that cause may be a just one.[14] For this reason, unannounced or (initially) covert disobedience can be preferable. Disobedience carried out covertly in the first instance to ensure that the act is successful may nonetheless be open and communicative when followed by an acknowledgment of the act and the reasons for taking it.[15] Second, the idea that, to be civil, disobedients must be willing to accept punishment ignores, first, that an unwillingness to accept punishment is not invariably a mark of incivility, such as when the very thing disobedients protest is the *punishment* for an offence, and second, that a willingness to accept punishment is not necessarily a mark of civility and fidelity.[16] Gandhi was a revolutionary and yet willingly went to jail many times.[17]

In contrast with Rawls, I hold that the civility of civil disobedience lies not in non-violence, publicity, or willingness to accept punishment, but in the conscientious, communicative motivations of civil disobedients. Civil disobedience involves not just a communicative breach, but a *conscientious* communicative breach of law motivated by steadfast, sincere, and serious, though possibly mistaken, moral

---

[14] Smart, Brian (1991) 'Defining Civil Disobedience' in *Civil Disobedience in Focus*. Hugo A. Bedau (ed.), London: Routledge, 206.

[15] Raz (1979), ch 14.

[16] Martin Luther King Jr saw the strategic value of being sent to jail: 'If you confront a man who has been cruelly misusing you, and say "Punish me, if you will; I do not deserve it, but I will accept it, so that the world will know I am right and you are wrong," then you wield a powerful and just weapon.' Washington, J. M. (ed.), (1991) *Testament of Hope: The Essential Writings and Speeches of Martin Luther King Jr*. San Francisco: Harper Collins, 348.

[17] For a defence of the view that willingness to accept punishment is necessary for conscientiousness and, hence, for civility, see Moraro, Piero (2007) 'Violent Civil Disobedience and Willingness to Accept Punishment' in *Essays in Philosophy* 8: 2, Article 6.

commitment. This combination of conscientiousness and forward-looking and backward-looking communicativeness constrains how civil disobedients may promote their cause, as I discussed earlier, and hence makes their conduct civil.

In sum, there are process-related constraints on civil disobedients that arise from their communicative conscientiousness. Those constraints have limits, though, since disobedients can sometimes find it unavoidable to use modest pressure or violence to get their issue onto the table. Only when they have an ear may they aim meaningfully to persuade authorities and society of their view. Also, disobedients' actions may have a coercing effect irrespective of their intentions since even constrained acts, such as illegal boycotts, illegal strikes, refusals to pay taxes, draft dodging, road-blocks, and sit-ins, can make it difficult for a system to function and thus can have a potent, non-reasoned effect on leaders' decisions. However, modest, incidental coercion need not muffle disobedients' moral plea in the way that radical protest can do, and so its use can be consistent with both the persuasive aims of civilly disobedient communication and a civil respect for their hearers. Radical protests are those acts of illegal dissent, including serious coercive violence, organized forcible resistance, militant action, intimidation, and terrorization, that also aim to communicate condemnation of policy, but lack the constrained conscientious communicativeness of civil disobedience.[18]

1.2 Civil disobedience and assistive disobedience

Civil disobedience differs not only from radical protest, but also, more interestingly, from what I will call, for lack of a better term, 'assistive disobedience'. Assistive disobedience is communicative, conscientious disobedience that is done not *for the purpose of* communicating condemnation of policy, but *because* it will communicate that condemnation. Here are some examples. When a doctor performs an illegal assisted suicide for a terminally ill patient, her act is not done, or should

---

[18] There are reasons not to label radical protest (or anything else) as 'terrorism'. Not only is the term inflammatory, but it is also bandied about by governments to capture an overly broad range of actions. Whereas 'civil disobedience' has developed as a more positive term that many people happily apply to their own protests, 'terrorism' is an epithet applied only to the actions of others. Given the highly negative connotations of this term, its philosophical usefulness is questionable. Less loaded notions of intimidation, forcible resistance, and severe violence offer greater space for a proper analysis of the justifiability of using such measures in political protest.

not be done, *for the purpose of* communicating condemnation of the law that prohibits the procedure. Rather, her act is done, or should be done, *for the purpose of* aiding the patient. Nonetheless, her act is communicative and conscientious when it is done openly and defended openly *because* that will communicate her condemnation of the law. Similarly, when animal liberationists rescue animals from laboratories, their act is not done, or should not principally be done, *for the purpose of* communicating disapprobation of the lawfulness of researching on animals. Rather, the act is done, or principally should be done, *for the purpose of* relieving the animals' suffering. But, their act is nonetheless *communicative* when it is done *because* releasing the animals will highlight the issue of animal suffering.[19]

The distinction between an act done *for the purpose of* having an effect occur and an act done *because* an effect will occur is a distinction between primary and secondary objectives where the latter is a constraint on the decision to act. As such, this distinction differs from Frances Kamm's Doctrine of Triple Effect, which she fleshes out with the example of throwing a party. She says, we intend to throw a party *in order to* have fun with our friends. But, we foresee that this will leave a big mess, and we do not want to have a party if we will be left with a mess to clean up ourselves. Yet, if we throw the party, it will have the effect that our friends will feel indebted to us and will help us clean up. Hence, we throw the party *because* our friends will feel indebted and *because* we will have help cleaning up. But, we do *not* throw the party *in order to* make our friends feel indebted or help clean up.[20] The 'because our friends will feel indebted' is a *condition* for having the party, not an intended objective in having the party. The mess is a foreseen, unintended, and undesired effect of the party, which would defeat our decision to have the party if our friends wouldn't help clean up.

This contrasts with cases of assistive disobedience since the 'because it will publicize the issue' *is* an intended objective for acting as well as a condition for engaging in the disobedience in the way that we do. If our chosen act would not publicize the issue, then we would undertake the act of rescue or assisted suicide in a different way that would publicize the issue.

---

[19] A third example might be selective refusal to go to war. I thank Larry May for highlighting this possibility.
[20] Kamm, Frances (2007) *Intricate Ethics*. Oxford: Oxford University Press, 95–6; 102–3.

So, in sum, through civil disobedience, we breach the law *for the purpose of* communicating our condemnation of a law or policy. Through direct civil disobedience, we additionally breach the law *for the purpose of* not lending ourselves to the wrong we condemn. We do not breach the law merely *because* it will communicate our condemnation. By contrast, through assistive disobedience, the conscientious doctor and animal rights defenders act *for the purpose of* aiding what they see as a suffering being, yet they do so openly and non-evasively *because* this will communicate opposition to laws against assisted suicide or animal research. And, the conscientious doctor and activists would not perform their acts in the way they do if those acts would not serve the aim of communicating condemnation of the law.

Although I have given two examples of assistive disobedience that are meritorious, not all acts of this kind are well-founded and well-motivated. For instance, a religious father might openly keep his daughters out of school *for the purpose of* protecting their minds from alternative ways of thinking and *because* doing so communicates his disapprobation for the teaching they would receive and the system that would have them attend school. His act is not meritorious, but, like the doctor's and the activists' acts, his act differs from civil disobedience in that the operative consideration motivating him is not a communicative one but a putatively assistive one. If the doctor, activists, or father were to act principally *for the purpose of* communicating their condemnation of the laws they oppose, then their acts would be radical ones indeed that fail to respect the beings they purport to assist. With such motivations, most likely, their acts would not be *civil* disobedience since they would lack both the civil disobedient's conscientious awareness of the need for moderation and her consistency in acting in genuine support of that to which she is committed.

One possible exception to this rule could be the following. Consider a famous doctor who works in a country where assisted suicide is legal and who has performed many assisted suicides in the past, but decides for whatever reason to stop doing so now while still thinking that the practice is morally permissible. Then a campaign springs up to make assisted suicide illegal in the country, and the famous doctor is asked to perform an assisted suicide to put the issue in the spotlight and to communicate condemnation for anti-assisted suicide propaganda. The doctor might decide to make an exception and perform the suicide *for the purpose of* communicating condemnation against the propaganda where she wouldn't otherwise perform the assisted suicide since she knows that others will do it.[21] In this case, the doctor acts in civil disobedience, not assistive disobedience, and the overall moral justifiability of her act may be questioned since, in one sense, her act manipulates the person seeking suicide. However, her act does not run afoul of the consistency and moderation requirements for conscientiousness in the way that the earlier examples do since, were other doctors not performing assisted suicides, she would do so, and would do so for the sake of the person seeking suicide.

By distinguishing civil disobedience from assistive disobedience, I do not mean to imply that civil disobedience is invariably the empty soapbox cousin of better-motivated acts of non-conformity. It is not. In some contexts, acting in order to denounce a perceived wrong is the best motivation that we can have. In other contexts though, particularly those in which our acts directly affect the interests of another being, we fail to respect that other being if we act upon them more to communicate our sense of injustice than to serve their perceived interests.[22] Although I focus for the most part on civil disobedience in this book, everything I say in support of it can be said in support of assistive disobedience of the variety that I have just distinguished.

2. Non-communicative Disobedience

In contrast with communicative disobedience, there is non-communicative or personal disobedience, which is a subset of the category of acts that I call *personal objection*. Such acts are often called 'conscientious objection', but I avoid that term for reasons that I have alluded to in the Introduction to this book and will specify further later on. Personal objection is a refusal to follow an injunction, directive, or law on grounds of perceived personal conviction. Although sometimes associated with pacifism (dating from the First World War), the practice of personal objection arises in numerous domains, from healthcare provision, civil service, retail work, and criminal justice, to family law, education, and personal attire in public. Examples include the

---

[21] I thank an anonymous reader for OUP for this case.
[22] Our act might also fail to respect the other person depending on what we sought to do ostensibly in her interests. The father's effort to protect his daughters from alternative points of view fails to respect them as persons with the autonomous reasoning capacities to deliberate amongst competing perspectives.

pharmacist who refuses to prescribe an emergency contraceptive pill, the religious patient who refuses an inoculation, and the soldier who refuses to redeploy.

Unlike civil disobedience and assistive disobedience, personal objection is not necessarily a breach of law. It might be a breach of a directive or order that falls short of law. In the case of military conscription, some legal systems regard non-selective pacifism as a legally legitimate ground for avoiding frontline military service. Moreover, even when personal objection is in breach of law, it differs from civil disobedience because civil disobedience is necessarily a *deliberate* breach of law, and personal disobedience is not. Personal disobedience is sometimes only incidentally a breach of law. In this respect, assistive disobedience is like personal disobedience. Think of the doctor performing an assisted suicide. It can be incidental to the act that it is in breach of law.

The most important difference between civil disobedience and assistive disobedience, on the one hand, and personal disobedience, on the other hand, is communication. Civil disobedience and assistive disobedience are *necessarily* communicative. Personal disobedience is not. When we engage in personal disobedience, we do seek to distance ourselves from the laws that we oppose, but we do not do so communicatively either *in order to* remedy or *because* it will remedy perceived injustices.

Personal disobedience can take either an evasive form or a non-evasive form. In its *non-evasive* form, it reflects our mere wish to act without interference in ways we take to be consistent with our commitments, and it is irrelevant to us whether our acts are seen by others or not. We neither seek to be seen nor seek not to be seen. And, we adjust neither our conduct nor our motivating reasons to avoid the consequences of our action. To the extent that there is any communication in what we do, it is incidental or accidental. Or, if we seek to communicate anything at all, it is that the law should not interfere with us in this domain. And, even that communication is secondary to our purposes, though it does indicate that, in one sense, our act is a *political* act that asserts our immunity from certain laws of the community.[23] Examples include the civil registrar who swaps assignments with colleagues to avoid performing same-sex civil partnership ceremonies; the grocery store employee who avoids shelving or processing the

---

[23] I thank Emanuela Ceva for highlighting this point.

sale of alcohol; the doctor who refuses to participate in the provision of abortions; the judge who refuses to hear gay couples' applications for adoption; and the religious person who refuses to wear or not wear legally regulated clothing in public.

In its *evasive* form, personal disobedience is a surreptitious, clandestine act that amongst other things is intended to ensure that there is no external interference from society. Here, we seek not to be seen to be acting as we are. Examples include religious people practising banned parts of their faith at odd hours and in secret locations, which has historically been the case, for example, for the practising of Juadaism; or religious parents concealing their child with curable diabetes to avoid her being taken to a doctor; or a US draft dodger covertly fleeing to Canada.

3. The Communicative Principle of Conscientiousness

The difference between the communicativeness of civil disobedience and the lack of it in personal disobedience signals a further difference in the quality of their conscientiousness. Of the two, only the civil disobedient may legitimately claim to appreciate that when we judge some conduct to be seriously wrong we must not only 1) avoid such conduct ourselves to the best extent that we are able, and 2) judge such conduct in others to be wrong as well, but also *ceteris paribus*, 3) be willing to bear the risks of honouring our conviction by not evading the consequences and sometimes taking positive action in support of it, and 4) be willing to communicate our conviction to others. As Antony Duff has noted in a different context, to remain silent necessarily casts doubt on the sincerity of our conviction that the conduct is seriously wrong.[24] This is what I call the communicative principle of conscientiousness. This principle lies at the core of my analysis of what counts as 'sincere moral conviction'. As the numbers suggest, this principle has four conditions:

1. a *consistency condition* that holds between our judgements, motivations, and conduct to the best extent that we are able;

---

[24] Duff, Antony (2001) *Punishment, Communication, and Community*. Oxford: Oxford University Press, 28.

2. a *universality condition* that holds between our judgements of ourselves and our judgements of others;
3. a *non-evasion condition* that we bear the risks of honouring our conviction, which means that we not seek to evade the consequences for reasons of self-protection, and, in some cases, take positive action when appropriate to support our conviction; and
4. a *dialogic condition* that *ceteris paribus* we be willing to communicate our conviction to others so as to engage them in reasoned deliberation about its merits. Our willingness to defend our conviction to others is a mark of both our non-evasion and our belief that our conviction is sufficiently credible that it can be given a reasoned defence.

The first condition has cognitive, affective, and conative elements. The second condition has cognitive and affective elements. The third has affective and conative elements. And, the fourth has conative and cognitive elements.

Given the conative elements of the communicative principle of conscientiousness, it has the advantage of being practically testable. That is, we can look at a person's conduct to see whether she satisfies the consistency, non-evasion, and dialogic conditions. This practical pay-off of testability means that this principle gives people who are charged with adjudicating others' conscientiousness, such as judges, medical tribunals, and military tribunals, more credible things to assess than mere assertions of conviction. Although I shall flesh out this communicative principle of conscientiousness in relation to civil disobedience and personal disobedience, it is a principle that stands independently of any particular practice. Each of the four conditions is potentially controversial and, therefore, I shall defend them each in turn.

3.1 Consistency

The consistency condition states that there must be consistency between our judgements, motivations, and conduct to the best extent that we are able. This means that we must avoid the conduct that we deem to be morally wrong, and engage in the conduct that we deem to be acceptable, right, or praiseworthy. For instance, if we deem it wrong to have extramarital affairs or wrong to go out in public bareheaded, then we must not have affairs or must not go out bareheaded to the best extent that we are able.

It is necessary to say something, first, about the pre-conditions for such consistency, and second, about the qualifier 'to the best extent we are able'. The English word 'conviction' derives from the Latin verb *convincere*, which means to convict, to convince, to prove, to conquer, or to demonstrate; it means to overcome in argument, to confute, to satisfy or persuade by argument or evidence.[25] Thus, *conviction* is the mental state or condition of being convinced, that is, of having a strong, settled belief or commitment founded on minimally satisfactory grounds. This does not mean that convictions must be correct, but it does mean that they must meet minimal standards of intelligibility, internal coherence, and evidential satisfactoriness.[26] Otherwise there is no determinate answer to what the content of the conviction is, and hence no way of assessing consistency,[27] and no way of deciding whether and how to be accommodating of it.

The qualifier 'to the best extent we are able' applies to simple cases such as entrenched physical or psychological inability. Suppose that you value friendship very highly and seek to do all you can to be a good friend. But, you also suffer from severe bipolar disorder and experience depressive and psychotic episodes during which time you are unable to be a friend at all. In honouring friendship as well as you can when you can, you show that there is consistency *ceteris paribus* between your judgements, motivations, and conduct to the best extent you are able.

The qualifier may also apply broadly to circumstantial inability. Suppose your child is sick and the only way to get aid to her is to go out in public bareheaded. It is contingently the case that you are unable

---

[25] The sense of 'to convince' that means 'to conquer' had another, now obsolete, meaning of overcoming or vanquishing by force, but that meaning was figurative, such as in 'I shall convince them by force of arms' or 'His two Chamberlaines will I with Wine and Wassal so convince,' (Shakespeare, William (1623), *Macbeth*, i. vii. 64). It was not a literal sense of 'to convince'. Also, the Latin root for 'to conquer' is *conquīrĕre*, which means to complete in seeking, to procure by effort, to gain, or to win. Cf *Oxford English Dictionary* (current online edition, September 2011.) Therefore, the etymological link between 'conviction' and 'conquering' need not be read as lending etymological support to a compulsion or overborne-will conception of *conviction*.

[26] By highlighting evidential satisfactoriness as a condition for conviction, I do not mean to take a stand on meta-ethical questions. Although I endorse an objectivist and broadly cognitivist view of morality, I do not take a stand on whether moral beliefs are natural or non-natural. Conscientiousness is not about the correctness of moral judgements, but about the consistency of moral judgements and the credibility of factual assumptions that have moral implications. Constrained by space, I shall take a minimal and commonsense view of what counts as evidential satisfactoriness.

[27] This is true not only for moral convictions, but also for factual and social convictions as well, the nature of which I specify on pages 35–6.

to care for your child and honour your commitment against going out bareheaded. Now this case is not as straightforward as cases of personal inability because, in choosing to go out bareheaded to get aid, it seems that you simply privilege your child's welfare over covering your head and hence are not wholeheartedly committed to the latter belief. Indeed, it seems to be an implication of the consistency condition that, at any one time, we can have only one really deep commitment because, almost inevitably, commitments will clash in practice (let alone in principle), and, almost inevitably, we will be forced to privilege one commitment A over another commitment B. And, since, in cases of contingent practical clashing, we could have chosen commitment B over commitment A but didn't, we cannot value commitment B as much as we value commitment A.

It may indeed be an implication of my view that, at any given time, only one thing could have overmastering importance for us as the thing we would not sacrifice for any other commitment.[28] That implication does not trouble me since what I defend in this book is the weighty claim that society must not only take seriously, but also accommodate (where possible) people who act on the basis of conscientious conviction. It does not matter for that thesis whether we can have more than one overmastering commitment at a time. Moreover, the implication that we cannot does not mean that we cannot have other deep commitments at all. We *can* have other commitments, and can only hope that they never come in conflict practically, or that, if they do conflict in their demands on our conduct, they won't conflict in their demands on our attitudes and beliefs. For some commitments at least, this could be true. Aung San Suu Kyi and Nelson Mandela undoubtedly continued to love their families after they devoted themselves to realizing democracy in their respective countries. Their feeling of love for their families never had to be sacrificed for the sake of their democratic ideals even though their conative efforts to care for their families as parents and spouses certainly were sacrificed.

Moreover, we could adopt a more nuanced, context-sensitive approach to how we privilege different commitments in action. In context 1, we might privilege commitment A. In context 2, we might privilege commitment B. And, this *might* not fall afoul of the consistency condition if commitment A is not particularly salient in context 2, and commitment B is not particularly salient in context 1. So, suppose that

---

[28] I thank Rafael Cejudo Córdoba for pressing me in conversation to address this issue.

to get aid for your child you must go outside bareheaded but only along a dark backstreet frequented solely by women whom you do not mind seeing you bareheaded since it is not a core part of your conviction that women not see you bareheaded. In the context of the backstreet, the core of your commitment to covering your head is not undermined, and hence your conduct satisfies the consistency condition. The more rigid, absolute, and demanding your declared conviction is, the less easily you can adopt a context-sensitive approach to consistency.

A final question for the consistency condition concerns the duration and persistence of our commitment. For how long must our judgements, motivations, and actions align to the best extent that we are able for us to have a genuine conviction? How stable and unwavering must this alignment be? Must we never have doubts about our commitment? Must we never flag or fail in our conduct, putting the capacity qualifier aside? These would be heavy demands, but it is undoubtedly a feature of convictions that they change slowly and gradually, and are thus unlike ordinary beliefs or attitudes, which can rapidly be revised.

Although we tend to be impressed with sincere conviction when we think we see it, we also tend to be reluctant to attribute sincere conviction even when there is evidence of it over time. For example, consider the case of Stanley 'Tookie' Williams, a Los Angeles gang leader convicted in 1979 for four robbery-related murders and sentenced to capital punishment. For several years, he continued to lead a gangster life in prison, assaulting guards and fellow inmates and attempting escapes, which resulted in six and half years in solitary confinement. In the mid-nineties, however, Williams began to renounce his former life. He became an anti-gang activist, wrote many children's books against gang life, received a President's Call to Service Award from George W. Bush, and reportedly was nominated five times for the Nobel Peace Prize. In 2005, then California Governor Arnold Schwarzenegger decided not to commute Williams' sentence, arguing that the evidence of his redemption was questionable given, amongst other things, his continued insistence on his innocence, his refusal to give evidence against former fellow gang members, and his dedication of *Life in Prison* to several people with violent histories including George Jackson.[29] On a nuanced interpretation, none of

---

[29] Kershaw, Sarah (2005) 'Governor Rejects Clemency for Inmate on Death Row' *The New York Times*, 13 December 2005: <http://www.nytimes.com/2005/12/13/national/13tookie.html>.

these things need be in tension with a genuine commitment to redemption and peace. Assuming that Tookie's efforts *were* genuine, we may ask if a 10 year commitment is really insufficient to satisfy the consistency condition for sincere conviction, despite the contrast with his past acts and allegiances. To say that it is insufficient seems to set an impossibly high standard for genuine conviction, and seems to reject the alterability (and redeemability) of people.[30]

3.2 *Universality*

The universality condition requires us to make a universal judgement that the act we deem to be wrong is wrong not only when we do it, but also when others in similar circumstances do it.[31] Taken at face value, this condition seems to imply both monism and insufficient context-sensitivity, that, to be conscientious, we must make universal *all things considered* moral judgements. Hence, if we judge that it is wrong to eat meat, then we must judge it wrong all things considered for anyone to eat meat, even if other people's lives hang in the balance. This is a patently implausible view of the universality condition not only because it rides on an absolutist account of morality, which I reject, but also because it implies that, if we are sensitive to competing moral considerations, we cannot be sincere and serious in our

---

[30] Avishai Margalit is eloquent on this point: 'Even if there are noticeable differences among people in their ability to change, they are deserving of respect for the very possibility of changing. Even the worst criminals are worthy of basic human respect because of the possibility that they may radically reevaluate their past lives and, if they are given the opportunity, may live the rest of their lives in a worthy manner... Even though it is likely that she will continue living this way, this likelihood should not be turned into a presumption, because in principle an evildoer has the capacity to change and repent. This capacity implies that she deserves basic respect as a human being who should not be "given up on", precisely because there is a chance, no matter how small, that she will repent.' Margalit, Avishai (1996) *The Decent Society*. Cambridge: Harvard University Press, 70–5. Cited in Tasioulas, John (2006) 'Punishment and Repentance', *Philosophy* 81, 279–322.

[31] The qualifier in the consistency condition—'to the best extent that we are able'—acknowledges the practical difficulties of aligning our conduct with our convictions in all cases. Circumstances, others' conduct, our experiences, and our past decisions can all impede us in the effort to act in accordance with our deepest convictions. This ability qualifier also acknowledges that, given the pluralistic nature of morality, persons who have morally defensible sets of convictions will be unable in many cases to honour more than one or two of the values to which they are properly committed. The consistency condition raises a question about the *tu quoque* argument that, if we are engaging in (or have engaged in) a certain type of conduct, can we condemn others who also engage in that conduct? I maintain that we can make the same moral judgement that they do *pro tanto* wrong that we can make about our own conduct.

convictions.[32] It implies that conviction is a matter of rigid, unthinking, brute passion, rather than reflective, sincere, and serious moral commitment. This passion-driven view is the wrong way to think about conviction as I demonstrate in Section 3.3.

A second, more modest interpretation of the universality condition, which I endorse, says that, to be conscientious, we must make universal *pro tanto* moral judgements as opposed to *all things considered* moral judgements. A *pro tanto* moral judgement says that some act is wrong to a certain extent, but outweighing or overriding moral reasons may vindicate that wrong and make it not wrong *all things considered*. Thus, if we judge an act to be wrong, we must judge that it is *pro tanto* wrong not only when we do it, but when others do it too. And, this does not entail any particular conclusion about how we or others should act all things considered. So, if we judge that it is wrong to eat meat, we must judge that it is *pro tanto* wrong for anyone to eat meat. But, additional considerations must be taken into account to conclude that we or anyone else act wrongly all things considered by eating meat since we may be starving or we may have starving children to whom we feed it. This modest interpretation of the universality condition accommodates both context-sensitivity and moral pluralism. And, it recognizes that people may justifiably (or excusably) differ in how they respond to morally difficult problems in light of their differing and often role-related responsibilities (cf Chapters 2 and 3).

The universality condition may, however, be problematic in a different way since it seems to cast doubt on the depth and sincerity of any community-based convictions we have. Suppose there is a religious community, the Mournish, who believe that they should plant a flower whenever a member of their faith dies. The universality condition seems to say that, unless a Mournish person believes that people outside her faith do wrong by disregarding the flower-planting ritual, she cannot have a sincere conviction that she should practise it herself.

The answer to this little puzzle lies in distinguishing conscientiousness as deep *moral* conviction from other types of conviction, such as factual conviction and social conviction. We can believe that the Earth is round and that people who believe otherwise are mistaken, without believing that they do moral wrong by being mistaken, and without

---

[32] Winch, Peter (1965) 'The Universalizability of Moral Judgements' in *The Monist* 49: 2, 196–214.

thereby raising doubts about our own belief that the Earth is round. Similarly, if we are the Mournish, we can believe that our community should practise the flower-planting ritual as an expression of our faith and social identity, and we can believe that other people are mistaken or unfortunate in not being party to our ritual, without believing that they do moral wrong in not planting flowers for the dead, and without thereby raising doubts about our conviction that we should practise this ritual as a social group. Indeed, this is how many religions do approach their rituals.

To this, a critic might respond that, even though a Mournish member may think non-members do no wrong by neglecting the flower-planting ritual, she probably thinks that *members* of her community do do wrong when *they* neglect this ritual, and this suggests that non-universality still lurks in her moral judgements, which implies either that her convictions cannot be conscientious or that the universality condition is false.

In reply, the content of her judgements is what matters. Suppose the Mournish change their ritual from flower-planting to 24-hour chanting. The committed Mournish member now believes that her fellows do wrong in not chanting for the dead, but no wrong in not flower-planting, whereas before they did wrong in not planting and no wrong in not chanting. Her *individual* judgements of her fellows' conduct are not moral judgements because they blow with the community's ritualistic winds. Yet, these judgements may well be driven by a more enduring, abstract, content-dependent judgement—that community members should honour the rituals of their community—or that some tribute should be paid to people when they die—which is universalizable as a moral judgement. (Its correctness or incorrectness as a moral judgement is, of course, another matter.)

There is a practical pay-off to the universality condition for conscientiousness, namely, that it allows us to be sceptical about the convictions of a person who is happy to have others do what she will not do herself and who will free-ride on their willingness to do it. We can be sceptical of the draft dodger who is happy for others to go to war in his place, and the civil registrar who happily asks colleagues to perform the same-sex civil partnership ceremonies assigned to her, and the doctor who refuses on principle to perform abortions, but happily refers women to other doctors. In each of these cases, the person refusing to act benefits from others being willing to do what she will not do. For instance, the registrar benefits from her colleagues being willing to pick up those assignments that she judges to be morally wrong; she depends on them not having the same scruples that she has.[33]

This practical pay-off seems to have a sting in its tail since it appears to invite us to be rigid in our moral outlooks. For instance, it appears to invite the doctor to refuse to provide referrals on the grounds that abortions would be equally wrong if performed by anyone else. But, this sting is a phantom pain since the universal judgement required for conscientiousness is a *pro tanto* judgement. The doctor who views abortions as morally wrong can be conscientious about that conviction while nonetheless appreciating the moral considerations in favour of providing the procedure, which could override or outweigh the reasons against it, and all things considered justify either her or another doctor in providing an abortion. When it comes to universality of judgement, the difference between the conscientious person and the hypocrite lies in their reasoning and their attitude towards others' conduct.[34]

3.3 Non-evasion

The non-evasion condition is one practical test for conscientiousness. It requires that we bear the risks of honouring our convictions, which means that we do not seek to evade the consequences and, in some cases, take positive action to support our convictions. It is through our consistent non-evasion of the costs that we signal we are neither inconstant nor hypocritical. This condition is, of course, broadly context sensitive. It is often important to stand up for our beliefs in a public forum. But, for reasons of respect or sympathy, it's not usually important to stand up for our beliefs when we're invited over to someone's house for dinner.[35]

---

[33] It is true that such benefiting does not in itself expose a lack of genuine conviction. Since there are colleagues willing to perform the same-sex ceremonies, the test for the registrar's sincerity would have to be a counterfactual one: Would she be willing to bear the risks of non-conformity if there were no colleagues there to perform the ceremonies for her? I thank Joe Horton for identifying this counterfactual test.

[34] For a discussion of the practice of referring patients who seek an abortion, see McLeod, Carolyn (2008) 'Referral in the Wake of Conscientious Objection to Abortion' in *Hypatia* 23: 4, 30–47. Anti-abortion advocates argue that referrals make objectors complicit in the performance of acts they find morally objectionable. McLeod argues that the referral requirement is not a genuine compromise for anti-abortion doctors, and hence pro-choice advocates must offer a better argument for the referral requirement. She argues that the better argument for the referral requirement lies in showing that abortion is morally permissible.

[35] I thank Adam Slavny for highlighting this point.

One model of non-evasion, noted at the beginning of this chapter, is Sir Thomas More as he is presented in *A Man for All Seasons*. Another is Socrates as he is presented in the *Crito* awaiting his death in prison. In general, disobedients need not meet such high standards of self-exposure to be non-evasive. To satisfy the non-evasion condition, it is enough that they act communicatively and thereby take the risk of being arrested and punished or socially censured. They need not act to *ensure* that they are punished.

A critic might raise three objections against the non-evasion condition. First, why, for conscientiousness, must we be willing in all cases to accept burdens to honour our convictions? Suppose there are two equally effective ways to communicate our commitment, one of which brings burdens for us and one of which does not. In order to be conscientious, must we take the burdensome option?[36] And, if so, why?

One reply is that there are always burdens in communicating our views to others, most notably the burden of risk that, through our communication, we will damage some of our interests. We might alienate allies, injure our reputation, or invite concrete burdens such as punishment. Therefore, it is a moot point to ask why we must take the burdensome option. All options are burdensome.

This reply is not satisfying because some ways of communicating will be more burdensome than others. Thus, the question is: to be conscientiousness, must we take the *more* burdensome option? In reply, in principle, to be conscientious, we do not need to take the more burdensome of two equally effective options. However, there can be an epistemic advantage to our doing so in that we can ensure that no doubt is cast on the sincerity of our conviction. Such doubt is cast when we take the less burdensome, smoother-sailing option because, by doing so, we raise doubts about our motivations, and consequently doubts about our sincerity.[37]

Second, a critic might argue that the second part of the non-evasion condition—the willingness to take some positive action to support our conviction—is too strong because it runs counter to the deontological

---

[36] I thank Tom Porter for raising this question.

[37] In some cases, it may seem that a genuinely burdensome option is not available to us. For instance, Ireland passed laws against blasphemy, which reportedly many people tried to break in order to test the laws in court. They have had difficulty getting themselves arrested, as the police appear to be disinclined to enforce these laws. I thank Brian Carey for noting this point.

principle that the moral duties we have not to act wrongly are more stringent than the moral duties we have to prevent others from acting wrongly. According to this principle, a person could be fully committed (rightly or wrongly) to a moral belief that some act is wrong without ever forming an intention to prevent others from engaging in that act.

In reply, little weight could be put on the asserted 'convictions' of a person who does not think that, in at least *some* cases, she should be willing to act positively to prevent others from doing what she regards as seriously wrong. She need not be willing to act thus in all cases since, as shown on page 35, the universality condition pertains to *pro tanto* judgements and the consistency condition allows for context-sensitivity. Nevertheless, other people's morality is more often our business than dominant liberal positions tend to acknowledge. A story that nicely illustrates this is of the Dalai Lama, who was reportedly once asked: What would you do if a guy came at you pointing a gun? The Dalai Lama is said to have replied that he would shoot the man in the knees and then go over and comfort him. This response may be interpreted as saying that he would incapacitate the attacker as much to protect the attacker from the horrific act of killing as to protect his own life. Given that it is permissible to strike out in such a case for reasons of self-defence, why would it be any less permissible to strike out both for the reason of self-defence and for the reason of protecting the attacker from an opprobrious act?

Third, a critic might argue that the non-evasion condition is not content-insensitive and, thus, it arbitrarily rules out some beliefs from being potentially conscientious. For example, it seems to rule out the conscientiousness of evasive commitments such as a hermit's commitment to not engaging with other people.

In reply, first, it is true that the communicative principle of conscientiousness is not wholly content-insensitive. But, this is due to the content-sensitive nature of *conviction* given the logical and evidentiary constraints on genuine convictions noted earlier. The hermit who believes she is morally required to avoid contact with others cannot hold that *unqualified* belief as a genuine conviction because, to form that belief in the first place, she needed the support, protection, care, and guidance of other people. So, for her misanthropic belief to be a conviction at all, it must be tempered at least by a nod to socially dependent developmental needs.

Moreover, the example of the hermit misses its mark because the non-evasion condition turns not on what beliefs a person has (logical and evidentiary constraints aside), but on how she conducts herself in relation to those beliefs. If a hermit acts consistently with her belief that there is a moral requirement for adults to avoid other people, and she acts *for the reason* that she believes this, then she satisfies the non-evasion condition since she adjusts neither her conduct nor her motivations to avoid the costs of her belief. If, however, she modifies her conduct to avoid certain costs of her belief, then she is not consistently motivated and her belief does not satisfy the non-evasion condition.

More generally, there are three notable implications of the logical and evidentiary constraints on moral conviction. First, although emotional investment is an important part of conscientiousness, conscientious conviction is necessarily both cognitive and reflective. As noted earlier, my view of conscientious conviction contrasts sharply with one that construes moral conviction in terms of passion measured by how all-consuming it is. Hot-headed, unthinking, brute devotion is properly described as *obsession*, not *conviction*.[38] One implication of this distinction between obsession and conviction is that our own self-assessments and declarations of conviction are not authoritative. The mere assertion of deep, life-defining moral conviction or 'compulsion' is neither sufficient nor necessary for ours to be a genuine conscientious moral conviction. The necessary and sufficient conditions for conscientious moral conviction are, I maintain, those outlined in the communicative principle of conscientiousness.

Second, beliefs that fail to meet the logical and evidentiary standards for conviction cannot claim the degree of toleration or respect that genuine convictions might claim because they lack both the determinate content and reflection that confirm our psychological and emotional investment. Without determinate content and reflection, our declared convictions are flighty, capricious, incoherent things that warrant neither respect nor toleration from others.

If not much rides on a person's declared 'conviction', then its incoherence or kookiness need not trouble us since it does not raise a real problem of toleration. But, if that declared 'conviction' poses significant risks for others or the person herself, then its failure to satisfy the logical and evidentiary standards for conviction cannot be ignored.

---

[38] Of course, obsessions and uncritical faith can be useful, as studies of the placebo effect have shown.

For instance, the religious parents' belief that they will heal their child with curable diabetes through prayer alone, even though the evidence is that she is dying, and even though they would have taken her to a doctor had she broken her leg, is a belief that fails the combined tests of internal coherence and minimal evidential satisfactoriness. As such, it is not a genuine conviction let alone a conscientious moral conviction, and therefore cannot ground a claim to exemption from ordinary moral norms.[39] The same lack of (commonsensical) coherence dogs the anti-abortion activists who seek to endanger or kill abortion providers. Some such activists may be able to appeal coherently, if not credibly, to a third-party-defence for their violence, which would make their position internally consistent and *ceteris paribus* minimally evidentially satisfactory. But, other anti-abortion activists would not be able to give such an account, especially when their violence is indiscriminate, *ex post*, or motivated by vengeance. Of course, genuine convictions that do pass the tests of coherence and minimal evidential satisfactoriness also can pose significant risks to people, but they must be approached differently since they are not incoherent. (I develop these points later on.)

Finally, the logical and evidentiary standards of conviction give a further response to the earlier worry about universal judgement and rituals. Ever-adaptive beliefs, such as a Mournish's belief that each new ritual of the moment is morally obligatory *in itself*, need not be credited as genuine convictions since they fall below minimum standards of good reasoning and evidential satisfactoriness. We might say facetiously that the Mournish member who slavishly follows each new ritual is very 'conscientious' since her commitment is as inconstant as her leaders' ritualistic whims. By contrast, if she had the more settled belief that a Mournish member will rightly suffer social disapprobation if she

---

[39] In many US states, the law includes a religious exemption for child abuse and neglect that allows parents to appeal to religion or faith-based rituals as a legal defence for such abuse. In a 2008 case in Wisconsin, this defence was not available to a couple, as they were charged with second-degree reckless homicide, not child abuse and neglect, after allowing their 11-year-old daughter to slip into a coma and die due to curable juvenile diabetes while the family stood around her and prayed. The parents could have faced 25 years in prison, but were sentenced very leniently to six months' imprisonment respectively (one month per year for six years) and 10 years' probation. At the time of writing, the couple, Dale and Leilani Neumann, have appealed the ruling. The case is expected to go to the Wisconsin State Supreme Court. A fuller specification of 'evidential satisfactoriness' is, of course, required to legitimate my claim that cases of asserted religious exemption have little force when they fail to satisfy minimum standards of evidence.

continues with the old ritual and neglects the new, then her belief does satisfy the minimal logical and evidential standards to be a moral conviction.

3.4 Communication and dialogue

The dialogic condition for conscientiousness requires that we be willing to communicate our conviction to others in an effort to engage them in reasoned deliberation about its merits. Our willingness to do this shows both that we believe our conviction is sufficiently credible that it can be given a reasoned defence, and that we are sufficiently committed to it that we think it worth defending despite the potential risks to ourselves. Thus, the dialogic condition is another practical test for conscientiousness because a dialogic effort is evidence for the sincerity and seriousness of our conviction. And, a lack of a dialogic effort casts doubt on the sincerity of our conviction.

Additionally, our willingness to try to engage with others honours a link between integrity, conscience, and honest speech. Although sincere conviction is insufficient for integrity and conscience, it is a precondition for it.[40]

A critic might raise four objections against the dialogic condition. The first is that dialogic efforts are not a necessary condition for conscientious moral conviction because there are other, better ways to demonstrate conviction than by *talking* about it. The most obvious way is by *acting* on it. Intervening, thwarting, and sabotaging are all ways in which we can honour our judgement that certain conduct is seriously wrong.

In reply, although intervening, thwarting, and sabotaging are potential ways to honour our convictions in the short run, ultimately, on their own, they do not take other people seriously as reasoning moral

---

[40] In a recent paper, Matthew Pianalto outlines an account of moral conviction that also highlights the importance of dialogue, or 'discourse', as he puts it. Pianalto does not see a commitment to discourse as a necessary condition for moral conviction as I do. Rather, he sees it as a feature of *responsible* moral conviction. And he offers different arguments from mine for endorsing such a feature. Briefly, he offers, first, a consequential argument that a willingness to engage in discourse with others about our conviction 'serves as an aid to personal reflection, and sometimes (or perhaps often) as a corrective' since others bring a different perspective and knowledge-base to the assessment of our convictions, and second, a non-consequential argument that our convictions often affect other people, which means that they have something at stake in how we live and what we believe. Pianalto, Matthew (2011) 'Moral Conviction' in *The Journal of Applied Philosophy* 28: 4, 381–95.

agents with whom we can discuss the merits of our cause and whose conduct we should try to change through reasoned argument.[41] That said, the dialogic condition can be interpreted broadly to include *standing up* for our beliefs in an open or public way with the intention that this prompt others to reflect on the merits of our cause.[42]

The critic's second objection might be that, even if something like the dialogic condition were necessary for conscientiousness, it is too demanding for those of us who hold deeply unpopular views[43] or who are vulnerable, disadvantaged, or otherwise unable to engage in ordinary reasoned debate without undue personal cost.[44]

In reply, the dialogic condition is not as demanding as this suggests. First, it does not require that we succeed in defending or even in communicating our conviction to others. Rather, it requires that we appreciate the reasons to communicate our conviction and *ceteris paribus* that we intend to do so unless the reasons to communicate are outweighed by undue costs of communicating.[45] Having a sincere intention to engage others in a dialogue means that we do not wilfully immunize ourselves from their communicative efforts. Our readiness to heed and interpret them correctly is necessary for communication to occur. It also means that we consider whether our chosen *means* of

---

[41] As noted earlier in this chapter, part of being sincere and serious in our deep moral convictions is having a forward-looking aim of bringing about lasting changes in attitudes, behaviours, laws, or policies that reflect our convictions. This means that, necessarily, we must appreciate the reasons we have to seek rationally to persuade others of the merits of our view rather than either to coerce them to make changes or to remain silent and merely hope for the changes we ostensibly desire. The condition can accommodate anonymous acts and temporarily clandestine acts provided that the reasons for secrecy are not to avoid the personal consequences of detection, but rather, for example, to ensure success. To succeed in carrying out actions such as releasing animals from research laboratories or vandalizing military property, disobedients may have to avoid advance publicity. Such acts of civil disobedience nonetheless may be regarded as 'open' or 'non-evasive' when followed soon after by an acknowledgment of the act and the reasons for acting. Cf Raz (1979).

[42] I thank Larry May for drawing my attention to this issue.

[43] I thank Simon Caney for noting in conversation that the communicative principle of conscientiousness is more demanding for those people who hold unpopular views than it is for people who hold popular or tolerated views. In current conditions, it's much easier to protest against a despised war than it is to protest that white people should be privileged or that women shouldn't be given equal treatment in employment opportunities. The unpopularity of a view of course does not track its degree of plausibility. The point here is not that the communicative principle of conscientiousness is more demanding for people who have opprobrious views, but that it is very demanding for people who have unpopular views whatever the merits or demerits of those views.

[44] I thank Steve Cooke for highlighting these cases.

[45] I thank Christopher Bennett for helping me to refine this point.

communication—words, actions, images, body movements, facial expressions—and *modes* of communication—aggressively, violently, assertively, collectively, supportively—are likely to foster understanding in a way that is compatible with the reason-governed, reciprocal, and respectful nature of a dialogue. Both shunning and threats are incompatible with a commitment to genuine dialogue since they fail to recognize the other's communicative claim-rights and status. (I explore the conditions for genuine dialogue more fully in Chapter 7.)

Moreover, since communicative success is not required, the dialogic condition can be broadly position-sensitive. A willingness to communicate our convictions to others does not require that we try to engage all of society in deliberation. There are other ways to exhibit dialogic commitment. And, what we are required to do varies according to its burdensomeness for us. The communicative principle of conscientiousness is a *ceteris paribus* principle, and hence can be sensitive to the burdens of vulnerability, disadvantage, unpopularity, relative power, and relative cost of communication.

A third objection is that the dialogic condition makes no room for the person who holds a 'conviction' on the basis of believed revelation and who may well rightly think that others will not be willing to listen to her and certainly will not believe her view to be reasonable.

In reply, the dialogic condition does not rule out 'revelation'-based convictions because a person's view need not be accepted as reasonable for her to show, through her dialogic efforts, that she believes her view is reasonable. A person who believes something on the basis of 'revelation' would have to give arguments for accepting beliefs because they are acquired through a certain process, rather than because they have a certain content. Such an effort might fail the logical coherence and evidential satisfactoriness tests, but it would not run afoul of the dialogic condition.

A fourth, more general objection is that, by introducing the dialogic condition and non-evasion condition, I have so restricted the procedural requirements for moral convictions that I have secured the result that only liberal-minded people can have moral convictions, and this belies the ostensibly neutral and descriptive nature of my conceptual project.

In reply, the dialogic condition and non-evasion condition do not rule out radical positions. What they do do is place strict constraints on the *means* through which we may communicate our positions. For instance, it is reasonable to adopt a rough 'last resort' condition for any use of radical forms of communication. If a person is thinking about using violence to communicate her view, she must try much harder than she would ordinarily be expected to try to communicate her views through modest means. She must do much more than circulate a pamphlet and then, if ignored, take this as a licence to resort to serious violence. Although it is not possible to specify precise conditions for last resort, a commonsense notion of it is appropriate to set the bar for dialogic effort very high in cases where persons are tempted to resort to radical means of communication.

Two further issues arise for the dialogic condition, both of which relate to the undesirability of raising certain topics for deliberative discussion. The first is that there may be cases in which we would not wish to grant apparent standing to an offensive position by seeking to engage others in a dialogue about it. Two examples are the laws against sodomy in the American South and the South African Apartheid policy of assigning people a colour status and allowing them to apply for a change of colour status. The thought is that to engage with either policy at all, even to denounce it, would legitimate it as an, in principle, plausible position that could be reasonably debated.

This is a legitimate worry. However, by challenging such policies, we communicate to and for other people who are affected by them. For example, in Texas, if we are gay, we might speak up in part because we are not the only ones affected by the policy. And, the content of what we communicate may well be that there is no debate to be had.

The second issue is that, in some cases, the dialogic condition is disrespectful because it requires persons to raise their cause for collective deliberation even when, for them, the topic should not be discussed collectively. An example of this, highlighted by Leslie Green for different purposes, is sexuality in Muslim communities. Green notes that, when the BBC ran a radio programme in 2008 exploring contemporary British Muslims' views on sex and sexuality, the producers received complaints from some Muslim listeners that the programme failed to show proper respect for Islam. The producers replied that no disrespect had been shown since 'the subject was treated seriously, there was nothing salacious, diverse views were represented, none were mocked, and so forth'.[46] Yet, as Green notes, that was no answer to the listeners who considered the whole matter utterly private and

---

[46] Green, Leslie (2010) 'Two Worries about Respect for Persons' in *Ethics* 120: 2, 212–31.

off-limits for public consumption, especially among non-believers. 'The lively radio banter profaned the sacred and made some believers feel as if they were being treated as specimens rather than citizens. Respect, they felt, required a modest silence in this area.'[47]

This may seem like a tricky problem for the dialogic condition, but it is not. The complaints from the Muslim listeners who found the programme offensive confirm rather than deny the importance of dialogic effort for genuine conviction. In choosing to communicate their objection, they confirmed (to that extent) their conviction about the privacy of sexuality.

3.5 Implications

According to the communicative principle of conscientiousness, the least credibly conscientious agent under consideration in this book is the evasive personal disobedient, who *ceteris paribus* is both willing to adjust her conduct to avoid the costs of non-conformity and unwilling to raise her cause in the arena of collective deliberation. The slightly more conscientious agent—the non-evasive personal disobedient—does not adjust her conduct to avoid the costs of non-conformity, but, unlike the civil disobedient or assistive disobedient, makes no effort to raise her cause for collective deliberation. It is for this reason that I use the terms 'personal objection' and 'personal disobedience' rather than 'conscientious objection': *ceteris paribus* the conscientiousness of the personal objector can be doubted in light of the communicative principle of conscientiousness. The most conscientious agent here is the civil disobedient who paradigmatically acts in suitably constrained ways and bears the risks of being seen to defend her commitments. Her commitments might of course be wholly morally misguided, but she has the best case for being given whatever moral and legal protections we afford to conscientious disobedience.

This concludes my analysis of the communicative principle of conscientiousness. Before proceeding, let me make one cautionary note that follows from the last paragraph. We must not mistake any of the four elements of conscientiousness—consistency, universality, non-evasion, and dialogic effort—for something more meritorious than they are. We tend to be impressed by people who present themselves as caring deeply about something. And, we tend to be

---

[47] Green (2010), 212–31.

highly attentive to the consistency between their declarations and their conduct: Do they put their money where their mouth is? When they do, or seem to do, we tend to be highly responsive to their testimony about why we too should have the commitments they have. We tend to give them credit and rely on their testimony to gain confidence in things we do not know or have not yet experienced ourselves. These psychological facts about how we relate to people who are or appear to be conscientious should make us cautious because an assertion of moral conviction is not the same thing as actual moral conviction, and actual moral conviction is not the same thing as morally acceptable conviction. Therefore, we should not be too quick to attribute conscientiousness to someone. And, we should be attentive to the effect that our unreflective awe of conviction can have on any costs that the 'conscientious' person is asked to bear since those costs depend largely on how we respond to her. Even when we do plausibly attribute conscientiousness to someone, we should remember that this does not make her convictions or her conduct morally admirable. That said, as I argue in Chapters 4 and 5, it does positively affect how we ought to treat her since conscientiousness is linked to autonomy and dignity.

4. Ambiguities

There is an intricate relation between the descriptive notion of *conscientiousness* discussed in this chapter and the evaluative notion of *conscience* which I explore in the next chapter. I wish to close this chapter by noting an ambiguity in the treatment of these two concepts in one of the dominant liberal analyses of conscientious breach of law. In *The Authority of Law*, Joseph Raz describes *conscientious objection* in *objective* terms as:

a breach of law *for the reason* that the agent *is morally prohibited to obey it*, either because of its general character (e.g. with absolute pacifists and conscriptions) or because it extends to certain cases which should not be covered by it (e.g. conscription and selective objectors and murder and euthanasia).[48]

The phrase 'the agent is morally prohibited to obey [the law]' implies that, for an act to count as conscientious objection, first, there must be a

---

[48] Raz (1979), 263. Emphasis added.

genuine moral prohibition against following that law, and second, the agent must breach the law *for the reason* that it is morally prohibited. In other words, she must be both conscientious in her motivation *and* correct in her moral judgement that the law is morally wrong totally or in part. In a similar vein, Raz then says: '[Conscientious objection] is essentially a private action by a person who wishes to avoid committing moral wrong by obeying a (totally or partially) morally bad law.'[49]

By contrast, at other points (and in more recent writings), Raz characterizes *conscientious objection* in subjective terms as a violation of a law taken because the agent *believes* that obedience to the law contravenes morality.[50] He states that,

[The conscientious objector's] breach of law is committed because he *thinks* that it is morally wrong for him to obey the law on the ground that [as he believes] it is morally bad or wrong totally or in part.[51]

In a similar vein, Raz says that,

Conscientious objection is a private act, designed to protect the agent from interference by public authority... [The conscientious objector is] an individual asserting his immunity from public interference with matters he regards as private to himself.

The difficult case for evaluating how to treat conscientious objectors, Raz continues, is the case in which the conscientious objector proposes to act *wrongly* because he *wrongly* believes that the law is morally bad or wrong.[52]

Despite such shifts in language, it is the subjective, descriptive notion of personal conviction, and not the objective, evaluative notion of genuine moral responsiveness that Raz has in mind when he discusses conscientious objection and considers the implications of a good society recognizing a general right to conscientious objection. Briefly, Raz holds that such a general right would be problematic, as it would entail

---

[49] Raz (1979), 264.
[50] Raz, Joseph (2003a) 'Bound by their Conscience' in *Haaretz*, 31 December 2003.
[51] Raz (1979), 276. Emphasis added.
[52] Raz (1979), 276–8. As I noted in the Introduction to the book, an ambiguity in the understanding of conscience appears in international treaties, such as the Universal Declaration of Human Rights, where the concept of *conscience* figures prominently but is used both descriptively and evaluatively.

allowing persons to disobey the law for reasons of personal belief even when by doing so they act egregiously, such as the religious parents who decide not to take their severely ill daughter to a doctor for curable diabetes because they believe that healing should be done through prayer alone. Given the wrong and the harm that ensue in such cases, Raz says, the moral right not to be coerced by the law against our convictions is at most a *prima facie* right, that is, a defeasible right:

> It can be overridden to protect other values and ideals. This is inevitable, given that it is a right to do that which is in fact morally wrong which is given to people who will use it for that very purpose. To give it absolute importance is to prefer the morally wrong to the morally right whenever the agent has misconceived moral ideas however wicked.[53]

That said, operating in the background is the idea that, in at least some contexts, we should not be held liable for breach of duty (breach of law) if the breach is committed because we think the law is morally objectionable. A limited moral right not to be coerced to act against our own convictions is implied, Raz says, by an appropriate interpretation of humanism.[54] In Chapter 4, I endorse both a principle of humanism and a limited right to conscientious action, but argue that it should not be characterized as a right of *conscience* since that implies genuine moral responsiveness, but rather as a right of expression. As such, its scope is more limited than many liberal thinkers suppose. It also does not extend to many personal acts that negatively affect others' interests including those of our dependants. Moreover, in contrast with Raz, who takes a dim view of the idea of a right to civil disobedience, I argue that, to the extent that a principle of humanism implies that there is a moral right to engage in *conscientious* disobedience, this right applies more readily to civil disobedience than to personal disobedience.

Conclusion

This chapter has specified the core practices under consideration in this book, which are civil disobedience and personal disobedience. The former is a communicative breach of law. The latter is a

---

[53] Raz (1979), 281.   [54] Raz (1979), 286.

non-communicative and sometimes evasive breach of law. This chapter has also outlined the first of the two core concepts of this book, which is *conscientious moral conviction*. It has four key features: consistency, universal judgement, non-evasion, and dialogic effort. Together these comprise the communicative principle of conscientiousness, which underpins my view that the communicative practice of civil disobedience has better claims to the label of 'conscientiousness' than does non-communicative personal disobedience even though personal disobedience is commonly characterized as 'conscientious objection'. The notion of *conscientiousness* provides the conceptual foundation for one of the two strands of argument that I offer in this book in defence of civil disobedience. This conviction argument focuses, first, on persons as reasoning and feeling beings who are capable of forming deep moral commitments, and second, on the expressive and communicative efforts that such commitments imply.

Conscientious conviction is largely a descriptive property that is insufficient for *conscience*. This insufficiency is recognized in the objective, pluralistic account of conscience that I offer in the next chapter. It is also recognized, but not highlighted in more standard objective monistic accounts and subjectivist accounts of conscience. On a subjectivist account, conscience requires not just sincere and serious though possibly erroneous moral conviction about what is morally acceptable. It also requires the belief and attitude that our conduct *is* morally acceptable by our own lights. On an objective monistic account, conscience requires, in addition to well-founded moral conviction about what is right, the belief and the *reality* that our conduct is morally right. And, on the objective, pluralistic account that I defend, conscience requires genuine sensitivity to the pluralistic nature of morality and the moral quality of our conduct.

2
Conscience

Albert Einstein said of Mahatma Gandhi that 'Generations to come, it may be, will scarce believe that such a one as this ever in flesh and blood walked upon this earth'.[1] This quote captures just how extraordinary a figure Gandhi was in 20th century history. In his committed, non-violent, non-hating resistance of British rule in India, he achieved remarkable political change and offered an enduring model of serene goodness, which makes Einstein's quote so apt. Gandhi was someone who could say truly 'My life is my message'.[2] A similar statement may be made of Aung San Suu Kyi, the leader of the National League for Democracy in Burma, who was inspired by Gandhi, and who similarly adopted a stance of non-violent, non-hating resistance against the brutal dictatorship in Myanmar/Burma. Beginning in 1989, she endured the better part of 20 years under house arrest in isolation from her family before finally being released in 2010.

The lives of such people exemplify the second core concept of this book, which is *conscience*. This concept will occupy my attention in this chapter and the next. Let me briefly plot out the path of this chapter on the understanding that the details of my view may be oblique at this point, but hopefully will become clear as the discussion proceeds.

Recall from Chapter 1, that *conscience* is distinct from *conscientious moral conviction*. As I argued there, *moral conviction* is a largely descriptive property of deeply held though possibly mistaken moral commitment.

---

[1] Einstein, Albert (1950) *Out of My Later Years*. London: Thames and Hudson, 240.
[2] There is a dispute over whether Gandhi uttered this statement or wrote it down before leaving Calcutta for Delhi in 1947 in the hope of ending violence there between Hindus and Muslims.

It has the four features of consistency, universal-judgment, non-evasion, and dialogic effort. By contrast, as I will argue here, *conscience* is an evaluative property. It is a set of practical moral skills that stem from an inward knowledge of the workings of our own mind and heart. Having conscience means not just taking morality seriously (conscientiousness), but also being genuinely, self-consciously morally responsive. The moral reality that conscience makes us responsive to is, in my view, a fundamentally pluralistic one.

My conception of *conscience* seeks to respect the etymology of the English word 'conscience' which derives from the Latin *conscientia*—*con* (together) and *scientia* (knowledge)—meaning privity of knowledge or knowledge within ourselves. At the same time, my conception avoids both an amoral interpretation of this knowledge and a Christian interpretation of it.[3] In my view, for the inner knowledge and responsiveness of conscience to develop, we must cultivate practical wisdom, virtue, and objective moral integrity, but such knowledge and responsiveness are not the voice of God.

There are both conceptual and empirical grounds for the view of *conscience* that I espouse. The conceptual grounds are that inner *knowledge* of our own mind and heart requires, amongst other things, an absence of self-delusion including self-delusion about the moral quality of our own beliefs, intentions, and actions. This conceptual point gets us part of the way to an evaluative notion of *conscience*. The empirical grounds lie in the growing scientific evidence from the emerging field of contemplative neuroscience that a clear-headed absence of self-delusion is inextricably linked with the cultivation of wholesome states. There is evidence of an interdependence between cultivating wholesome states such as kindness, compassion, empathy, love, attention,

---

[3] The morally loaded concept of *conscience* was not one that animated ancient philosophers such as Plato and Aristotle. The concept of *conscience*, as we roughly understand it now, seems to have developed under Christianity, figuring in the writings of medieval philosophers and theologians such as Thomas Aquinas and Bonaventure, and acquired its special moral significance with the growth of Protestantism and then secular individualism. See Langston, Douglas (2001) *Conscience and Other Virtues*. University Park: Pennsylvania State University Press. John Skorupski observes that the English word 'conscience' originally included in its meaning what we now call 'consciousness' and 'self-consciousness'. It is only in the 17th century, in particular in John Locke's *Essay Concerning Human Understanding,* that the word 'conscience' came to be complemented by these other terms of 'consciousness' etc., and distinguished in meaning from them. 'Conscience' thus acquired its special moral meaning associated with moral seriousness, sincerity, self-assessment, and moral knowledge, while its other non-moral meanings became obsolete. See Skorupski, John (2010) 'Conscience' in *The Routledge Companion to Ethics*. London: Routledge.

generosity, and gratitude, on the one hand, and developing fuller and more accurate *practical* knowledge of the state of our own mind, body, intentions, and conduct, on the other. The evidence suggests that people who wholeheartedly cultivate wholesome states have a more accurate knowledge of how their own bodies and minds are functioning. They also have more accurate and detailed memories and perceptions of reality including perceptions of others' experiences.[4] Thus, conscience, as I characterize it, is not something that *all* people can claim to have and invoke as a shield against regulation or reproof.

One implication of my view of conscience is that there is no epistemic security in our untrained beliefs about our own mental states. Unless we cultivate wholesome states, we are neither infallible nor omniscient even in a qualified way about our own mental states. Indeed, until we have cultivated a considerable degree of conscience, we cannot know from our first-person perspective whether we are cultivating genuine conscience or mere conviction. (I expand on this point later.)

To develop my account, I shall begin by surveying some of the conceptions of *conscience* in the literature (Section 1). Although *conscience* is a somewhat neglected concept in contemporary debates, there are many different accounts of it in western philosophy. Some of these are objectivist. Others are subjectivist or relativist. Most of these accounts speak of our having '*a* conscience' almost like a body part that we have in the same way that we have a nose and a brain. Conscience is represented in these accounts as a guide, prompt, inner voice, inner

---

[4] For example, studies indicate that long-term meditation practice is associated with altered resting electroencephalogram patterns in the brain, suggestive of long-lasting changes in brain activity, and with changes in actual physical brain structure; fMRI scans of experienced practitioners of Insight meditation, which involves focused attention on internal experiences, indicate that they have thicker brain regions associated with attention, interoception, and sensory processing than do matched controls, including the prefrontal cortex and right anterior insula. Lazar, Sara W. et al (2005) 'Meditation experience is associated with increased cortical thickness' *Neuroreport* 28 November, 16(17), 1893–7. Also, studies indicate that the concern for others cultivated during loving-kindness-compassion meditation enhances affective processing particularly in response to sounds of distress, and that this response is modulated by the extent of persons' meditation training. The data indicate that 'the mental expertise to cultivate positive emotion alters the activation of circuitries previously linked to empathy... in response to emotional stimuli'. Lutz, Antoine et al (2008) 'Regulation of the Neural Circuitry of Emotion by Compassion Meditation: Effects of Meditative Expertise' in *PLoS ONE* 3:3, e1897. For a comprehensive bibliography of recent psychological and neurological research supporting my thesis, see Hanson, Rick with Mendius, Richard (2009), *Buddha's Brain*. Oakland: New Harbinger Publications.

policeman, critic, judge, or sentencer that either issues imperatives to us as 'demands of conscience' or holds us to account when we go astray, and that lets us know when we can rest easy, though not complacent, with a 'clear conscience'. Such characterizations can be misleading, simplistic, and unappealingly restrictive. First, conscience is a much more complex combination of skills, knowledge, experience, understanding, attitude, and effort than many of these accounts allow (Section 1). We should not speak of having *a* conscience any more than we should speak of having *a* rationality.[5] Conscience comes in degrees, and can be better developed in relation to some types of problems than others.

Second, there is more scope within *conscience* for celebration and goodwill towards ourselves than most accounts allow. We need not think that mere non-self-censure is the best we can hope to get from conscience. We can equally hope for delight and blissfulness (Section 2).

Third, given the complexity of practical reality, there must be an ever-refining alignment between conscience and experience that does not caricaturize conscience either as an infallible guide to objectively right action or as a relativistic, baseless source of self-satisfaction. Briefly, on infallibility, if the correct picture of morality is an objective and fundamentally pluralistic one as I think it is, then conscience could not be an infallible guide (or even a fallible guide) to morally *right* action as many defenders of an objective conception of *conscience* suppose, because the nature of morality precludes the possibility of unqualifiedly right answers to many fundamental moral questions. Rather, our conscience can improve as a guide to good conduct as our knowledge of our mind and heart develops. We can grow in our capacity to be self-consciously morally responsive where this includes being sensible of the irreducibly complex, pluralistic nature of morality.[6]

My effort to situate *conscience* within moral pluralism goes some way towards filling a gap in the literature. The pluralistic account of conscience is an under-explored account that can make sense of both the normative guidance of conscience and the commonsense notions of a *demand of*

---

[5] We can speak of having 'a conscience' in the same way that we can speak of having 'a knowledge', that is, we have a knowledge of something and we have a conscience of something.

[6] This discussion is about moral pluralism, not political pluralism.

conscience and a *clear conscience* (Section 2). There are other commonsense notions associated with conscience such as *liberty of conscience* that my view cannot accommodate. In my view, this kind of liberty is a liberty of *conviction*. And, there are still other commonsense notions such as a *right of conscience* that my view can accommodate, but understands differently from commonsense usage (see Chapter 4).

After defending a mundane notion of *conscience*, I show that we can extrapolate from it to a genuinely valuable ideal of conscience that is characterized by a sustained commitment to improving ourselves as moral beings, which is one element of a good human life (Section 3). This dynamic moral ideal of conscience as integrity and self-understanding contrasts with another putative moral ideal, which is the Virtuous Person. I show that the Virtuous Person is a questionable moral ideal for us when it is understood in static, immutable terms as a being of full and perfect virtue that necessarily lacks aspirations to improve morally (Section 4).

Although an ideal of conscience may seem distant from practical ethical debates about civil disobedience, there are potential practical pay-offs in explicating the features of this ideal. First, it opens up conceptual space for a richer and more generous view of conscience than those that see conscience principally as an *ex post* judge to whom we must answer and abase ourselves. Second, it offers a plausible alternative to popular subjectivist and relativist pictures of the commitments that a reasonably good society should accommodate. The conceptual and evaluative framework presented in what follows sets the stage for the discussions of responsibilities in Chapter 3, rights of conscience in Chapter 4, and the necessity defence in Chapter 6.

1. Common Conceptions of *Conscience*

Let me outline briefly some of the dominant conceptions of *conscience* in the literature. Two elements that are found either singly or together in most conceptions are 1) moral self-judgement, and 2) a (genuine or believed) source of moral knowledge.

1.1 Objective monistic conceptions

On the objective monistic conceptions of *conscience* defended by Joseph Butler and Immanuel Kant, the two elements of 1) moral self-judgement, and 2) source of moral knowledge are construed narrowly in self-directed, juridical terms.

For Butler, *conscience* is an unerring faculty of cool, reflective reason that dominates and orders our appetites, passions, and affections, thereby invariably directing human nature towards virtue while, regrettably, lacking the power to enforce its dicta. We must attend to our conscience to benefit from its infallible moral guidance.[7]

For Kant, conscience is backward-looking. Metaphorically speaking, it is our consciousness of an exacting internal tribunal or judge before which our thoughts accuse or excuse one another.

Every [person] has a conscience, and finds himself observed by an inward judge which threatens and keeps him in awe (reverence combined with fear); and this power which watches over the laws within him is not something which he himself (arbitrarily) makes, but it is incorporated in his being. It follows him like his shadow, when he thinks to escape. He may indeed stupefy himself with pleasures and distractions, but cannot avoid now and then coming to himself or awaking, and then he at once perceives its awful voice.[8]

Unsurprisingly, interpretations of Kant differ. Douglas Langston suggests that, for Kant, conscience possesses the duties that moral agents should follow to be morally good; and thus, Kant turns conscience into a universal moral judge whose judgements about duties are true not only for the agent whose conscience it is, but for all.[9] By contrast, Thomas Hill maintains that, in Kant's moral theory, *conscience* is not the same as *reason*, *judgement*, or *will*. 'It is not a moral expert with an intuition of moral truth or a moral legislator that makes moral laws or a moral arbitrator that settles perplexing cases.'[10] Rather, its role is restricted to that of an *ex post* 'inner judge' who scrutinizes our conduct and judges us

---

[7] Butler, Joseph (1983) *Fifteen Sermons Preached at the Rolls Chapel and a Dissertation upon the Nature of Virtue.* Stephen Darwall (ed.), Indianapolis: Hackett. Cited from Langston (2001), 80–2.

[8] Kant, Immanuel (1889 [1788]) *Critique of Practical Reason and Other Works on the Theory of Ethics,* trans. Thomas Kingsmill Abbott (4th revised edn). London: Kongmans, Green and Co., 321.

[9] Langston (2001), 83.

[10] Hill, Thomas (2002) *Human Welfare and Moral Worth, Kantian Perspectives.* Oxford: Oxford University Press, 280.

as guilty or innocent of either contravening our own reason-based judgement about morally right action or failing to exercise due care and diligence in forming the moral opinions that guided our action. Hill holds that, although Kant was willing to claim infallibility for conscience in its *ex post* analysis, the basic Kantian view of moral deliberation and judgement recognizes greater scope for error. Each of us must treat our final moral judgements as authoritative despite their fallibility. If we carefully make and rigorously follow our own best moral judgement, then we may live with a clear conscience even though this does not guarantee that our acts will be objectively right.[11]

1.2 Subjectivist conceptions

In contrast with the objective monism of Butler and Kant, other conceptions of *conscience*, such as the subjectivist conception offered by C. D. Broad, describe it more broadly and richly, though subjectively, as the combination of three related dispositions:

1. the *cognitive* disposition to reflect on, first, our own past and future actions to assess whether they are right or wrong, second, our own motives, intentions, emotions, dispositions, and character to consider whether they are morally good or bad, and third, the relative moral value of various alternative ideals of character and conduct;
2. the *emotional* disposition to feel remorse, guilt, and moral approval in respect of the moral characteristics which we believe these have; and
3. the *conative* disposition to seek what we believe to be good and to shun what we believe to be bad, and to do what we believe to be right and to avoid what we believe to be wrong, as such.[12]

In one sense, this conception of *conscience* is notably demanding with its tripartite dispositional requirements. In another sense, though, it is notably undemanding since none of these dispositions requires that we be either correct or justified in our moral judgements, feelings, and efforts. Indeed, in its starkest form, *conscience* thus conceived imposes no content restrictions on the objects that can animate us under the banner of morality. To have conscience in this view, it is enough that we believe we are reasoning, feeling, and acting as we should. It is worth

---

[11] Hill (2002), 281ff.
[12] Broad, C. D. (1973) 'Conscience and Conscientious Action' in *Conscience*. John Donnelly and Leonard Lyons (eds.), New York: Alba House.

noting, of course, that such a view of conscience can sit within either a subjectivist or an objectivist theory of morality. A moral theory might be subjectivist about conscience and objectivist about morality.

Although the radical content-insensitivity of a subjectivist account is undesirable partly because it drifts far from the etymological pier of *conscience* as inner knowledge of our own mind which requires the absence of self-delusion, nevertheless the multi-dimensional elements of this conception invite a more optimistic view of conscience than do the juridical conceptions of Kant and Butler. Here, a person who is developing conscience not only seeks to learn from past experience, but also reflects on how best to expand her own and others' moral horizons.[13] Here also, by giving an emotional dimension to conscience that is lacking in Kant's and Butler's conceptions, adequate space is given to its intuitive and affective elements: that burst of fellow-feeling, that jolt of horrified compassion at another's apparent plight, that instinctual spark of distressed empathy in the identification with another's apparent suffering.[14]

A less richly described subjectivist conception of *conscience* is put forth by John Rawls, who identifies a principle of equal liberty of conscience, agreed on in the original position, to secure the integrity of our moral and religious freedoms against the threat of an intolerant moral or religious majority. When reflecting on the space that the law should make for *conscience* so construed, Rawls states that there is a temptation to hold that the law must always respect the dictates of conscience. But, that cannot be correct, he says, since, as the case of the intolerant majority shows, the legal order must regulate our pursuits of our religious interests so as to realize the principle of equal liberty. And, it may certainly forbid religious practices such as human sacrifice; neither religiosity nor conscientiousness suffices to protect such practices. 'If a religion is denied its full expression, it is presumably because it is in violation of the equal liberties of others.'[15] Despite this check on 'full expression', Rawls' political liberal view of conscience is insufficiently demanding. It seems that, in principle, any sincere declaration of commitment can be as legitimate as any other, and give rise to the

---

[13] See Brownlee, Kimberley (2010b) 'Moral Aspirations and Ideals' in *Utilitas* 151: 3, 433–44.

[14] These descriptions of some of the emotions of conscience are drawn from Bennett, Jonathan (1974) 'The Conscience of Huckleberry Finn' in *Philosophy* 49, 123–34.

[15] Rawls, John (1971) *A Theory of Justice*. Harvard University Press, 205–8; 370.

expectation that no costs should be borne for having any particular commitment, equal liberty constraints aside, because liberty of conscience is so important.

In an even more radical vein, there are cultural relativist conceptions of *conscience* that, as Hill puts it, regard conscience as nothing but whatever cultural choice-guiding norms we happen to have internalized. Conscience is an instinctive, unreflective response to the socially instilled values of our culture, which disposes us on the basis of prudential self-interest to conform to group standards. In its extreme varieties, cultural relativist views of conscience are, Hill says, more than an empirical hypothesis about the origin of conscience in early socialization and the social function of the feelings attributed to it to maintain conformity. These views are distinctive in their deflationary stance on the nature and justifiability of moral beliefs. But, of course, the fact that cultural norms and standards differ and 'that people tend to internalize their local standards do not, by themselves, prove anything about objectivity in morals or any other field'.[16] Disagreements may be mere appearances; or they may be genuine but resolvable; or they may be unresolvable, but not undermine objectivity, as defenders of moral pluralism take pains to show.

Constrained by space, I shall not seek to discredit fully either a subjectivist conception or an objective monistic conception of *conscience*. My reason for not challenging the subjectivist conception is that it highlights a genuinely important piece of conceptual and evaluative territory, namely, the territory of the descriptive property of conscientious moral conviction that I explored in Chapter 1, and which I show later is linked to autonomy. My quarrel with the subjectivist conception is that it regards that territory as the sum total of what it means to have conscience, which leaves unacknowledged the equally important conceptual and evaluative space of genuine, self-conscious, moral responsiveness.[17] My reason for not challenging the

---

[16] Hill (2002), 287–8.
[17] Michelle Madden Dempsey has suggested in correspondence that there is a possible parallel between the subjectivist conception of *conscience* and the legal positivist conception of *law*. For the legal positivist, law is valid (ie it exists) in virtue of its sources, not its merits. Yet, even the legal positivist will acknowledge that this account of law's validity does not begin to provide a full account of the nature of law. Similarly, a subjectivist conception of *conscience* might claim that conscience exists in virtue of its subjective formation and acceptance by the one whose conscience it is, that is, it exists in virtue of the fact of its being posited by the individual. Yet that account does not begin to provide the sum total of what it means to have conscience.

objective monistic conception is more strategic. To discredit this kind of conception, it would be necessary to wade into longstanding debates about the correct view of the nature of morality, which cannot be pursued satisfactorily in this space. Rather, I shall put aside monism and analyse *conscience* within a pluralistic moral framework, on the grounds that the latter project is a neglected one which, given the prominence and plausibility of moral pluralism, is worth pursuing even if no final resolution can be reached about the correct view of morality.

A conception of *conscience* situated within moral pluralism sits at a distance from the conceptions just discussed, which, despite their divergences, share some features that a pluralism-situated conception might seem to lack. First, these conceptions are each attentive to the psychological pressure of the 'awful voice' of conscience, which we feel in exigent cases as an absolute, unyielding duty to do what is right.

Second, partly in consequence of this, these conceptions each provide conceptual space for the commonsense notion of a *demand of conscience*. In subjectivist conceptions, such a demand draws its force from the psychological pressure that we feel toward our (possibly mistaken) convictions of what morality requires. In objective monistic conceptions such as Butler's or Kant's, a demand of conscience would combine the act that morality actually requires with our heightened sensitivity to its moral force. And, in a more modest, objective monistic conception such as Hill's, a demand of conscience would be the act that our final reflective moral judgement takes to be morally required.

Third, each of these conceptions can make sense of the commonsense notion of a *clear conscience*, and can specify conditions under which we may have one. A clear conscience results, on the subjectivist conception, from acting as we genuinely believe is right and required, and on the objective monistic conception from acting rightly and virtuously or (in Hill's view) acting as our final, reflective moral judgements would have us act.

By contrast, it is less obvious that these core notions surrounding conscience can be given plausible treatment within a fundamentally pluralistic moral framework.[18] Moral pluralism comes in different

---

[18] Moral pluralism is marked by discontinuities in our measurements of value. Elinor Mason highlights the following points on this. First, moral pluralism is about the structure or shape of morality. As such, it cuts across the distinctions between objectivism, relativism, and subjectivism. A pluralist theory can be either objective or non-objective since pluralism is about how many elements are fundamental, and not about the meta-ethical status of those elements. Second, although moral pluralism is often contrasted with the three traditional

strengths of course. This means that some of the challenges for situating conscience within it depend on the particular account of moral pluralism that we embrace. The central tenets of the account that I shall work with here are as follows: 1) there are several different, fundamental moral values that 2) are not reducible to a single ultimate value and 3) cannot be lexically ranked or 4) added together without discontinuities including incommensurabilities, and 5) will, in consequence, often conflict in practice requiring the sacrifice of one for the sake of another; yet, despite this, 6) reason-vindicating choices can often be made between these irreducibly plural values. I appreciate that other versions of moral pluralism deny incommensurability, and still others accept incommensurability and deny that reason-vindicating choices can be made between irreducibly plural values. The variety of moral pluralism that I am working with is a strong one, though not the strongest. I have chosen it because it is credible, but also more importantly because it does not solve in advance the questions that confront the effort to situate conscience within a pluralistic moral framework.

Now, a critic might doubt whether, within the pluralistic framework I have outlined, conscience can play those useful roles of option-ranker, guide, director, task-master, prompt, and judge, which both subjectivist and objective monistic accounts attribute to it. If morality is shaped by competing moral demands and incommensurable moral values, then what is a *demand of conscience*? If morality is marked by tragedy, regret, and moral residue, then what is *a clear conscience*? And, if

approaches to morality—deontology, consequentialism, and virtue ethics—it is compatible with each of these three ways of thinking about morality because there are different ways of thinking about what the fundamental elements are. Those elements may be seen as good(s) to be realized in the world in the way that consequentialists or virtue ethicists approach morality, or they may be seen as sources of moral obligations, imperatives, rules, and principles in the way that deontologists approach morality. They may also be seen as a combination of these things. Third, pluralism can operate at different levels. Some versions of it are foundational; some are normative; some are decision-procedural. The real contrast for moral pluralism is moral monism. The question is whether there is a single, overarching good or principle under which all others can be subsumed. All pluralist theories deny this. Fourth, moral pluralism highlights the fact that there are discontinuities in our measurements of value. Such discontinuities come in different strengths, the most extreme form of which being incommensurability or incomparability—when two values cannot be ranked at all. As Mason notes, pluralists disagree over both whether pluralism entails incommensurabilities, and, if it does, on what incommensurability entails for the possibility of choice. I endorse the view that there are incommensurabilities, but deny that this means rational choice is impossible. For an excellent discussion of these and other core features of moral pluralism, see Mason, Elinor (2011) 'Value Pluralism' in *The Stanford Encyclopedia of Philosophy* (Fall 2011 edn), Edward N. Zalta (ed.): <http://plato.stanford.edu/archives/fall2011/entries/value-pluralism/>.

the notion of *a clear conscience* is intelligible, could there be realizable conditions under which we could have one? Also, if morality admits of no unqualifiedly right answers to fundamental moral questions, then what is the normative status of whatever guidance conscience purportedly gives? Indeed, by what criteria could conscience guide us at all since whatever ranking of fundamental value options conscience might yield would stand in contrast with the actual unrankability of those values (a fact to which we would be sensitive if we have adequate conscience), and since whatever standards conscience might establish could not be those of 'right' action without this implying a disingenuous, wilful, or schizophrenic blindness to the reality of inescapable moral pluralism? In short, what meaningful role, if any, can conscience as self-conscious moral responsiveness play within moral pluralism?

These various worries are less troubling than they appear. It is undeniable that, in adopting a pluralistic moral framework, I am giving up the advantage of relative simplicity, which is the prerogative of monism. But simplicity can just be bluntness and crudity dressed in a tailsuit. Although more complicated than monism, moral pluralism has the advantages of subtlety and context-sensitivity. These assets can be drawn on to show that pluralism can accommodate 1) *demands of conscience*, 2) scope for error, and 3) *a clear conscience*. Let me examine each in turn.

2. Conscience and Moral Pluralism

2.1 *Demands of conscience*

Having conscience does not entail moral infallibility. Rather, it entails genuine, self-conscious, moral responsiveness, which comes in degrees. If we have an adequate degree of conscience in a given area, then our decision-making in that area will be informed by a genuine appreciation for the legitimacy of different values. However, our decision-making is not thereby imperfect. This is because there is no perfect, utopian commensuration of values with which our efforts may be compared. Therefore, when our adequate degree of conscience leads us to identify a given value as overridingly important—as a moral demand of conscience—we can recognize it as such while being sensible of the competing values that will be forfeited in honouring it.

In broad terms, the moral demands that we should privilege, and that we will privilege if our conscience is adequately well developed, are those that track the moral responsibilities that are ours. And many, if not most, of our moral responsibilities are ours in virtue of our moral roles. A *moral role* gives rise to specific kinds of moral reasons that apply, in virtue of their content, to us as the holder of the role.[19] When we come to hold a given moral role, this affects our moral responsibilities in significant ways. Some reasons now apply to us that did not apply to us before. And, some reasons that may have applied to us before as ordinary reasons now apply to us as categorical mandatory reasons (duties). And some reasons that may have applied to us categorically now apply either only as ordinary reasons or not at all. Drawing on Joseph Raz's examples, the moral reason to care for our child applies, in virtue of its content, only to those of us who are parents. Other moral reasons apply in virtue of their content only to those of us who are pregnant women or trained swimmers and lifesavers, or trained healers and carers, or the adult children of elderly parents. In each case, the moral role identifies the typical or characteristic moral functions required of the holder by the interactions, relationships, and undertakings that define that moral role.

Our moral roles can come to be ours in a variety of ways. First, some moral roles become ours voluntarily and others become ours nonvoluntarily. We need not choose to be a parent to come to have the special moral responsibilities that go with being a parent. Second, some moral roles become ours formally and others informally. We need not make a formal acknowledgment of friendship and its commitments to come to have the special responsibilities of a friendship. Third, some roles come to be ours individually and others come to be ours collectively with other people. The assumption of such moral roles can often be the result of coordination problems and situational differences. For instance, we may collectively have a moral responsibility to feed and clothe a group of starving people. But, I have a responsibility to feed and clothe one subset and you have a responsibility to feed and clothe another subset owing to our relative proximity to each subset and the efficiency of coordinating our collective responsibilities. Finally, some moral roles come to be ours immediately and others come to be ours over time from continued behaviour and developed expectations.

Despite the variety of ways we can come to have moral roles and the multiplicity of forms those roles can take, when our conscience is

---

[19] See Raz, Joseph (2004) 'Incorporation by Law' *Legal Theory*, 10, 1–17.

adequately developed, we will typically recognize when we hold such roles and will be responsive to the special responsibilities they generate. (I develop my account of moral roles and their responsibilities in Chapter 3. Broadly speaking, I take a commonsense, humanistic view of the kinds of roles that are genuine moral roles.)

As this suggests, there is an importantly personal dimension to the moral demands of conscience in that they will vary according to our moral roles, responsibilities, and value-commitments. By embracing the values and responsibilities that make for goodness or excellence in one moral domain, such as parenting or nursing, we may have to put aside the values that would make for excellence in other moral domains, such as mediation or dispensing justice. Nelson Mandela committed himself to freeing black South Africans from oppression and, as a result, neglected his wife and children. He was separated from them for 27 years and then returned to them as father of the nation. Similarly, Aung San Suu Kyi has devoted her life to realizing democracy in Burma. Due to her extended house arrest, she was unable to be a mother to her sons or a wife to her husband whom she could not visit in the UK when he was dying because of the risk that the military regime would not let her back into Burma.

Moreover, by incorporating certain values fully into our lives through our moral responsibilities we may become *unable* to cultivate or internalize fully the values essential for other morally valuable ways of living. This is the reality, Raz observes, of competitive moral pluralism; it recognizes not only the validity of distinct, incompatible moral values, but also the validity of moral values that, given human nature, tend to encourage intolerance of other values and virtues.[20] And yet it is in this competitiveness that we find the answer to the concerns about guidance and decision-making. Our sustained and deeply-held allegiance to certain fundamental values and moral responsibilities, which are ours in virtue of our moral roles, skills, and circumstances, enables us non-arbitrarily to settle contests between competing values. Excepting emergencies in which our normal moral responsibilities and values may have to be put aside, our moral roles and value-commitments inform our ability to act in morally acceptable ways. This is because *ceteris paribus* we are better placed to act well in relation to the values we have internalized than in relation to

---

[20] Raz, Joseph (1986) *The Morality of Freedom*. Oxford: Oxford University Press, 404.

those we have not, and we are better placed to realize the values we have internalized than are people who have not internalized those values.

Thus, the personal dimension of conscience, that is, the unique inner heart and mind of morality, can explain in part the sense of urgency and categoricity that attends a moral demand of conscience. It is when our moral responsibilities and values come under serious threat that we should feel the urgent psychological pressure of conscience. However, if our conscience is sophisticated and well developed, this psychological pressure will not prompt us to run roughshod over others' chosen values or morality in general. The personal dimension of conscience is informed by a sensitivity to the value of tolerating, respecting, and, if possible, appreciating other morally acceptable commitments and roles, which our own values otherwise may lead us to judge unfavourably. Thus, the personal dimension of conscience is very different from the subjectivism of descriptive conscientiousness even though the psychological pressure of the two may feel the same. The pressure may feel the same because, first, bad rules and commitments can be as difficult to adhere to as good ones can be, and second, the first-person experience of conscientiousness may be indistinguishable (much of the time) from the first-person experience of cultivating conscience.[21]

On this last point, as I noted at the outset, one implication of my view of *conscience* is that there is no epistemic security in our untrained beliefs about our mental states. Unless and until we cultivate wholesome states, such as loving kindness, compassion, gratitude, attention, awareness, and generosity, we are neither infallible nor omniscient even in a qualified way about our own mental states. Consequently, most of us will be unable to determine whether we are cultivating conscience or merely cultivating conscientious conviction. This fact about our first-person experience can explain in part our sensitivity to people who assert 'conscience' in defence of bizarre and offensive practices. They cannot know from their first-person perspective whether it is conscience or just conviction that they have cultivated. I assume, though, that once we have cultivated conscience to a significant degree, we will have sufficient wisdom to discern that we are indeed becoming genuinely morally responsive.[22]

---

[21] Although his conception of *conscience* differs from mine, Jonathan Bennett rightly notes that 'The problem of conscientiousness can arise as acutely for a bad morality as for any other: rotten principles may be as difficult to keep as decent ones.' Cf Bennett (1974), 123–34.

[22] I thank Eve Garrard for highlighting these points.

Finally, as noted earlier, the personal dimension of conscience is broadly sensitive to emergencies in which values that we are not personally invested in, such as perhaps the non-contingent basic needs of strangers, have a pressing claim on our attention. In such emergencies, if we have adequate conscience, we feel much the same urgency to protect those needs that we feel in more personal cases to protect the values we espouse. So for example, if others' basic subsistence needs are being grossly undermined by current laws, and the values we prize such as free expression are not being undermined, then *ceteris paribus* we should place greatest weight on the demands that basic subsistence generates irrespective of our other moral responsibilities. And we will do so if we have adequate conscience. (I return to the topic of non-contingent needs in my discussion of the necessity defence in Chapter 6.)

As this suggests, conscience is operative both in the identification of our *pro tanto* duties and in the assessment of our all things considered duty. A moral demand of conscience begins as a genuine *pro tanto* moral duty to which we are cognitively and motivationally responsive. But, since we can feel the force of more than one value-commitment, it is our intuitive or deliberative appreciation that one duty must be prized before others that translates it *ceteris paribus* into our all things considered moral duty.

2.2 *Scope for error*

The '*ceteris paribus*' of the last sentence is an acknowledgment of the fact that our conscience is not always well developed. Having conscience means being self-consciously morally sensible and responsive but, in its mundane form, it is inevitably incomplete and erratic. It comes in degrees. We can be skilled at addressing some kinds of moral problems, and unskilled at addressing others. We can improve in our efforts over time or we can regress and become apathetic or hateful. As Hill notes, we can be distracted by prevailing social norms; we can be given poor moral training as children; we can be subject to fears and prejudices or inculcated into false ideologies; we can be emotionally fragile or threatened, all of which can imitate or distort the guidance of conscience, especially if we have dulled it by frequently disregarding it.[23]

---

[23] Hill (2002), 284.

Thus, although, in my view, there is a non-negligible, minimum threshold of moral responsiveness that must be satisfied for us to have conscience, nevertheless there is considerable scope for variation along a continuum of practical skill. And, consequently, there is considerable scope for error in the moral efforts that flow from our conscience according to the degree to which we have it. Let me note four kinds of errors that can occur: 1) a conative error, 2) a cognitive and conative error, 3) a cognitive and affective error, and 4) an affective error. I will flesh out these different errors with the help of the Red Cross, Thomas Stockmann, Huckleberry Finn, and a callous driver.

First, although we may correctly identify a given moral value as a value and reasonably make a commitment to it, nonetheless we may do much that is wrong by honouring it at the expense of other values that we may or may not have embraced. For example, suppose that either out of group-loyalty or the instrumental value of neutrality such as that observed by the International Red Cross, we remain silent when we see torture taking place. We are not in the same position as the one who tortures, but we have disregarded the stringent moral demands of an emergency that *ceteris paribus* should be overriding demands of conscience.[24] As the poet Ella Wheeler Wilcox puts it, 'To sin by silence, when we should protest, makes cowards of men'.[25] This error is principally a conative error, but it can stem from deeper cognitive or affective inadequacies in our conscience.

Second, although we may correctly identify a given moral value as a value and justifiably rank it before other values in a given context, it does not follow that the act we take in support of it best honours it. In Henrik Ibsen's play *Enemy of the People*, Dr Thomas Stockmann assumes incorrectly that he will be heeded and appreciated when he informs his town that the popular new tourist baths, which he helped to build, are contaminated with waste from the local tannery and making tourists sick. He is correct in thinking that it would be morally wrong to allow the baths to stay open unchallenged; and he is correct in thinking that he is correct on this point. But, he is mistaken in thinking that his belligerent whistleblowing against the contamination will best honour the moral values of safety, respect, and common good. He would have

---

[24] Of course, the neutrality and mission of the International Red Cross could be jeopardized if they spoke out against torture in public.
[25] Wheeler Wilcox, Ella (1914) 'Protest' in *Poems of Problems*. W. B. Conkey, 154.

done better to choose less antagonistic means to alert the town to the danger. In acting as he does, he honours the value of honesty (and adheres to that extent to the communicative principle of conscientiousness), but at a high price to other values. His error, such as it is, is a conative and cognitive error.

I do not mean to imply that our morally legitimate efforts must always succeed for us not to err in our exercise of conscience. It would be odd to say that German citizens who wholeheartedly opposed the Nazis during the 1930s did not have adequate conscience because they failed to prevent the Nazis from coming to power and engaging in atrocities. Rather, my thought about the Stockmann case is that the error in his practical moral reasoning lay in his belief that he would be heeded and that his efforts would promote the moral values that he creditably endorsed.

Third, although we may correctly identify a moral value as a value, it does not follow that we self-consciously appreciate that correct identification. In essence, our degree of conscience may be such that we are led, mistakenly, to believe that our planned act is morally wrong, and yet nonetheless believe justifiably that it is demanded of us. An example of this is Huckleberry Finn's decision that he'd rather be damned than return Jim to slavery. 'Alright, I'll go to Hell', he says. Huck genuinely believes that he does an unmitigated wrong in not exposing Jim, but decides that he does not care. His act is not one of natural wisdom, but of promise-keeping and dedication to a friend.[26] Yet, of course, Huck acts in the only morally acceptable way open to him. Undeniably, he correctly identifies and acts on the moral values of friendship, respect, and decency even though he does not self-consciously recognize them as such because they are not acknowledged as such by his society.[27] His unacknowledged act of conscience is an

---

[26] Cf Gopnik, Adam (2010) 'The Man in the White Suit' in *The New Yorker*, 29 November 2010. Also cf Bennett (1974).

[27] What Huck describes (mistakenly) as his 'conscience' is his feeling that he ought to return Jim to slavery. Twain presents the moment vividly: 'Jim said it made him all over trembly and feverish to be so close to freedom. Well, I can tell you it made me all over trembly and feverish, too, to hear him, because I begun to get it through my head that he was most free—and who was to blame for it? Why, me. I couldn't get that out of my conscience, no how nor no way. It got to troubling me so I couldn't rest; I couldn't stay still in one place. It hadn't ever come home to me before, what this thing was that I was doing. But now it did; and it stayed with me, and scorched me more and more. I tried to make out to myself that I warn't to blame, because I didn't run Jim off from his rightful owner; but it warn't no use, conscience up and says, every time, "But you knowed he was running for his freedom, and you could a paddled ashore and

intuitive, spontaneous one as such acts often are. Although his conscience is not fully developed since he is not self-conscious of the value of the moral demand it highlights, his case affirms a side-benefit of a rich view of moral responsiveness, namely, that we need not be philosophers to act in morally acceptable ways on morally acceptable grounds. Huck's error is principally a cognitive error. It is an affective error only to the extent that his conscience leads him to feel guilty for acting well.

Fourth, a different kind of emotional misresponse from Huck Finn's is one in which the degree of conscience we have does not give rise to appropriate emotions of regret and distress when the results of our conduct turn out badly even though we acted as well as could be expected. Consider the example of a driver who is proceeding with all due care but who cannot avoid hitting a child who has just run out into the street. The driver acts as well as can be expected of her, but nonetheless has inadequate conscience, in my view, if she responds to the tragedy as a bystander might do and not as the principal party who was causally involved in the tragedy.[28] There are two reasons for this. First, there is an epistemic difference between the driver and the bystander; the driver must confront the fact that there could always be a doubt about whether she could have done more to avoid an accident. She chose to get behind the wheel in the first place. Second, there is a positional difference between the driver and the bystander. The situation for the sympathetic bystander watching the event differs from that of the principal agent who has to make a decision and face the

---

told somebody." That was so—I couldn't get around that noway. That was where it pinched. Conscience says to me, "What had poor Miss Watson done to you that you could see her nigger go off right under your eyes and never say one single word? What did that poor old woman do to you that you could treat her so mean? Why, she tried to learn you your book, she tried to learn you your manners, she tried to be good to you every way she knowed how. That's what she done." I got to feeling so mean and so miserable I most wished I was dead... My conscience got to stirring me up hotter than ever, until at last I says to it, "Let up on me—it ain't too late yet—I'll paddle ashore at the first light and tell." I felt easy and happy and light as a feather right off. All my troubles was gone.' But, then, when it comes time to act, Huck hears Jim say: '"Pooty soon I'll be a-shout'n' for joy, en I'll say, it's all on accounts o' Huck; I's a free man, en I couldn't ever ben free ef it hadn' ben for Huck; Huck done it. Jim won't ever forget you, Huck; you's de bes' fren' Jim's ever had; en you's de only fren' ole Jim's got now."..."Dah you goes, de ole true Huck; de on'y white genlman dat ever kep' his promise to ole Jim." Well, I just felt sick...' and he doesn't give him away. Twain, Mark (1884) *The Adventures of Huckleberry Finn*, ch 16 (various edns).

[28] This example is borrowed from Postema, Gerald (1980) 'Moral Responsibility in Professional Ethics' in *NYU Law Review*, 55, 63–90.

effects of it. Examples include Jim's decision in Bernard Williams' *Jim and the Indians*,[29] and the warrior hero Arjuna's decision in Amartya Sen's example from the Indian epic the *Mahabharata*, who faces a war in which he knows he will kill many of his friends and family for whom he has affection.[30] These persons must live with the effects of the causal chains to which they contribute. The driver's error in the above case is principally an affective error. Even if it is true that she could not have acted otherwise and so is right to think the accident not her fault, she displays a lack of emotional recognition of the tragic nature of the event and her causal role in it.

2.3 A clear conscience

The notion of *a clear conscience* is a confusing one not least because it feeds into the idea of our having 'a' conscience like an object or body part that we possess and yet speak of as an entity somehow divorced from ourselves. What the notion of *a clear conscience* gets at, I take it, is a sense of moral ease and non-self-censure. The question here is: What does such a sense of moral ease mean under conditions of fundamental moral pluralism since in most, if not all, cases we cannot hope to act *rightly* without moral residue? Perhaps the moral of the story of moral pluralism is that moral ease is not so much unachievable as unintelligible. Given the ongoing inevitable complexity of moral life, perhaps we cannot make sense of the idea of resting easy as moral agents since there will always be values left unhonoured and duties left undone. Perhaps, we must persist in a permanent state of moral unease.

This overly bleak assessment can be rejected. First, there is nothing mysterious or unintelligible about the notion of moral ease within moral pluralism. Such ease is simply the state of being justifiably at peace with ourselves about our conduct, attitudes, and beliefs, which we can have when there is congruity between our well-founded beliefs about how we ought to act, ie moral demands of conscience, and how we are acting. In a catchphrase, the reality of pluralism is not our fault. Provided that we act with and for morally justifying reasons, we may

---

[29] Smart, J. J. and Williams, Bernard (1973) *Utilitarianism: For and Against*. Cambridge: Cambridge University Press.
[30] Sen, Amartya (2000) 'Consequential Evaluation and Practical Reason' in *The Journal of Philosophy* 97: 9, 447–502.

be morally at ease. So, to return to the examples of Nelson Mandela and Aung San Suu Kyi, each can feel morally at ease in neglecting his or her family since each acted for undeniably morally undefeated reasons by leading the democratic movements in their respective countries.

A critic may then ask, however, what would a state of moral *unease* be on this account? What would a 'troubled' or 'unclean' conscience be? The answer turns on the moral reasons that apply to us in virtue of our moral responsibilities. If a parent develops adequate conscience, he will rightly be troubled if he is neglecting his child for anything less than morally undefeated reasons. If a doctor develops adequate conscience, she will rightly be troubled if she is mistreating her patients.

Second, far from maintaining a state of perpetual moral unease or a state of unease punctuated by brief moments of reprieve, the multi-dimensional notion of *conscience* as self-conscious moral responsiveness allows us to celebrate our praiseworthy conduct, attitudes, and intentions. In the fullest sense, having conscience means being sensible of the greatness of our capacities for moral goodness, love, and kindness. It means taking pleasure in our moments of supererogation and virtuousness. It means celebrating any progress we make in moral development.

This rich image of conscience aligns with a core idea in the Buddhist tradition. Although Buddhism reputedly lacks a notion of *conscience*,[31] it does have a concept that aligns with my celebratory view of conscience. That notion is called the *bliss of blamelessness*. It captures what I regard as the best of what the mistaken phrase of 'a clear conscience' tries to articulate. The bliss of blamelessness is the happiness that comes from leading a life of objective integrity as well as we can.[32] And, in my view, such a life is made possible only through the cultivation of conscience as inner knowledge and moral responsiveness.

In what follows, I argue that, in its richest form, conscience is a genuinely valuable moral ideal for persons. As such, it is a model that we may use to orient our mundane efforts to improve as moral beings.[33]

---

[31] Chryssides, George (1999) 'Buddhism and Conscience' in *Conscience in World Religions*. Jayne Hoose (ed.), University of Notre Dame Press, ch 7.
[32] Baraz, James (2010) *Awakening Joy*. New York: Bantam, ch 5.
[33] The next section elaborates some ideas in Brownlee, Kimberley (2010a) 'Reasons and Ideals' in *Philosophical Studies* 151: 3, 433–44; and Brownlee, (2010b). See also Coady, C. A. J. (2008) *Messy Morality*. Oxford: Oxford University Press, ch 3.

3. An Ideal of Conscience

Let me first explicate the concept of an *ideal* since it is key to the full account of conscience I want to offer, and since ideals often figure in decisions to disobey the law. The concept of an *ideal* will also help to disambiguate conscience from what may appear to be a related, if not overarching, ideal of perfect virtue. I shall explain the difference between conscience and virtue. I shall also show that an immutable being of full and perfect virtue is an implausible moral ideal for us as persons.

An ideal is a model of an advanced state, excellence, or perfection around which we can orient our attention and seek to effect substantial changes in perspectives and practice. Ideals can guide us in the development of our attitudes, motivations, beliefs, reasoning, conduct, relationships, dispositions, and general character. Many ideals are paradigmatically personal in nature, such as athletic excellence, musical virtuosity, intellectual achievement, good parenting, true friendship, enlightened spirituality, and personal goodness. Other ideals are paradigmatically collective or public, such as lasting peace, global prosperity, and common good.[34] An ideal that is personal in nature may nonetheless be 'public' in the sense that it is dependent on other people for much of its meaning and for much of our success in cultivating it. Also, the effects of cultivating personal ideals are not limited to our associates and ourselves, but instead can contribute to the common wealth of the community.[35]

Some ideals are genuinely valuable. Others are not. Commonsense examples of genuinely valuable ideals include those I have just listed. Commonsense examples of disvaluable ideals include supreme domination, racial purification, and religious purification.[36] When an ideal is genuinely valuable, we have reason to admire both it and people's

---

[34] This distinction between personal ideals and public ideals picks out the identity of the typical pursuer of the relevant ideal without restricting that identity to any one kind of pursuer. Two or more people can strive together to realize a parenting ideal. An individual as an individual can be committed to a public ideal of community peace or social justice.

[35] Similarly, many so-called public ideals have a personal dimension in that, although common to the community, they influence, inspire, and affect the individual as an individual. To judges, for example, justice has a distinctly personal dimension. See Coady (2008), ch 3.

[36] In this discussion, I adopt a commonsensical view of genuine values. For an examination of the nature of value, see Raz, Joseph (2003b) *The Practice of Value*. Oxford, Oxford University Press; and Raz, Joseph (2001) *Value, Respect and Attachment*. Cambridge, Cambridge University Press.

efforts to cultivate it. When an ideal is not genuinely valuable we have no reason to admire either it or people's efforts to cultivate it as such.

The fact that we have reason to admire others' cultivation of a genuinely valuable ideal does not mean that we have reason to cultivate that ideal ourselves. We may admire the musical virtuoso or the world-class athlete without having reason to incorporate those ideals into our own comprehensive views of a valuable life. That said, not all ideals are optional. Some ideals have a claim on the attention of all of us. Commonsense examples are justice, truth, and goodness. To this list, as I will argue, we should add conscience.

When an ideal, be it valuable or disvaluable, has our deep commitment, it necessarily grips our imagination, claims our esteem, and forms a core focus of our lives. It motivates us to aspire not only to realize it, but to cultivate it *constitutively* in a manner in keeping with its spirit, and to do this even though it is presently unrealizable for us and may ultimately remain so. This description identifies at least four key features of ideals that distinguish them from both ordinary values and ordinary goals. These four features are: comprehensiveness, aspirationality, constitutive cultivation, and unrealizability. Some of these features have been explored by C. A. J. Coady and Nicholas Rescher. I elaborate them in this section with some revisions. Each of these features is, I argue, an attribute of conscience in its richest form.

3.1 Comprehensiveness and aspirationality

Our sincerely chosen ideals influence key domains of our lives in a way that has a comprehensive effect on our thoughts, actions, and feelings.[37] Ideals can be the animating objects of a life that is perceived both by the person living it and by others as meaningful. In this, ideals differ from ordinary goals, which need not be comprehensive, all-consuming, or (when valuable) meaning-giving. An educated person's ideal of intellectual achievement has a deeper and more comprehensive effect on the shape of her life than do her mundane goals of exercising regularly, reading good books, or getting a degree, even though, of course, the latter things can contribute to the cultivation of the former. Some of the scholar's mundane goals are contingent manifestations of non-contingent, constitutive elements of her ideal such as learning and improving. But, there is a multiplicity of ways in which learning and

---

[37] Coady (2008), 51–2.

improving may be instantiated. She need not take a degree or read good books to become knowledgeable. Moreover, there also can be different and possibly irreconcilable ideals of intellectual achievement. For example, different personality types and habits of mind are suited to different kinds of intellectual excellence. And, different strategies and attitudes towards learning are needed to cultivate these different kinds of excellence. As noted earlier, these attitudes can be competitive and prevent full appreciation of the values central to other admittedly valuable ideals. Finally, for any one ideal of intellectual achievement, there can be a multiplicity of ways in which that ideal might be cultivated (a fact that is true of many goals as well). And, there can be a multiplicity of constitutive elements of that ideal, not all of which are necessarily compatible with each other in practice.

A second core feature of ideals is their aspirationality. Our ideals orient our attention not only by informing our choices, but also by becoming the objects of our aspirations. We make our ideals the objects of our deepest longings and strivings for what is presently beyond us. Our *genuine* aspirations are the longings we have for things that are not only presently beyond us, but also evaluatively greater than some aspect of our current situation.[38] The attitude of aspiration distinguishes our relation to our ideals from our relation to our ordinary goals, which do not require of us the committed striving that ideals require. For example, a gardener may have an ordinary desire to achieve her ordinary goal of pruning her roses this week. No greater commitment is required.

Conscience exhibits both of the features of comprehensiveness and aspirationality. It can grip our imagination and claim our esteem. And, we tend to think that a life in which conscience is prized is a meaningful life. Indeed, the realm of conscience overlaps with the realm of great moral figures. We tend to be awed by both literary and historical figures such as Antigone, Socrates, Jesus, Gandhi, Rosa Parks, Martin Luther King Jr, Aung San Suu Kyi, and Liu Xiaobo, who are thought to be wise, to have great moral courage, and to be able to say creditably, 'Here I stand, I can do no other'.[39] Also, less positively, we tend

---

[38] That said, the phrase 'presently beyond' should not be taken to imply that an ideal is somehow literally 'beyond' or above those who espouse it. Given the constitutive nature of ideals, an ideal can be deemed 'presently beyond' us while lying within us as something that, in principle at least, can be cultivated.

[39] This declaration is attributed to Martin Luther.

to show deference to persons who *claim* to be led by conscience, irrespective of whether we have good reason to think they are, which, as I noted in Chapter 1, shows just how impressed we can be by mere assertions of deep moral conviction.

3.2 Constitutive cultivation

Coady observes that, when we are genuinely committed to an ideal, we do not simply take ideal-neutral steps to bring about the ideal in some remote future. Rather, we act now in light of our ideal and in keeping with the spirit of our ideal. The ideal comes to exist in us to a greater or lesser degree as we seek to live it.[40] In other words, the core behaviour that we undertake to cultivate our ideal is to varying degrees constitutive of that ideal itself and not merely an independent, instrumentally useful means for pursuing it. The expert musician comes increasingly to embody an ideal of virtuosity as she seeks to live it.

This echoes Aristotle's conception of *virtue*, which relies on a distinction between purely instrumental promotion of an end and constitutive promotion of that end. For Aristotle, the exercise of the virtues promotes the good of man in the constitutive sense.[41] Exercising the virtues is not a contingent, preparatory, or instrumental part of coming to live a good life. It is constitutive of such a life. This non-contingent, constitutive connection holds between all ideals (valuable or not) and the core conduct that we take to cultivate the ideals to which we are deeply committed. The activities that we take to cultivate our ideals will become increasingly constitutive of those ideals as we come to embody them to a greater or lesser degree.

Of course, we can cultivate ideals non-constitutively by, for example, philanthropically funding others' efforts to realize our ideals. As philanthropists, though, we are dependent on the efforts of those we fund to engage in the constitutive cultivation of the ideals. We cannot cultivate an ideal of global social justice, for example, unless the Oxfam volunteers that we fund actually engage in the constitutive acts of providing relief and support to victims of famine, disaster, and war. We may be just as psychologically invested in the ideal as the Oxfam

---

[40] Coady (2008), 57.
[41] cf Aristotle *Eudemian Ethics* (1228a ff). Aristotle's position, as summarized by Alastair MacIntyre, is that the good of man is constituted by a complete human life lived at its best, to which the exercise of the virtues is a central part. MacIntyre, Alasdair (1981) *After Virtue*. Notre Dame: University of Notre Dame Press, 139–40.

volunteers are, but our efforts to realize it are derivative of their constitutive cultivation of the ideal.

In the case of conscience, we can seek to cultivate it instrumentally by, for example, seeking to educate our children about moral matters. But, the cultivation of conscience in ourselves requires practical, constitutive cultivation because we cannot become genuinely, self-consciously morally responsive without gradually incorporating moral sensibility, virtue, and integrity into our lives.

3.3 Present unrealizability

There are at least two dimensions to the present unrealizability of ideals. The first concerns the *degree* of unrealizability. How likely is it that the present unrealizability will lift? The second concerns the *kind* of unrealizability or the reason for the unrealizability. Both of these dimensions vary across ideals. The degree to which an ideal is unrealizable is influenced by factors such as the circumstances and abilities of the parties aspiring to that ideal as well as the kind of ideal it is. For instance, some ideals are ideals for some people (a novitiate's spiritual ideal might be to resemble the Dalai Lama), but not ideals for other people (the novitiate's spiritual ideal is no ideal for the Dalai Lama himself). Other ideals are presently ideals for all people who would cultivate them (such as the ideal of global prosperity), but may become realizable in the future through changes in technological, economic, and cultural conditions. Still other ideals are presently unrealizable for all people and may well remain so (such as the philosopher's ideal of truth) even though they are, in principle, practically realizable. This last example is offered by Coady, who notes that it is possible that a philosopher might always make only true claims and sound arguments, but in all probability she will not succeed in doing so.[42]

The second dimension of unrealizability is a matter of kinds. Ideals differ in the ways in which they are unrealizable and the reasons for their unrealizability. One kind of ideal I call a *sustainability ideal*. Such an ideal requires us to sustain indefinitely a certain attitude, disposition, mode of conduct, state of affairs, or combination thereof. Even if the requisite attitude, disposition, conduct, or state of affairs is readily realizable, it is an ideal if its ongoing maintenance is unsustainable.

---

[42] Coady (2008), 59–61.

For example, although an ordinary adult may momentarily realize the elements that make a good parent, nevertheless 'being a good parent' in a comprehensive sense is an ideal for ordinary adults because, in all likelihood, they cannot sustain at all times the requisite combination of attitudes, dispositions, and conduct that make a good parent. To realize the ideal, the parent would have to have been a good parent yesterday, be a good parent all day today, be one tomorrow, and so on. For another example, being committed to improving ourselves morally is a sustainability ideal for most of us because the constituent element of *being committed* to moral cultivation is realizable in a single moment, but its ongoing maintenance is not.

A second kind of ideal I call a *great moment ideal*. It is a presently unrealizable but broadly specifiable event, objective, or experience. For example, Mandela and the ANC strove for decades to realize democracy in South Africa. 'It always seems impossible until it is done,' is how Mandela characterized it. Then, in 1994, the great moment of a democratic election was realized. For another example, for Aung San Suu Kyi and the National League for Democracy, the great moment of realizing democracy in Burma is, at the time of writing, still an ideal. But it is an ideal for which a glimmer of possibility begins to shine, through Aung San Suu Kyi's election in 2012.

A third, richer kind of ideal I call an *ongoing progress ideal*. This is an ideal of continued development of constituent elements. One example is improving as a parent. A person could always be a *better* parent than she is now or has been before. There may be no upper bound to parental virtuosity or, even if there were, that bound may lie beyond the present abilities of any actual parent.[43]

Although ideals lie along a spectrum of unrealizability in terms of both degree and kind, they are a distinct conceptual category from deep impossibilities such as living forever, travelling back in time, or giving birth to oneself,[44] which defy the imagination. Deep

---

[43] The degree to which a given ideal is unrealizable depends at least partly on the kind of ideal it is. It is reasonable to think, for example, that an ideal of sustaining realizable elements lies closer to the realm of the realizable than an ideal of successfully or progressively realizing not readily realizable elements. Sustaining the attributes of an adequately good citizen may be a more realizable ideal than sustaining those of a good parent, and sustaining the attributes of a good parent may be more realizable than momentarily achieving the attributes of a great parent, and momentarily realizing those elements is more readily realizable than sustaining them.

[44] I have borrowed this example from John Gardner.

impossibilities defy the imaginative contemplation of how to endeavour with appropriate focus to realize them. By contrast, ideals originate in the use of the imagination as models of advanced states, excellence, or perfection that can animate us to achieve greater things than we believed possible.[45]

When specified fully, conscience, with its value-oriented cognitive, affective, and conative dimensions, lies beyond what is readily realizable for most, if not all, of us in light of its difficulty both as an exercise in sustainability and as a project of ongoing development. There are plausible ideals of conscience of each of the three kinds just noted: sustainability ideals of conscience, great-moment ideals of conscience, and ongoing-progress ideals of conscience. The three interrelated dispositions of conscience that shape any one of these ideals are the following:

1. the *cognitive* disposition to reflect on, first, our own past and future actions to assess whether they are right or wrong, second, our own motives, intentions, emotions, dispositions, and character to determine whether they are morally good or bad, and third, the relative moral value of various alternative ideals of character and conduct;
2. the *emotional* disposition to feel remorse or approval in respect of the moral characteristics that these actually have; and
3. the *conative* disposition to seek what is good and to shun what is bad, and to do what is morally justifiable and to avoid what is morally unjustifiable.

As my discussion suggests, what is an ideal of conscience for one person can differ from what is an ideal of conscience for others. This is because, first, what comprises an ideal of moral responsiveness will vary from

---

[45] That said, it is too simple to say that imaginability tracks practical possibility and that imaginative opacity tracks intractable impossibility or necessary hypotheticality because some cases of genuine impossibility, such as my jumping 100 feet in the air, are readily imaginable and some cases of imaginative opacity, such as the experience of sleepwalking, are not only practical possibilities, but actualities. For a discussion of imaginative opacity and necessary hypotheticality, see Brownlee, Kimberley and Stemplowska, Zofia (2010) 'Trapped in an Experience Machine with a Famous Violinist: Thought Experiments in Normative Theory', *MANCEPT Working Papers* <http://www.socialsciences.manchester.ac.uk/disciplines/politics/about/themes/mancept/workingpapers/documents/TrappedianExperienceMachinewithafamousViolinist/pdf>. There is a more general ambiguity about ideals as objects of the imagination, which is their status in the landscape of value. Since they originate in the mind, can they be genuinely valuable in any mind-independent sense? The answer lies in thinking about more concrete objects of value. A great poem is conceived in the mind. So too is a stunning painting or a moving concerto. There is no reason to deny that these things are of value simply because they are products of human cognition and creation. The same is true for a genuinely valuable ideal generally conceived; it originates in the imagination but is a model of genuine excellence.

person to person given the personal dimension of conscience, and second, what is unrealizable will vary from person to person given the differences in persons' moral development. For example, whereas a plausible ideal of conscience for a psychopath (though he is unlikely to embrace it) would be to cultivate ordinary moral judgements and acceptable conduct, a plausible ideal of conscience for a moral exemplar such as Gandhi would be highly sophisticated and impressive.

3.4 Value

The value of genuine ideals of conscience seems difficult to deny. If we were to realize an ideal of conscience, we would reflect better than we do on the moral quality of our past actions, emotions, intentions, attitudes, and beliefs. We would also reflect better than we do on our plans for future action as well as alternative possible ideals of character and conduct. And, if we realized a fairly sophisticated ideal of conscience, we would seek to learn from past experience; we would consider how best to expand our moral horizons; we would cultivate a future-oriented awareness of possibilities for moral development; we would live much of our life in a range of wholesome states including kindness, compassion, generosity, forgiveness, and love; and, we would attend to other persons' opportunities to flourish. In short, we would have integrity.

The absence of a commitment to cultivating conscience invites moral inattentiveness, carelessness, indifference, apathy, emotionally stunted growth, self-delusion, and short-sightedness. These are all at odds with integrity, self-respect, and moral development. For these reasons, ideals of conscience have a claim on the attention of us all. Let me now consider three objections to my account.

4. Conscience and Virtue

One possible objection to an ideal of conscience is that it subsumes all of personal morality under its banner.

In reply, having conscience, even in an ideal form, would not give us either omnipotence or omniscience about morality. In principle, we could have a richly developed conscience and still act wrongly all things considered because we never have complete knowledge of all relevant facts, and because we cannot control the full effects of our actions. Since we have imperfect information, we may come to have some attitudes and emotions that are unfounded, though they are in-keeping with how we ought to feel and think if facts were as we think they are and we have done all that can reasonably be done to be fully aware of the relevant facts.[45a]

This objection may be recast as a second objection that the ideal of conscience identifies no distinctive conceptual space from that occupied by an ideal of virtue.

In reply, first, conscience undoubtedly shares some important features with virtue. One of them is its calculative elusiveness.[46] Like spontaneity, virtue, and many other moral qualities, conscience is calculatively elusive because it cannot be deliberatively internalized or calculated over at a first-order level without self-defeat. As Philip Pettit notes with the example of spontaneity, to be spontaneous is to be uncalculating, and no calculative pyrotechnics can allow spontaneity to be deliberatively internalized. In Jon Elster's phrase, it is an essential by-product, not something that can be pursued in our individual choices.[47] The same is true of conscience. To be conscience-driven means that we do not act directly for the sake of conscience, but rather we act because we love someone or because some need is pressing. To be responsive to conscience is to be aware but uncalculating.

However, second, although conscience shares features with the ideal of virtue, it is not synonymous with at least one standard version of that ideal. That version is full and perfect virtue, and it requires both something more than moral responsiveness and something other than ongoing commitment to, and progress in, the cultivation of moral ability. In its purest manifestation in the Virtuous Person, full and perfect virtue does not allow for the possibility of error, something which the ideal of conscience can accommodate.

In other writing, I have raised doubts about the intelligibility of the putative moral ideal of an immutable and perfect Virtuous Person who has a deeply entrenched, multifaceted mindset and disposition to act in

---

[45a] This kind of imperfection is distinct from the error that Huck Finn makes because, even if the facts were otherwise, it's not the case that Huck ought to feel he should return Jim to slavery.

[46] As Philip Pettit and Geoffrey Brennan say: 'The lustre which unselfconscious involvement gives to behaviour is an example of a calculatively elusive consequence. It is a benefit which is reliably produced by the unselfconscious predisposition but which evaporates under a regime of sustained action-calculation.' Cf Pettit, Philip and Brennan, Geoffrey (1986) 'Restrictive Consequentialism' in *Australasian Journal of Philosophy* 64: 4, 438–55.

[47] Elster, Jon (1983) *Sour Grapes*. Cambridge: Cambridge University Press, ch 2. Cited from Pettit, Philip (1988) 'The Consequentialist Can Recognise Rights' in *The Philosophical Quarterly* 38: 150, 42–55.

the right way at the right time on the basis of the right reasons with the right attitude, intentions, and expectations. First, the intelligibility of such a being may be doubted on value pluralism grounds. That said, I do not doubt the intelligibility and possibility of virtuous persons with a small 'v' and small 'p' as mutable beings struggling for goodness.

Second, irrespective of its conceptual intelligibility, the Virtuous Person appears to be implausible as a *moral* model for us as persons because it necessarily lacks an aspiration to improve morally because moral improvement is not presently 'above' such a being. Moral improvement is simply not possible for such a being. Yet, an aspiration to improve morally is, as I argue elsewhere, an important part of a morally good life for persons, and thus is a requisite element of a plausible moral ideal for persons.[48]

Without the possibility of aspirations to improve morally, the Virtuous Person begins to look like a deep impossibility. It is difficult to imagine what form a being who possessed full and perfect virtue and consequently lacked moral aspirations would take. It is difficult to imagine how such a being would conduct herself.

Put more gently, the Virtuous Person may be likened to an angel in that she would be good, but not in the way that humans are good. If angels existed, they would necessarily lack one type of goodness that humans have, namely, the goodness that comes from having to struggle to be good. A true angel could not be good in this way because she could never have to struggle to be good, and thus could not understand this kind of goodness because she would not be of a nature to experience it.[49]

Now, a critic might say that this analogy with angels shows that I have used a caricature of the Virtuous Person. The Virtuous Person is, if nothing else, a *person*, and hence comes with all of the temptations, foibles, and eccentricities that make persons persons. So, the Virtuous Person must fall along the same spectrum of goodness as wise persons, such as Jesus, the Buddha, Gandhi, and Suu Kyi, since she must have

---

[48] Cf Brownlee (2010b).

[49] I thank Steve de Wijze for assistance in thinking about the nature of angels. As an aside, in other writing, I also suggested that, assuming its intelligibility, the Virtuous Person could not even act as an advisor to us because she would have no understanding of what it is like to be less than perfectly virtuous. Yet, herein may lie one moral aspiration for a Virtuous Person, namely, the aspiration to come to understand what it is to be less than virtuous so that she may guide us in how to act and how to improve morally. One challenge to this thought is that such understanding might not be possible, in principle, for the Virtuous Person to acquire, in which case she could have no aspiration to achieve it just as we can have no aspiration to fly by flapping our arms.

the essential properties of persons. So, the 'full and perfect virtue' of the Virtuous Person must be 'the fullest and most perfect virtue that human beings are capable of realizing', which could fall short of, and be different from, the virtue of angels and gods.

It is possible to acknowledge this response while still maintaining that the Virtuous Person is an impossibility in itself and not a model for persons. The reason, which I have not highlighted in other writing, is that the concept of the *Virtuous Person* assumes there is an upper bound to each and every one of the virtues that persons can cultivate. It assumes that there is a 'full and perfect virtue *for persons*'. But, there is no reason to think that all virtues have a built-in upper limit. Virtues such as loving kindness or compassion might be limitlessly progressive ideals. And, there need not be a built-in upper limit to our capacities to cultivate such virtues. Indeed, in the Buddhist tradition, which gives a rich articulation of kindness and compassion, these virtues are said to be unlimited. Hence, speaking of such virtues in terms of 'full and perfect virtue' is like speaking of the largest number in the unbounded infinity that is the natural numbers. Consequently, there can be no model for persons that embodies the fullest virtue of which persons are capable since there is no necessary limit to the virtues of which persons are capable.

A final, more general objection to ideals of conscience asks why we should talk about ideals at all. Why not focus on the more mundane degrees of conscience that we can presently realize? Or, indeed, why not focus on descriptive conscientiousness? My response is that an ideal of conscience provides the background explanation for why liberal societies should take mundane conscience seriously. The ideal reveals the full value of this kind of personal capacity. It makes clear what it is that societies should embrace, respect, and even exhort their members to cultivate.

But, the worry may be weightier than this. The worry may be that any ideal, even a valuable ideal such as conscience, invites over-zealous dedication and single-minded fanaticism about what is valuable, which breed both hostility towards other concerns and a willingness to sacrifice all for the sake of the chosen ideal.

In reply, in the case of conscience, the worry about fanaticism is overstated since fanaticism is at odds with the very nature and value of the ideal of conscience that we are cultivating if we are cultivating it constitutively. The cognitive and affective states of self-conscious moral responsiveness are based on a deep inner knowledge of our own mind and heart. As such, they are incompatible with the blind, reckless passion of fanaticism. Conscience brings clarity and open-mindedness, which dispel blind passions and unreasonable commitments.

Conclusion

In this chapter, I have fleshed out the second core concept of this book, *conscience*. I have rejected both a theistic conception of *conscience* as the voice of God and a subjectivist conception of *conscience* as personal inclination. I have instead endorsed a non-theistic, objective conception of *conscience*, and have situated it within a pluralistic moral framework. In my view, *conscience* is a moral property of genuine, self-conscious, moral responsiveness. It makes us broadly aware of the actual moral quality of our own and others' conduct. To develop this responsiveness, we must cultivate practical wisdom, virtue, and objective moral integrity. In its richest form, the cultivation of conscience is the cultivation of a genuinely valuable, non-optional moral ideal. Such an ideal can inform how we, as a society, ought to view acts of non-conformity that are animated by conscience. In the next chapter, I specify the moral place for conscience within a reasonably good society.

3

Responsibilities

> Your Representative owes you, not his industry only, but his judgment; and he betrays, instead of serving you, if he sacrifices it to your opinion...
>
> —Edmund Burke[1]

Moral exemplars such as Gandhi and Aung San Suu Kyi, discussed in the last chapter, are not just diamonds pressed out of brutal regimes. Such exemplars can also be found in democracies, though the stakes are generally lower in democracies and hence the achievements less dearly bought. One example, which I discuss in what follows, is that of anaesthesiologists in California who refused to oversee capital punishment by lethal injection. Their refusals led to a state moratorium on capital punishment. That case contrasts with those of unreflective conformity with formal expectations. A tragic example of the latter is the case of two UK community support police officers who saw a child drowning in a pond and instead of wading in to save him radioed for a trained crew to come to the scene. In the interim, the child died. The officers were praised by their superior for following standard procedure, but censured by UK society and leaders for not doing what anyone morally should do, never mind the job.

This chapter continues the analysis of conscience by considering what normative force our moral responsibilities have when they

---

[1] Burke, Edmund (1774) 'Speech at the Conclusion of the Poll'. 3 November 1774; WS 3, 69.

bump up against the formal expectations of society.[2] These expectations typically include following the law, carrying out our institutional functions, and respecting the norms of the community. The relation between such expectations and our moral responsibilities is particularly significant not in the brutal societies of Gandhi and Aung San Suu Kyi, but in reasonably good societies, to which many western liberal democracies might approximate. A reasonably good society is one in which the institutional framework: 1) is founded on morally legitimate principles and values that 2) function by and large as intended, and 3) are standardly thought to trump whatever values support non-conformity with formal expectations.[3] In such a context, we may ask whether the guidance of conscience would depart from formal dictates in anything but an emergency. And, if it would, whether we should follow conscience or formal norms.

In this chapter, I defend two interrelated theses (Sections 1 and 2). The first is a broadly Aristotelian thesis that we might call the gap thesis:[4]

The gap thesis: Even in a reasonably good society, there is an ineliminable conceptual and evaluative gap between the formal codifiable dictates of normatively legitimate offices and positions, and the broadly non-codifiable moral responsibilities of the moral roles that underpin and legitimate those positions.[5]

---

[2] This chapter elaborates some of the ideas in Brownlee, Kimberley (2010d) 'Responsibilities of Criminal Justice Officials' in *The Journal of Applied Philosophy* 27: 2, 123–39. An ally for some of my views is Arthur Applbaum in (1999) *Ethics for Adversaries*. Princeton: Princeton University Press. Applbaum is more sanguine than I am about the legitimating power of reasonable *ex ante* consent. Another ally for some of my views is Sheppard, Stephen (2009) *I Do Solemnly Swear: The Moral Obligations of Legal Officials*. New York: Cambridge University Press. In this work, Sheppard argues that officials must act morally, not just legally. This thesis was once an unquestioned view but is now subject to an all-too-common distrust about moral concepts, in general, and the role of universal judgements in public life, in particular. Sheppard, as he himself openly acknowledges, provides no theoretical exploration of, or defence for, the normative judgements that he advances in the book.

[3] The view that dominates legal theory and political science debates presumes that some general obligations must arise from legal norms and be reconciled with political realities either by subsuming moral norms under legal norms or by defending a space for moral wrongdoing—dirtying one's hands—in the name of public good. Cf Kadish, Mortimer R. and Kadish, Sanford H. (1973) *Discretion to Disobey: A Study of Lawful Departures from Legal Rules*. Stanford: Stanford University Press; and Luban, David (1988) *Lawyers and Justice: An Ethical Study*. Princeton: Princeton University Press. See also Walzer, Michael (1973) 'Political Action: The Problem of Dirty Hands' in *Philosophy and Public Affairs* 2: 2, 160–80.

[4] Cf Aristotle, *Nicomachean Ethics,* Book V, ch 10.

[5] By the gap thesis, I do not mean that the moral universe of a formal position is a hermetically sealed moral environment. Rather, I mean that the normative rules of any formal position will give morally inadequate guidance to its occupant.

Commonsense examples of normatively legitimate offices and positions are judge, doctor, legislator, juror, journalist, police, and citizen.[6] Examples of the moral roles that underpin and legitimate those positions are mediator (in the case of judge and jury), educator (in the case of judge, doctor, and journalist), carer (in the case of doctor and citizen), guard and guardian (in the case of police, judge and citizen), and coordinator (in the case of legislator, police, and citizen).

Given the rigidifying and generalizing nature of formal institutions, we will be called on even in a reasonably good society to engage in morally problematic practices as a matter of course that are in tension with the responsibilities of the moral roles that legitimate our offices.[7] This leads to the second thesis, which is the moral roles thesis:

The moral roles thesis: When the moral responsibilities of the moral roles that underpin and legitimate formal positions diverge non-trivially from the formal expectations of those positions, it is morally obligatory *ceteris paribus* to depart from formal expectations and to adhere to our moral responsibilities.

There are two ways to interpret the moral roles thesis. The morally less controversial interpretation says that we should do what we ultimately have most reason to do. The morally more controversial interpretation says that we should adhere to the moral reasons that govern our moral roles and responsibilities even if this is at the expense of doing what we might ultimately have most reason to do. I argue that, except in extreme emergencies, the latter version of the thesis holds true. I call this the priority of special responsibility principle. The moral roles thesis is offered here both as a *ceteris paribus* decision-making procedure and as a standard for morally acceptable conduct.

---

[6] The idea that *citizen* is a formal position in society on a par with legislator, judge, or juror may seem non-obvious, but it is the case. Even if we construe the notion of *citizen* broadly not in terms of nationality, but in terms of recognized society membership, it is nevertheless a politically and legally recognized status that brings with it formal demands. These typically include tax payment, jury duty, conscripted duty in emergencies, and adherence to law, as well as more subtle formal expectations such as political participation, voting, knowledge of the law, and contribution to the development of law. The demands on the citizen in the reasonably good society may not include all of these things, but they will include at least some of them on the assumption that the reasonably good society is a liberal democracy.

[7] In this context, the term 'moral role' is used in a technical sense to distinguish it from an 'office' or 'formal position'.

After fleshing out both the gap thesis and the moral roles thesis, I respond to some likely objections that pertain to decision-making competence, democratic processes, burdens of judgement, voluntarism, valuable institutions, and value pluralism (Section 3). The first three of these objections target the credentials of the moral roles thesis as a decision-making procedure. The latter three target its credentials as a standard for morally acceptable conduct.

In combating these objections, I articulate an important principle for a reasonably good society, which I call the *minimum moral burdens principle*. According to this principle, society must ensure as well as it can that the offices it establishes to address important concerns do not place unduly heavy moral burdens on any would-be occupants of those offices.

More generally, in combating these objections, I show that, *no matter what our formal position is*, non-conformity with formal dictates and, particularly, suitably constrained, conscience-driven communicative disobedience of law, is not by nature threatening to democratic processes and valuable institutions. Instead, it often best honours the spirit of the moral values that underpin our formal positions.

1. Formal Expectations and Moral Responsibilities

1.1 Competing views of discretion and expectation

In liberal theory and practice, there is some recognized latitude in the formal expectations of some official positions, notably the positions of police and prosecutor. In common law systems, there are generally recognized norms of police discretion and prosecutorial discretion. By contrast, there are only grudgingly recognized norms of jury discretion (ie jury nullification). And, there are no recognized norms of prison guard discretion, soldier discretion, or citizen discretion. Given these differences, one might think that, only when the demands of our position are underdetermined, as in the case of police and prosecutors, should we employ first-order moral reasoning about how best to act. When our position grants us little or no formal discretion, such as in the case of foot soldiers or prison guards, non-conformity with directives in all but the most extreme cases would constitute a threat to the valuable institutions of which our position is a part.

A second, related view one might take is that those of us who are lower down the institutional ladders (including ordinary citizens) are more likely to make mistakes in first-order reasoning since we have limited access to relevant information and less time to make decisions because our positions are not constructed to allow us to make certain kinds of judgements. David Estlund takes this view when he argues that the prison guard, who knows a convicted person is not guilty, is morally obligated nonetheless to incarcerate him, and the soldier, who knows that the war he fights in is unjust, is morally obligated nonetheless to follow orders in that war. Estlund bases this claim on a commitment to honest, competent, legally legitimate, though necessarily fallible, institutional processes and procedures. He says that, when the political and institutional processes that produce these expectations are duly looking after the question of whether the suspect is guilty and the war is just, the prison guard and the soldier would be wrong to substitute their own private verdicts and thwart the state's will even though the state has made a mistake.[8] Estlund's argument appeals to the knowledge-seeking nature of the formal processes and their greater epistemic reliability over private judgement under certain conditions.

Such views are unappealing because, as I argue later, they depend on questionable assumptions about both the appropriate distribution of discretion and officials' relative access to relevant information.[9] And, for those officials to whom convention grants some discretion, the question remains whether they are morally required sometimes to step beyond what that discretion formally licenses them to do or, indeed, to disdain to do what that discretion licenses them to do.

A third view one might take says that those of us who are *higher* up the institutional ladder or most visible on the ladder, such as judges,

---

[8] Estlund, David (2007) 'On Following Orders in an Unjust War' in *The Journal of Political Philosophy*, 15: 2, 213–34. For instance, about the prison guard, he says, 'The trial procedure can be a legitimate and competent method for officially trying to punish the guilty without punishing the innocent, even if it is fallible. In that case, the jailer can be permitted and required to leave that job to others, such as the judge and jury, and simply be the jailer.' However, Estlund does acknowledge that these pre-conditions for deference to the state are substantial, and both the prison guard and the soldier will need to think for themselves about whether those conditions are met.

[9] As Jeff McMahan argues, it is possible for ordinary soldiers to assess whether the war in which they are being called on to fight is an unjust one. For instance, if their mission is ostensibly a humanitarian intervention, are the 'oppressed' people that they are riding in to save living peaceably with their 'oppressors'? If so, that is one indicator that the proposed war may be unjust.

legislators, military commanders, and executives, have the most stringent duty to 'follow orders'.[10] Non-conformity with formal expectations by these officials, unlike non-conformity by less scrutinized ones, may threaten valuable institutions by undermining general confidence in the workings of those institutions. As Joel Feinberg observes, the high court judge is not protected by the same degree of secrecy as the mere juror. Nor can she so easily escape sanctions afterwards, being subject to impeachment and subject to social pressure to give an account of each judicial decision and mode of argument.[11] The same is presumably true of the military commander in comparison with the lowly soldier.[12] But, the potential costs of non-conformity for the judge or commander, and for people's confidence in these institutions, must be weighed against the costs of general conformity with formal dictates, including costs that should weaken people's confidence in these institutions.

A fourth view one might take focuses not on the highness or lowness of an office, but on the institutional context in which that office is situated. One might argue that, whereas unjust institutions cannot generate obligations, the just institutions of a reasonably good society can generate moral obligations for *all* officials to adhere to formal dictates. One might argue that when our offices are voluntarily assumed within institutions that are not unjust we have a moral obligation to adhere to formal dictates.[13]

---

[10] In this discussion, the terms 'duty' and 'obligation' are used interchangeably. The term 'responsibility' captures essentially the same content as 'duty' or 'obligation', but is reserved here to refer to those duties that are distinctively ours (not everyone's) in virtue of our moral roles, skills, and circumstances, which are, by nature, not universal to all.

[11] Joel Feinberg argues that: 'The conscientious judge's situation is quite different [from that of the ordinary citizen or the juror], especially when he is a judge in the nation's highest appellate court... the judge does not have legal power of the same degree of effectiveness as that of the ordinary citizen or the juror. Paradoxically, the higher we climb in the court system, the less effective power to breach official duties do we find. I suspect that is because the duties themselves, at that level, are regarded with awe and thought to be of maximum or supreme stringency.' Feinberg, Joel (2003) *Problems at the Roots of Law*. Oxford: Oxford University Press, 17. Michelle Madden Dempsey has observed in conversation that Feinberg's view may conflate strong discretion with weak discretion. Although, contra Ronald Dworkin, judges may exercise strong discretion (in determining standards of reasonableness, for example), they nonetheless may lack weak discretion to be the final arbiter on a case; social pressures will limit a judge's weak discretion to say whether some conduct satisfies a given standard.

[12] However, when problems occur, there seems to be a tendency in the military to deflect blame to those lowest in the hierarchy. The US military and government response to the abuses perpetrated at Abu Ghraib prison is a case in point.

[13] Cf Hardimon, Michael O. (1994) 'Role Obligations' in *The Journal of Philosophy* 91: 7, 333–63; and Simmons, A. John (1996) 'External Justifications and Institutional Roles' in *The Journal of Philosophy* 93: 1, 28–36.

In reply, there can be injustice in institutions even when those institutions themselves are not unjust. It is unjust for a doctor to be asked to provide nothing but abortions because her colleagues refuse to participate in providing them. But, it is certainly not unjust to have a healthcare system in which abortions are readily available to women and it is not unjust to accommodate, where possible, those doctors who wish to refuse to provide them.

A fifth view that one might take draws from the amorphous set of ideas known as political realism to highlight concerns about fanaticism and authoritarianism.[14] But, such a view can easily collapse into skittish, under-theorized political realist worries about either the relevance of morality in political life or the very idea of morality. Although political, social, and legal realities undeniably pose challenges for moral reasoning about public life, they do not entail the rejection of moral reasoning. Rather, they affirm the importance of rigorous moral reasoning.

In what follows, I argue that, irrespective of the highness, lowness, or visibility of our official positions, and irrespective of the goodness of the institutional framework in which we operate, the gap thesis and the moral roles thesis hold true. I maintain that, in a reasonably good society, the case for setting up a given office must rest on the value of the underlying moral roles that that office seeks to embody, and hence there can be no general *pro tanto* moral obligation to conform with the formal demands of the office since those demands can depart from the responsibilities of the moral roles that underpin them. This opens the door to the idea, contra Estlund, that a soldier has no general moral obligation to deploy and may often have an obligation to refuse to deploy or to refuse to carry out orders in war since deploying or following orders can depart from and threaten the genuine moral responsibilities that legitimate the office of soldier. For the same reason, a police officer may have an obligation to decline to arrest a known

---

[14] According to C. A. J. Coady, this collection of views known as political realism, which lack a clear and consistent set of theoretical precepts, can be distinguished by some strands of belief: 1) a certain opposition both to idealism and to morality in international affairs, 2) an opposition to moral self-inflation, and 3) a concern for both national interest and the stability of the international order. Coady argues that political realism is often misunderstood by both its critics and its defenders as opposing any inclusion of morality within international politics, when it could be most plausibly presented in terms of opposition to certain distortions in morality that deserve the epithet 'moralism', such as excessive righteousness or moral self-aggrandizement. Cf Coady, C. A. J. (2008) *Messy Morality: The Challenge of Politics*. Oxford: Oxford University Press.

offender even though instructed to do so. A prosecutor may have an obligation routinely to dismiss a certain type of charge even though there are sufficient legal grounds to proceed to trial. A jury may have an obligation to acquit an obviously guilty defendant or a defendant with a certain background. A prison guard may have an obligation not to enforce a lawful sentence of incarceration. And, an ordinary citizen may have an obligation to instigate an illegal boycott, to release classified documents that come her way, or to refuse to pay her taxes. If we have adequate conscience, then we will be responsive to these non-codifiable moral responsibilities even when this leads us to disobey the law.

To set the stage for my defence of the gap thesis and moral roles thesis, I begin by fleshing out the notion of a *moral role* that was introduced in Chapter 2 and contrasting it with the notion of a *formal office* or *position*. I explicate moral roles as the things that provide the moral foundation for most of our moral responsibilities and for any normatively valid office or position that a reasonably good society might establish.

1.2 Moral roles

When we come to hold a given moral role this affects our moral responsibilities in significant ways. Some moral reasons now apply to us that did not apply to us before. Some moral reasons now apply as categorical mandatory reasons (moral obligations) that previously applied as ordinary reasons. And, possibly, some moral reasons now apply as ordinary reasons that previously applied as obligations.

Some moral roles have clear forms, precise features, and broadly well-defined spheres of responsibility. For example, the specific moral role of raising a particular child gives us special moral responsibilities to care for, educate, protect, feed, clothe, house, and love that child. By contrast, other moral roles, such as healer, protector, advocate, educator, or mediator, have less precise features and pick out broader categories of moral responsibility the general nature of which can be deduced from linguistic intuitions about the paradigm activities given in the titles of these roles—'carer' is linked to caring, 'healer' to healing, 'protector' to protecting, and so on. Indeed many of these latter roles combine together in different ways to comprise more clearly defined roles such as parent, partner, and friend.

As noted in Chapter 2, there are various ways in which we can come to have a given moral role. Some roles typically come to be ours through voluntary assumption, such as the role of partner. Others can come to be ours voluntarily or non-voluntarily such as that of friend. Some roles we can acquire by ourselves and some we acquire jointly with others. Some we can acquire in a single instance, through a promise, and some we acquire over time through gradually built-up expectations.

Often our assumption of moral roles is the result of coordination problems and situational differences. In a war zone, I may have a responsibility to feed and care for these children and you may have a responsibility to feed and care for those children. And the allocation of responsibility may be due to chance or to our relative proximity to each group and the efficiency of coordinating our efforts.

In what follows, I focus my attention on those moral roles that credibly underpin and inform the formal, legally-entrenched offices and positions of a reasonably good society.[15] My analysis of the relevant moral roles is structured by an investigation of their interplay with the normatively valid offices that they legitimate.

1.3 Offices and positions

In contrast with a *moral role*, an *office* or *formal position* is a formally recognized post governed by formal rules. The offices and positions established by a reasonably good society are, by definition, founded on normatively valid principles, and they function by and large as they are intended to do.

They are structured to embody as well as possible within that society's institutional history the moral roles—categories of moral responsibility—that are necessary to address the society's fundamental concerns. These concerns include the security of the society and its members from external and internal threats; the reasonable prevention

---

[15] Quite possibly, 'parent' is a formal position in society. Legal guardian certainly is. Friend is not, at least not in contemporary western society, and it is an interesting question to consider whether we would do well to establish legal contracts of friendship in the same way we establish legal contracts of life-partnership. In the novel *Snow Flower and the Secret Fan*, author Lisa See describes the (possibly fictional) old Chinese relationship of *laotong* (the word 'laotong' means 'old same' or kindred spirit), which is a lifelong intimate, non-sexual relationship between two unrelated women. She says that these relationships were more intimate than marriages since, unlike marriages, they were voluntarily undertaken by the young girls of a certain social standing who were granted permission to form such connections. In See's story, set in 19th century China, a pair of young girls from good families are matched together to form a lifelong intimate friendship, formalized by oaths and a written contract. Cf See, Lisa (2005) *Snow Flower and the Secret Fan*. London: Random House.

of serious wrongdoing; the appropriate redress of wrongdoing; the care for members' health and well-being; and the cultivation of noble ends including the scientific, cultural, and social life of the society as well as ideals of justice, peace, respect, and common well-being. The overlapping categories of moral roles that must be formalized to address such concerns presumably include protector, guardian, educator, producer, coordinator, researcher, mediator, counsellor, advocate, adjudicator, healer, and carer.

My view grounds the defence for setting up a given office in the value of the moral roles that *that* office aims to embody. Thereby, my view contrasts with the more orthodox view that the defence for establishing a given office is that it is necessary to keep the legal system running as a whole, and it is the good functions performed by the system *as a whole* that justify individual offices. According to the orthodox view, what justifies the duties and the rights incurred by members of the police, for example, is not that they perform the service of protecting, but that they perform a subset of the tasks that need to be performed in order for the legal system as a whole to be capable of protecting its members. It is for this reason that, normally, members of the police should not consider departing from formal dictates because they cannot effectively protect citizens by themselves; they can only effectively contribute to the coordinated effort through which the legal system protects its citizens.[16]

I take a narrower approach than the orthodox view. I do this because some of the reasons to establish normatively legitimate offices are independent from the reasons to secure a formal system of interlocking offices. If we start with the credible assumption that there are certain key tasks that need to be performed, that is, we need healers, carers, parents, producers, educators, and coordinators, then we can acknowledge the reasons we have to formalize such roles into offices irrespective of the reasons to set up a grander system capable of effectively discharging all of these tasks. In short, if for whatever reason we could not get a complete functioning system in place, we would still have reasons to have doctors, teachers, and farmers.

All that said, my view can accommodate the fact that there is a plurality of legitimate ways in which a society may work to embody important moral roles through its creation of different offices within a

---

[16] I thank an anonymous reader for OUP for fleshing out this alternative.

formalized web of interlocking expectations. Given this plurality of legitimate ways to structure a system, the chosen structure of a system will shape to some extent the special moral responsibilities that we have as its office-holders. For example, moral roles such as mediator and educator, which amongst other things underpin the formal office of judge, will be fleshed out by the parameters of this office as it exists within a given system. Consequently, the specific actions required of judges to honour the special responsibilities of their moral roles will vary according to the institutional arrangements of the system.

The special moral responsibilities that apply to a given office-holder do not, however, reduce to a general *pro tanto* content-insensitive moral obligation to conform with the formal expectations of the office. As office-holders, we may have an obligation to do as our office demands in a given case, but not necessarily because our office demands it since, even in a reasonably good society, formal, codifiable expectations will inevitably diverge from our actual moral responsibilities (the gap thesis). This is due to both the inbuilt rigidity and generalizing character of formal expectations and the contingencies of practical operations. Let me articulate three dimensions of this gap.

1.4 *The gap thesis*

First, even in a reasonably good society, we will be called on formally to do morally problematic things as a matter of course, such as threaten people, attack people, make laws that harm people, lie to people, detain people, isolate people, charge people with offences, make judgements on people's guilt, sentence people to be punished, impose punishments on people, deprive people of their resources, and perhaps, in extreme cases, incarcerate people and possibly kill people. (I assume that there would be some sort of criminal justice system even in a reasonably good society, though it may exist only for egregious offences, and punishment may take far milder forms than those used in existing societies.)

Second, even in a reasonably good society, occasions will arise where our understanding as an office-holder is clearly greater than that reflected in the formal expectations of us. For example, if we are a prison official, we may well understand the severity of incarceration and its likely effects on offenders much better than do the legislators who enact its lawful use, the judicial officials who sentence its imposition, or the ordinary citizens who champion its value.

Third, even in a reasonably good society, there remains the possibility for error (such as false positives), for improper bias in our fellow office-holders, and for non-institutional social injustices to filter into people's experience within institutions. We can often be stymied in our good faith efforts to act justifiably by the errors and prejudices of other members of the institutional structure. For example, a judge cannot control the fact that black persons may be far more likely to come before her for a given offence than white persons are despite comparable levels of offending.

As these three points indicate, the realities of formalized structures are such that general adherence to formal norms is deeply morally problematic. Although the moral values that fully legitimate *certain* office-dictates are the same as those that entail the special moral responsibilities underlying that office, those values do not legitimate the codification of such office-dictates. In other words, the codified office-dictates that those values are presumed to entail are not entailed by those values in some circumstances.[17] This does not deny that there are values and principles, such as procedural norms of generality and predictability, which can at least partially legitimate the codification of some dictates. But, those procedural norms are distinct from, and subordinate to, the substantive, context-sensitive, and non-codifiable moral responsibilities of underlying moral roles. This is because those procedural norms, often grouped together under the heading 'rule of law', are compatible with a substantively unjust system, and thus cannot block codified office-dictates from deviating from what is morally acceptable.[18]

As a consequence, when morally problematic factors infect some office-holders' decisions, this can modify our own special moral responsibilities within our own official sphere (the moral roles thesis). This is because the moral roles that underpin our own position will not make it our responsibility to do what is morally indefensible, such as, say, proceed with a criminal case against a person who has been the victim of grave injustice or imprison a clearly innocent person whom others have lawfully convicted. If our office demands such acts under some more general directive, then the only morally acceptable course may be non-conformity. Similarly, in more mundane cases, when we

---

[17] I thank Hillel Steiner for helping to clarify this point.
[18] See Raz, Joseph (1979) 'The Rule of Law and its Virtue' in *The Authority of Law*. Oxford: Clarendon Press.

clearly have a better understanding of the character and consequences of a given order than that reflected in the order itself, this too modifies our moral responsibilities in ways that can lead us not to conform with formal expectations. What form our non-conformity legitimately may take will be discussed in Section 2.

1.5 The moral roles thesis

The moral roles thesis is advanced here both as a decision-making procedure and as a standard for morally acceptable conduct. Let me examine it first as a decision-making procedure.[19]

No moral role makes it our general responsibility to forbear from engaging in first-order moral reasoning about formal expectations. Instead, in our decision-making, we always have a responsibility actively to engage in first-order moral reasoning and to privilege it above formal expectations when the latter depart from genuine moral responsibilities. This is most apparent in situations where conformity with formal norms rightly elicits condemnation. Consider the case I noted at the start of this chapter of the two British community support police officers (CSOs) who tried to save a child drowning in a pond not by attempting a rescue, but by radioing for a trained emergency crew to come to the scene as their professional code instructed them to do. While the officers were praised by their superior for following proper procedure, they were censured by the community and by former Home Secretary David Blunkett, who stated that, 'What was appropriate in this circumstance for a uniformed officer would be appropriate for CSOs as human beings, never mind the job.'[20] I would put the point slightly differently, citing not just the CSOs' status as human beings, but their special moral responsibilities as CSOs. When deciding how to act, they should have considered not the rulebook, but their responsibilities to protect the members of their community.

In the same spirit, Feinberg argues that, what morality requires of us in morally difficult circumstances is not something to be mechanically determined by an examination of our office. We must on some

---

[19] The next two paragraphs closely follow Brownlee, Kimberley (2012a) 'Conscientious Objection and Civil Disobedience' in *The Routledge Companion to Philosophy of Law*. Andrei Marmor (ed.), London: Routledge, 534–5.
[20] BBC News (2007) 'Blunkett Criticises Pond Officers' *BBC News* (22 September). Retrieved from: <http://news.bbc.co.uk/2/hi/uk_news/england/manchester/7008077.stm>.

occasions have the courage to rise above all that and obey the dictates of conscience.[21] And, this is not restricted to lower level officials or ordinary citizens. Joseph Raz rightly observes that, 'Sometimes courts ought to decide cases not according to the law but against it. Civil disobedience, for example, may be the only morally acceptable course of action for the courts.'[22] In such cases, departing from formal expectations, such as the CSOs wading into the pond after the child or a judge refusing to convict an offender on evidence obtained under torture, is most in keeping with the spirit of the office and its underlying moral responsibilities.[23]

Several objections might be raised against the moral roles thesis as a decision-making procedure. They focus on democratic processes, the burdens of judgement, and the parameters of decision-making competence. I address these objections in Section 3. For now, let me specify the moral roles thesis as a standard for morally acceptable action.

Except in extreme moral emergencies, we act in morally acceptable ways when we adhere to the moral responsibilities that are ours in virtue of our moral roles, even though doing so may mean we act other than we have most reason to act all things considered. This is the *priority of special responsibility principle*. One reason for adhering to the moral roles thesis in all but emergencies is coordination. We do not hold our moral roles in isolation; and, in the vast majority of cases, we should not try to do each other's moral jobs. So, while we may depart from formal dictates in order to honour our underlying moral

---

[21] Even more spiritedly, Henry David Thoreau declares that: 'The mass of men serve the state thus, not as men mainly, but as machines, with their bodies. They are the standing army, and the militia, jailers, constables, posse comitatus, &c. In most cases there is no free exercise whatever of the judgment or of the moral sense; but they put themselves on a level with wood and earth and stones; and wooden men can perhaps be manufactured that will serve the purpose as well. Such command no more respect than men of straw or a lump of dirt. They have the same sort of worth only as horses and dogs. Yet such as these even are commonly esteemed good citizens. Others—as most legislators, politicians, lawyers, ministers, and officeholders—serve the state chiefly with their heads; and, as they rarely make any moral distinctions, they are as likely to serve the Devil, without intending it, as God. A very few, as heroes, patriots, martyrs, reformers in the great sense, and men, serve the state with their consciences also, and so necessarily resist it for the most part; and they are commonly treated as enemies by it.' Thoreau, Henry David (1991 [1848]) 'Civil Disobedience' in *Civil Disobedience in Focus*. Hugo Bedau (ed.), London: Routledge. Despite its rhetorical flair, Thoreau's claim resonates with my claims about ideals of conscience in Chapter 2 as models for how a reasonably good, liberal society should think about conscience.

[22] Raz, Joseph (1994) *Ethics in the Public Domain*. Oxford: Oxford University Press, 328.

[23] See, Greenawalt, Kent (1987) *Conflicts of Law and Morality*. Oxford: Clarendon Press, 281.

responsibilities, we should not generally depart from our underlying moral responsibilities in order to do what there is, on balance, most reason to do. For example, a diplomat who seeks, without exploitation or coercion, to get the best trade deal for her community honours the moral responsibilities that she has to her community, but may well not act as she has most reason to act all things considered. She acts unfairly by doing what she can to get a good deal for her people while knowing that it may not be a good deal for others. Her doing this is morally acceptable, though, if she acts in the knowledge that the other society has its diplomats too, who are *competently* representing its interests. Just as she should not try to do the moral jobs of other office-holders in her community, so too she should not try to do the moral jobs of office-holders from other communities. Simply, she may act to represent the interests of her people, subtly understood, which includes attending to their reputation and their future interests in other interactions.

By contrast, in morally *extreme* circumstances, coordination can be either too costly or impossible. When it is, we should seek to do the best we can morally all things considered. When the other society does not have diplomats competently representing its interests, and the trade deal will spell disaster for that society, our diplomat should look beyond her ordinary role-related moral responsibilities to act as there is most reason to act.

In non-morally-difficult circumstances, the moral roles thesis may be limited to occasions in which we, the official, *clearly* will better act as the moral reasons that apply to us would have us act when we attend to those reasons directly and not to the rules governing our office. When we will not clearly act better by attending to those reasons directly, we would do best (in a reasonably good society) to adhere to the rules governing our office, given that the likely costs that interference would impose on us and others may be higher than allowing a minor injustice to occur.[24] For example, the reasons that apply to a law enforcement officer include reasons to protect society from dangerous persons, to communicate the appropriate community disavowal of serious wrongdoing, to promote both restoration of victims and reconciliation amongst affected parties, and to enhance people's confidence in public institutions. In non-morally-difficult circumstances, it is only when attending to these reasons directly will *clearly* better enable us to honour

---

[24] I thank an anonymous reader for OUP for clarifying this point.

them that we should attend to them directly, though it may lead us to depart from formal expectations.[25]

There are several objections to the moral roles thesis as a standard for morally acceptable conduct. They focus on voluntarism as a source of moral obligation, valuable institutions, and the pluralism of our moral roles and responsibilities. I tackle these objections in Section 3. For now, let me consider the implications of the moral roles thesis for both society and individuals.

1.6 Implications for society

It is not enough for society to make provisions for us to excuse ourselves from adhering to formal demands that are especially onerous for us. Certainly, in many cases, society should do that. But, the point is that society should strive as well as it can to avoid setting up institutional frameworks to address important concerns that place overly heavy moral burdens on any would-be occupants of those institutions. This is the minimum moral burdens principle. One example of its application is the case of the California doctors that I noted at the beginning of this chapter.

In US states such as California, doctors have refused to carry out the function of overseeing executions by lethal injection because their assigned tasks are not just to reduce the condemned person's suffering, but also to intervene to facilitate death if the person wakes up. This task runs afoul of the minimum moral burdens principle, as it deeply conflicts with doctors' special responsibilities as healers and carers to promote people's well-being. As a result of doctors' refusal to perform this function, a moratorium was imposed on capital punishment in California.[26] It would be no solution to set up a special medical office of 'execution overseer' because such an office would be, by nature, excessively morally burdensome for any would-be occupant.

A related objection can be raised against doctors' function of treating offenders in high-security prisons whose conditions are often marked

---

[25] Raz's normal justification condition for authority states that the person subject to the putative authority would better conform to reasons that apply to her anyway if she intends to be guided by the directive than if she does not. See Raz, Joseph (2006) 'The Problem of Authority: Revisiting the Service Conception' in *Minnesota Law Review* 90, 1003–44. I assume that, in a reasonably good society, Raz's independence condition—that [an official's] judging for herself how to act is not more important than conforming to reason—is satisfied.

[26] Gels, Sonya (2006) 'California puts Execution off after Doctors Refuse to Help' *The Washington Post*, 22 February.

by brutality, degradation, and deprivation. This requires doctors to oversee and be party to punishments that are highly detrimental to offenders' well-being. (Such brutal institutional structures are equally at odds with the spirit of the moral roles of guardian and protector, which legitimate the offices of prison guard and police.)

From the examples I have given, it might seem that the minimum moral burdens principle applies more to real societies like ours than to a reasonably good society since the latter would probably not use capital punishment or harsh justice. Even so, a reasonably good society is not an ideal society and the people in such a society are real people not all of whom are reasonable.[27] And, such a society would still have to make decisions about how to address big problems as well as procedural decisions about who is to perform which tasks in handling those big problems. Amongst other things, there is the issue of contingencies. An office might not be unduly morally burdensome by nature, but become so over time if other people refuse to perform their share of the burdensome tasks. For example, if all other doctors in a hospital refuse to provide abortions, one doctor may spend most of her time performing this morally charged procedure. Coordinating and sharing around the morally troubling tasks is one matter that even the reasonably good society must address.

As this implies, it does not follow from the minimum moral burdens principle that society may never ask us to engage in morally problematic conduct. Society may legitimately ask a civil registrar to conduct civil partnerships for homosexual couples despite her religious scruples so as to ensure non-discriminatory provision of a secular alternative to religious marriage. Similarly, society may legitimately ask its medical professionals to provide adequate, non-discriminatory healthcare services irrespective of their convictions about the moral merits of different procedures, medications, or patients. And, in those rare times of genuine crisis, society may legitimately call on its members

---

[27] Even in a reasonably good society, a soldier might be asked by a superior to engage in an action when the superior hasn't assessed all the relevant information, or when the superior has ulterior motives, or when the justness of the cause could be disputed. The formal office of soldier will not rule out either following ill-motivated orders if there are grounds for those orders or following ill-informed orders if the relevant facts track roughly what the orders assume. But, the soldier who is attentive to his protective and defensive responsibilities should be sensitive to his superiors' intentions and to their efforts to engage in fact-finding. His superiors' errors might not legitimate an outright refusal, but non-conformity is a nuanced enterprise that comes in degrees (as I discuss in this chapter).

to go to war. (Saying that society may legitimately expect morally problematic conduct from its members does not imply that we, the members, have no moral rights to refuse to oblige our society. I pursue this issue further in Chapter 4.) The minimum moral burdens principle simply requires that society pay close attention both to the institutional structures that it sets up to address important concerns and to the specification of the offices that comprise those institutions, so as to minimize the moral burdens that it imposes on its members, and thereby reduce the occasions in which non-conformity is the only morally acceptable course of action.

Of course, society's success in addressing its significant challenges is usually not a binary state of 'yes we did' or 'no we didn't' succeed in addressing them. Instead, it is a continuum. We address one type of challenge fairly well and another type poorly. We address one challenge well along one dimension and badly along another. So, in articulating the minimum moral burdens principle, it is necessary to acknowledge the issue of trade-offs. Society should aim to make the moral burdens as minimal as possible relative to a certain standard of satisfactoriness in addressing the challenge. Fortunately for the minimum moral burdens principle, there is evidence that often less morally demanding institutions are equally good, if not better, at addressing core challenges than are harsher, more morally demanding institutions. Criminal justice systems are a case in point.[28]

1.7 *Implications for individuals*

One challenge for me might be that the minimum moral burdens principle seems to condemn my own account of formal offices since I place heavy moral burdens on the occupants of institutional offices to engage in first-order moral reasoning to figure out how best to honour

---

[28] European penal systems tend to eschew the harsher methods of Anglo-American systems and some non-western systems in favour of practices that respect offenders' sense of honour and dignity, give those in prison a voice about their conditions, assign to them transparently meaningful responsibilities related to reparation, and enable them to retain many of their familial responsibilities (in some jurisdictions, families can live with prisoners). Assigning a wrongdoer specific responsibilities to care for, protect, support, and provide for victims and society directly connects the communication of blame and the suspension of normal relations with the wrongful conduct. Thus, it is not only less morally burdensome for the officials charged with carrying out lawful punishment, but also more defensible than the coercive, dismissive, and dehumanizing responses that isolate wrongdoers from victims and society. Cf Whitman, James Q. (2005) *Harsh Justice: Criminal Punishment and the Widening Divide between America and Europe*. New York: Oxford University Press.

their special moral responsibilities. By contrast, the orthodox view of formal offices seems to satisfy the minimum moral burdens principle by holding that, except in extraordinary circumstances, officials need only comply with what they are told to do.

It is true that an implication of the moral roles thesis for us as individuals is that, at all times, we must reflect on the moral merits of the formal expectations we face. The police officer must reflect on the merits of the call to use certain interrogation techniques. The prison guard and parole officer must reflect on the merits of the order to incarcerate someone. The prosecutor must reflect on the merits of the charges brought forward by police. The soldier must reflect on the justness of an order in war. The citizen must reflect on the policies that her resources go to fund and the actions taken by her government in her name. If adhering to formal expectations will lead us better to conform to the moral reasons that apply to us in virtue of our moral roles, then our judgement should lead us to accept those expectations as authoritative. But, if the formal expectations are substantially unjust, or if, in some other cases, we clearly will not better conform to the moral reasons that apply to us by adhering to expectations, then our judgement should lead us not to accept those expectations as authoritative.

But, I do not see this as running afoul of the minimum moral burdens principle because, assuming a certain level of competence in reasoning, it is not overly burdensome to ask us to reflect on morality. It is overly morally burdensome to ask us to do horrible things in the name of social order when non-horrible things would suffice. I return to this point in my discussion of the competence and epistemic limitations objection (Section 3).

Despite these wide-ranging implications, the offices of a reasonably good society retain normative importance because they identify broadly the limits of persons' spheres of responsibility when the system is functioning well. When fundamentally important moral roles are formalized as well as they can be into offices structured to address the most significant concerns of the society, and when the occupants of these offices honour their own moral responsibilities largely as they should, then all occupants must respect the efforts of their colleagues and not seek to do each other's jobs. When, however, some people do not fulfil the moral responsibilities that are theirs in virtue of the roles that underpin their offices, this affects the nature of others' moral responsibilities. It widens the gap between formal expectations and genuine moral responsibilities.

2. The Forms and Purposes of Non-conformity

When that gap is non-trivial, non-conformity with formal expectations may be our only morally acceptable course of action. But, of course, non-conformity takes many forms, and not all of those forms will be morally acceptable given our special moral responsibilities. The general forms of non-conformity include the following: 1) partial conformity with a formal expectation; 2) full non-conformity with that expectation (such as civil disobedience, assistive disobedience, or personal disobedience); 3) verbal challenges of the expectation; 4) efforts to reform the structures and practices that give rise to that expectation; 5) recusal; 6) resignation; and 7) emigration from the society.

These general forms of non-conformity divide into more concrete varieties that tend to serve different purposes. At least four broad purposes of non-conformity come to mind: 1) informing, 2) dissociating, 3) disrupting, and 4) self-expressing. Civil disobedience and whistleblowing typically serve the purpose of informing others about some issue. Civil disobedience also serves the purpose of dissociating us from the law or policy we oppose. Recusing ourselves or resigning in protest tend to serve both the purpose of dissociating and that of disrupting. When our continued participation in a process is necessary for it to go forward, in the way that the anaesthesiologists' participation was necessary for capital punishment in California, then recusal or resignation can be an effective way to abort the process. Another way to disrupt a process is to thwart it from within. Death penalty administrators tend to disrupt the capital punishment process by taking so-called 'go slow' days much of the time.[29] More extreme ways to disrupt processes are with threats,

---

[29] In a recent paper, Bernard E. Harcourt states that: 'Another important but rarely discussed factor that promotes abolitionist reforms [of capital punishment] are ordinary acts of resistance by those who are either knowingly or unconsciously uncomfortable with capital punishment or truly opposed to the death penalty. These men and women—a clerk at the county courthouse, an employee at the local police department, a secretary in the prosecutor's office, sometimes even a judge or law clerk—slow death penalty cases down and effectively undermine the machinery of death.' He then continues that 'In several death penalty cases that I have been involved as a litigator, I have encountered more than just inertia—more than just laziness or distraction. I have experienced almost intentional or deliberate delay by men and women in all categories of life who take it on themselves to stall a death penalty prosecution by ignoring it. It is these acts of resistance—one could say unconscious minor acts of sabotage—that render the death penalty simply ineffectual in many states. The deliberate resistance of doctors to participate in the mechanics of capital punishment is the conscious and public manifestation of these forms of resistance, but the phenomenon tends to be far more unconscious and, as a result, pervasive.' Harcourt, Bernard

coercion, and terrorization. Finally, other forms of non-conformity may be ineffective in informing, dissociating, or disrupting, but nonetheless serve the more personal purpose of expressing moral consistency. The lowly soldier may be unable to leave his unit, garner wider attention, or abort an unjust mission. Yet, through whatever modest forms of non-conformity are available to him, he may serve the expressive purpose of confirming to himself both his genuine moral responsibilities and his conscience-driven efforts to act on them.

Although the four purposes just identified—informing, dissociating, disrupting, and expressing—are neither mutually exclusive nor collectively exhaustive of the purposes of non-conformity, they offer a way both to distinguish seemingly similar activities and to assess their moral merits when pursued by different people in different contexts. Those moral merits are informed by at least two considerations: 1) our special moral responsibilities in light of the moral roles that underpin our position, and 2) the likely costs of our chosen mode of non-conformity for individuals and the society. Let me apply these considerations to some cases.

In general, it would be more morally acceptable for police officers to contest objectionable demands made of them by political agents than to hold a general strike or to resign en masse. The reasons are, first, that the moral responsibilities of the moral roles of protector, guard, guardian, and investigator shape the moral permissibility of the types of non-conformity that a police officer can engage in to challenge unjust or ill-informed directives. Second, responding through mass renunciation of the office would leave the society without a functioning security system. It would be at odds with the moral responsibilities underlying the position of police officer.

By contrast, it may be more morally defensible for doctors to resign or refuse to assume offices in abusive detention facilities than simply to contest administrative decisions about those facilities and, when that contestation fails, to conform to the demands of the office. Here again, the reason relates to the moral responsibilities of the roles of healer and carer as well as the likely impact of resignation. This comparative judgement is contingent on the circumstances surrounding doctors'

E. (2008) 'Abolition in the U.S.A. by 2050: On Political Capital and Ordinary Acts of Resistance' *John M. Olin Program in Law and Economics Working Paper Series*. Retrieved from: <http://www.law.uchicago.edu/Lawecon/index.html>.

resignation being such that their resignation would not result in substantially more suffering for inmates. When it would result in more suffering, this speaks against resignation and in favour of other, perhaps more radical, forms of non-conformity such as thwarting the process.

It is small comfort to the people suffering under an unjust policy to know that an office-holder had no wish to be part of it. As Feinberg observes in the context of judging, a judge who resigns in order to retain his integrity makes a poor hero. While the action may require considerable moral courage, it is of little help to those who suffer under the institution unless his participation in that institution is necessary for its continued operation.[30] The more positive view of resignation nonetheless has some force: we should neither support a practice nor benefit from a practice that violates other persons' basic rights. And, it is only when our participation in that practice is unavoidable that we should focus on reforming the practice from within instead of distancing ourselves from it. To be genuinely conscience-driven in such cases, our resignation would, most likely, have to be supplemented by other acts that highlight the injustice.

Let me look at some lower level offices. In general, a jury's covert nullification of a judge's instructions would be on balance more morally defensible than its showing open disregard for a judge's instructions since covert nullification does less damage to the reasonably good institution of fair and responsible trials. Similarly, in general, it would be more morally defensible for a prison officer quietly to release a convicted innocent person early than it would be for her publicly to disregard a judge or jury's lawful decision of incarceration. That said, even in cases where covertly releasing a convicted person would be morally acceptable, releasing that person nonetheless may not be what the prison officer ought to do if it will make the convicted person's life worse overall. (It is worth noting that, in some cases, no ranking of the acceptability of different non-conforming acts is possible or necessary. Sometimes any conscience-driven departure from the expectations of an office will be morally preferable to conformity with a directive given the objectionable character of such conformity.)

Some of these examples might seem problematic given the clandestine nature of the non-conformity, which we preserve to avoid

---

[30] Feinberg (2003).

nullification of our efforts. Such secrecy can seem troubling, as it violates typical norms of transparency and predictability: justice must be seen to be done. It also seems to run afoul of the communicative principle of conscientiousness identified in Chapter 1, according to which conscientiousness requires non-evasion. Since conscientiousness is a necessary condition for conscience, deliberately clandestine acts of non-conformity appear not to be the fruits of conscience.

In response, the kernel in the above adage about justice and transparency is that justice is not done *unless* it is seen to be done, which is false. Justice can be done without being seen to be done. Indeed, sometimes justice cannot be done if what is done is seen to be done. The examples of clandestine non-conformity noted earlier are precisely those instances in which what is just cannot be done publicly because publicity would negate the just decision by bringing other elements into the mix. In general, it is better to do justice even when it cannot be seen to be done than it is not to do justice. Transparency is one important value, but it is not the only important value. Doing justice, when we can, allays the worry about the communicative principle of conscientiousness because the person who runs afoul of that principle is the person who can protest or redress an injustice, and bear the risks that go with that, but does not do so.

Let me now take up the objections that I identified in Section 1, beginning with those that target the moral roles thesis as a decision-making procedure. These objections focus on decision-making competence, democratic processes, and the burdens of judgement. I then turn to those objections that target the moral roles thesis as a standard for morally acceptable behaviour. These objections focus on voluntarism, valuable institutions, and value pluralism.

3. Objections and Replies

3.1 Competence and epistemic limitations

This first objection concerns our competence to make first-order judgements. A critic might argue that I have over-intellectualized the requirements for acquitting ourselves well in an official capacity. The critic might say that, for many of us, given the nature of our office or the limits of our reasoning abilities, we would better conform to the reasons that apply to us if we do not engage in first-order moral reasoning, but routinely act on and for the reason that we are *directed* to act. This objection applies in particular to those less powerful parties, such as whistleblowers and soldiers, whose acts can have significant impact but who lack certain kinds of information.

In reply, I acknowledge that, in a reasonably good society, an incompetent or improperly biased person would better conform to the reasons that apply to her if she routinely follows formal expectations and acts for the reason that she is directed so to act than if she gives primacy to her own judgement. However, what she does by routinely adhering to formal expectations will often fall well below what she has a moral obligation to do, and so, in failing to reason well about the merits of the demands on her, she does not act well, even though she acts better than she would do if she attended to her own judgement directly. As this reply indicates, I reject any straightforward version of 'ought implies can', but that should be evident already from my defence of the ideal of conscience in Chapter 2.

A further reply is that our capacities to engage in good first-order moral reasoning and judgement can be strengthened or weakened by how much space society gives us to cultivate our reasoning and judgement. Our capacity to cultivate conscience is shaped at least partly by the practices of our society. As Gerald Postema argues, a sense of moral responsibility and sound practical judgement—which I call *conscience*—depend not only on the quality of our training, but also on our ability to draw on the resources of a broader moral experience, which in turn requires that we seek to achieve a fully integrated moral personality. Postema argues that practical judgement is both a disposition and a skill that must be learned and continually exercised. 'It is important,' he says, 'if we are seriously to consider matters of moral responsibility in professional contexts, that we pay attention to the conditions of development of this disposition and the exercise of this skill.'[31]

The decision-making incompetence objection might, however, be re-presented in terms of a concern for equality that requires those of us who are competent in our official capacities not to arrogate to ourselves licence to follow our own first-order reasoning when our colleagues cannot do the same given their circumstances, limited access to information, or limited reasoning abilities.

---

[31] Postema, Gerald (1980) 'Moral Responsibility in Professional Ethics' in *NYU Law Review*, 55, 63–90.

In reply, this re-presentation of the objection has the counterintuitive implication that, unless all of us are able to act morally as well as each other, the demands of equality require that those of us who are able to act well do not morally outperform those who are not. Given this counterintuitive implication, we may put this objection aside. Concerns about equality can, however, be put more forcefully in terms of the value of democratic decision-making processes.

3.2 Democratic processes

On the assumption that a reasonably good society would take a liberal and democratic form, a critic might argue that my view disregards the importance of democratic decision-making processes. In particular, my view seems dismissive of the distinctive issues raised by *officials* in contrast with ordinary citizens. Non-conformity by officials seems to be a much more serious rejection of democratic procedural principles than non-conformity by ordinary citizens either in personal disobedience or in civil disobedience. In relation to ordinary citizens, there is a worry that they improperly arrogate to themselves licence to disregard the law in defiance of democratic processes; the slogan for the objection is 'No man is above the law'. But, when applied to officials, the objection seems much more forceful on the grounds that public office-holders improperly arrogate to themselves licence to interfere in democratic decision-making processes in more serious ways than those typically available to ordinary citizens.[32] There are three possible replies to this objection.

First, the division that this objection sets up between ordinary citizens and officials is a false one or at least an overdrawn one since all of us, irrespective of our powers and formal expectations, are subject to morality. It is important, where possible, to challenge the practice of depersonalizing discussions about authority and governing. The terms 'the law', 'the state', 'the government', and 'authority' all downplay the extent to which the formal institutions of a society are run by people, whose actions call for moral justification as the actions of ordinary individuals who are subject to morality.

If I am correct that the distinction between 'ordinary citizen' and 'official' is overdrawn, then the objection against officials not adhering to legal demands is no stronger than that objection against ordinary

---

[32] I thank Jeremy Waldron for sketching out this objection.

citizens. And, my response to the latter, which I flesh out more fully in Chapter 5, is that civil disobedients often play a vital role in democratic processes. As Daniel Markovits notes, civil disobedience can sometimes correct a democratic-deficit where discussion on a particular issue has stalled or been silenced.[33] Similarly, it can help to redress the comparative injustice of the imbalance of political power between minorities and majorities.[34] Granting minorities some space to continue to challenge democratically taken decisions through suitably constrained civil disobedience after the votes are counted is not an attack on democracy; it is reflective of democracy (see Chapters 4 and 5).

Second, we may put aside the fact that we are all subject to morality and focus on the fact that we are all citizens, where 'citizen' is construed not in terms of nationality, but more broadly as 'recognized members of a community'. We may hold other offices in addition to that of citizen, but we all hold at least that one office of citizen and our moral responsibilities that underpin our positions as citizens need not be seen as, by nature, secondary to our other moral responsibilities.[35]

Third, it is worth noting that even if the distinction between ordinary citizens and officials were credible, we can question the claim that individual officials are routinely in a position to interfere in democratic processes in more serious ways than ordinary citizens are. And, even if they are, we can question whether their doing so is morally problematic if what they do is more just than that which the dictates of their offices would have them do. For instance, in some cases, decisions are urgent or time-sensitive. In those cases, it may be impossible to appeal to the democratic will of society to amend formal expectations before departing from them.

3.3 Burdens of judgement

The democratic procedures objection might be reformulated as a political liberal concern about legitimacy. A critic might say that some problems are genuinely difficult ones to address, and consequently people may reasonably disagree about how best to address them. Therefore, even if we, the official, have the best answer to

---

[33] Markovits, Daniel (2005) 'Democratic Disobedience' in *Yale Law Journal* 114, 1897–952.

[34] Lefkowitz, David (2007) 'On the Moral Right to Civil Disobedience' in *Ethics* 117: 2, 202–33. Cf Brownlee, Kimberley (2008) 'Penalizing Public Disobedience' in *Ethics* 118: 4, 711–16.

[35] I thank Zsuzsanna Chappell for highlighting this response.

some problem, it would be disrespectful for us to take a decision outside the ordinary processes of political legitimacy.

One response to this objection lies in the quotation from Edmund Burke with which I opened this chapter. Burke continues his statement by saying: 'If government were a matter of Will on any side, yours, without question, ought to be superior. But government and Legislation are matters of reason and judgment, and not of inclination.' Therefore, it is not disrespectful to adopt decision-making procedures that serve the aims of reason and judgement even if those procedures sometimes take us outside the ordinary processes of decision-making.

A second, partially concessive response begins by acknowledging that we care about ordinary processes of political legitimacy because we care about disrespect, and then notes that there is a variety of ways in which we can choose not to conform fully with formal expectations when non-conformity is morally required of us. Thus, our act of non-conformity need not wholly depart from the declared agenda of the formal democratic process. And, in general, we might seek to adopt forms of non-conformity that disrupt that process as little as possible.

Let me now turn to the three objections against the moral roles thesis as a standard for morally acceptable conduct. These objections concern voluntarism, valuable institutions, and value pluralism.

3.4 Voluntarism

A critic might say that, in a reasonably good society, we *voluntarily* assume an office or position and hence have a *pro tanto* content-insensitive moral obligation to conform to formal expectations because we have sworn, consented, or otherwise committed ourselves to carrying out its functions. By accepting a job as an academic, journalist, soldier, magistrate, judge, lawyer, or president, we commit ourselves to carrying out its functions, and to do otherwise would be to act in morally unacceptable ways. At least four replies to this objection present themselves.

First, the voluntarist argument does not apply straightforwardly to many of the contexts under consideration here including office-holders who are conscripted into service, such as jurors and draftees, or who are conscripted into action such as national guards, or who inherit their office and for whom extricating themselves from that office would be particularly difficult, such as monarchs or peers.

Second, the voluntarist presumes that promise-keeping has a general moral application that trumps other kinds of moral duty even when the conduct promised entails the performance of deeply objectionable acts. This presumption is deeply implausible. Amongst other things, no decision to take up an office could be so well-informed, so prescient, that it could bind us to follow the dictates of the office no matter what issues arise.

Third, as the analysis of the moral roles thesis showed, what it means to carry out the function of a normatively legitimate office is not to be determined by a painstaking itemization of its formal rules, but by a full appreciation of the spirit and underlying moral justification for the office.

Fourth, one cannot defend an expectation of conformity with formal dictates by pointing out that we need not assume a particular office if we don't want to (conscription aside) and that we are, in most cases, at liberty to resign our office or leave the society. And, one cannot defend an expectation of general conformity by making provisions for us to excuse ourselves in cases where adhering to formal expectations would be especially onerous for us.[36] The reason is the one given in Section 1. When a society establishes an office that, despite gross moral imperfections, provides the only way to address an important challenge, there are genuine moral reasons for appropriately qualified members to assume the office, which makes their situation particularly unenviable (as the case of the California doctors shows).[37] Thus, as the minimum moral burdens principle states, society must ensure as well as it can that the offices it establishes do not place overly heavy moral burdens on any would-be occupants.

3.5 Valuable institutions

A second objection concerns the preservation of valuable institutions irrespective of their democratic foundations. A critic might say that non-conformity by at least some officials poses a threat to necessary

---

[36] For an examination of related issues, see Tasioulas, John (2003) 'Mercy' in *Proceedings of the Aristotelian Society* 103: 2, 101–32.

[37] For a discussion of some related issues, see Green, Leslie (2007) 'The Duty to Govern' in *Legal Theory*, 13, 165–85. Green observes, for example, that 'however we understand "necessary tasks," they are likely to carve out a duty to govern that is much narrower than the claims of modern states or the scope of legitimate governance'.

and valuable institutions and public goods, and hence is morally unacceptable.

This charge is levelled in just war theory debates against thinkers who argue that soldiers should refuse to fight in an unjust war and should refuse to follow unjust orders in an otherwise just war. Jeff McMahan's responses to the charge are worth summarizing, as they can be applied *mutatis mutandis* to other political contexts:

> It is often suggested that if some soldiers or draftees refuse on moral grounds to fight in an unjust war, this could compromise the efficient functioning and perhaps even threaten the survival of valuable institutions to which these people would rightly be committed. But even if this is true, those who create, serve, and are served by valuable institutions must themselves bear the burdens when those institutions malfunction, thereby causing or threatening unjust harm to others. It would be unjust to impose the costs of their own mistakes or wrongdoing on others.

Moreover, McMahan continues:

> ...the consequences for just institutions of people refusing to fight in unjust wars are unlikely to be calamitous... Victory in an unjust war may serve the national interest but is likely on balance to have a corrupting effect on just institutions... those who refuse to fight in an unjust war might in the long term actually benefit their country's institutions by setting a precedent that would help to deter those in positions of authority within the institutions from initiating further unjust wars. It is also possible that those who refuse to participate in an unjust war could prompt the institutions to shield themselves from the instability that such challenges can cause by adapting themselves to anticipate and accommodate instances of conscientious refusal to fight. The enhanced institutional flexibility would almost certainly be healthy and would presumably involve more generous provisions for conscientious refusal to fight.[38]

In less morally extreme contexts, analogous arguments apply to those of us who conscientiously do not conform to unjust demands.

---

[38] McMahan, Jeff (2004) 'The Ethics of Killing in War' in *Ethics* 114, 693–733.

One apparent difference, however, between the context of war and other domains of political life is killing. McMahan gets mileage for his defence of non-conformity from the fact that what is at issue in war is killing and indeed the killing of innocent people, whereas following unjust orders in other contexts will typically involve far less serious consequences.

This difference is undeniable, but the arguments McMahan makes take a general form. First, those who set up, serve, and are served by an institution must take responsibility for it when it malfunctions. This speaks to the minimum moral burdens principle because one cause of malfunctioning is undue burdensomeness. It is not doctors in California who threaten the valuable institution of criminal justice when they refuse to oversee executions by lethal injection. Rather, the decision-makers and their supporters who adopted execution as a mode of punishment must take responsibility for choosing to address the significant problem of serious wrongdoing through an institution that is likely to malfunction due to its injustice. Second, indeed, the doctors who refused to oversee lethal injections served the long-term interests of their state's institutions by setting a precedent that resulted in a moratorium on capital punishment. Third, in any arena of political power, refusal to participate can prompt institutional leaders to shield the institutions from possible instability by adapting them to anticipate and accommodate non-arbitrary refusals, and this would bring the advantage of flexibility. Therefore, McMahan's arguments can be applied to many other institutions, most notably criminal justice, because, in those realms, there is the potential for grave injustice even if the institution does not involve killing.

3.6 *Value pluralism*

A final problem concerns how we are to act on the moral roles thesis given the assumed reality of fundamental moral pluralism. First, most, if not all, of us hold more than one position or office in society, the underlying responsibilities of which will at times conflict. We are citizens and parents, judges and spouses, doctors and jury members, legislators and siblings. Second, each of our normatively valid offices is underpinned by more than one moral role, the responsibilities of which may be discontinuous. For example, the office of judge is underpinned by several moral roles, including mediator, educator, adjudicator, and guardian. Third, any one moral role is presumably comprised of various moral responsibilities that cannot be ranked under an overarching moral value independent of those that shape the moral role itself. In this minefield of pluralism, how are we to know how to act when we privilege our office-legitimating moral roles before formal expectations? Which office may we privilege? Which underlying moral role may we privilege? Which moral responsibility may we privilege? These questions are related to those that arose about conscience generally in Chapter 2.

In that chapter, I used the notion of a *moral role* itself to respond to worries about moral pluralism at a general level. I argued there that, when we come to hold a given moral role, this affects our moral responsibilities in significant ways since certain moral reasons now apply to us as categorical mandatory reasons (duties) that did not apply to us before. I argued that, when we are confronted with conflicting values and duties, we should privilege, and indeed will privilege if our conscience is adequately developed, those that track the special moral responsibilities that are ours in virtue of our moral roles, skills, and circumstances.

This line of argument, while plausible in the general context of moral decision-making, is not helpful when the pluralism at issue is amongst the moral responsibilities of our moral roles themselves. This is the kind of conflict that would confront the California doctors if the lethal injections would proceed without them. They would have to decide either to oversee capital punishment by lethal injection or let the procedure go ahead without medical oversight. The same kind of conflict confronts doctors who have to decide whether to treat offenders in high-security prisons since the prisons won't close if they refuse to give treatment. And, this kind of conflict confronts the prison officers who have to decide whether to baulk at, or proceed with, subjecting offenders to conditions that can render them unable to reintegrate into society since the prisons won't close if there are fewer officers to run them. If the society is responding to the challenge of serious criminal wrongdoing with execution and solitary confinement (though it is doubtful that such a society would be reasonably good), and if these practices will continue even in the absence of adequate medical care or official oversight, then the doctors and prison officers have role-related moral responsibilities both to be party to these practices and to refuse to be party to them. The problem is to specify how these officials should view the conflicts amongst their moral responsibilities.

Given the nature and pervasiveness of moral pluralism, no final solution can be reached in such dilemmas. However, a non-arbitrary, though imperfect, solution can be sought in at least two, and possibly three, places.

The first place is the deliberative democratic process itself. Here this process is richly understood to include ongoing engagement in deliberation through conventional and non-conventional means (such as civil disobedience) to refine society's interlocking web of formal expectations to minimize the moral burdens that institutions place on office-holders. I invoke the deliberative democratic process here to perform a subtler task than the initial one of establishing offices that embody necessary categories of moral responsibility. This subtler task is to reflect on how to revise offices when necessary to address conflicts amongst the underlying moral responsibilities. It is in this spirit that I proposed the minimum moral burdens principle. When a society has various options open to it to address a pressing challenge such as serious wrongdoing, it should choose those options that impose the most modest moral burdens on the would-be occupants of the institution. And, if an institution and its offices, once established, does come to impose undue moral burdens on its office-holders, then the society should reflect on how best to revise those offices to neutralize the moral conflict as much as possible.[39]

When many office-holders refuse to perform certain tasks, and appeal to the very spirit of their office to legitimate their refusals, this signals that the minimum moral burdens principle may not be satisfied and that revision of the office or institution may be required. Herein lies the second source of an imperfect solution to the pluralism of moral responsibility: the consensus of the relevant office-holders as persons who are knowledgeable about the moral challenges they face. Broadly speaking, soldiers on the ground, prison officials in the system, and doctors in the hospital have a practical appreciation of the moral challenges they face. If a sufficient number of them representing sufficiently diverse backgrounds come to a consensus that a given formal expectation generates overly costly competition amongst their special moral responsibilities, then their concerns should be given particular weight. Of course, there is not always a consensus among such 'experts'

---

[39] For instance, assuming that a reasonably just society has various viable options open to it when deciding how to respond to serious criminal wrongdoing, it should opt *ceteris paribus* for a system of criminal justice that imposes the minimal set of moral burdens on its office-holders. Put bluntly, even if it were true that capital punishment is the just response to some offences, there may be no conditions under which a criminal justice system could reasonably ask of its members that they impose such a punishment.

about what their moral burdens are. And sometimes there is a consensus, but that consensus is not a convincing barometer of moral burdensomeness because its members do not represent a sufficiently diverse group of people.

A third possible source of an imperfect solution is a coordination principle. Such a principle is not put forward as a more ultimate moral principle, but rather as a mechanism for reflecting on the overall performance of the interlocking web of moral responsibilities in our society. A coordination principle would aim as well as possible to ensure that we do not confront significant clashes of moral responsibility when we carry out our official functions. It would seek to ensure that a doctor does not have to operate on her daughter, and a judge does not hear a case in which his nephew is the defendant, and a legislator is not involved in making laws that closely affect her spouse or, indeed, her financial backers.

My reason for flagging these dilemmas is not only to address the value pluralism objection, but also to show that this issue sits at a distance from, but is easily conflated with, issues of personal moral conviction. Persons may make assertions of moral responsibility that they declare to be reflective of their underlying moral roles but that are actually at odds with the spirit of their moral roles properly understood. This distinction between personal conviction and the pluralism of responsibility is an important one that can readily be made in the abstract, but will be contentious in concrete cases. As I noted in the Introduction to this book, I cannot hope to settle longstanding debates about the morality of concrete cases such as reproductive services for women, parental responsibility, and war. Therefore, when I give examples to elucidate my views, I do so knowing they will be intuitive only to those who share my intuitions.

Conclusion

In this chapter, I argued that the moral roles that legitimize formal offices have overriding moral importance even in a reasonably good society. In defence of this view, I advanced both the gap thesis and the moral roles thesis. I also articulated a principle that is implied by these theses, namely, the minimum moral burdens principle. According to this principle, society must deal with its big challenges by trying as well as possible to set up offices that are not overly morally burdensome for any would-be occupants of those offices. My arguments in this chapter raise doubts about both the standard distribution of formal discretion across offices and the normative validity of some of the offices that presently exist in societies, such as that of high-security prison doctor. My arguments also show that it can often be morally obligatory to resort to conscience-driven, communicative disobedience irrespective of our office and the goodness of our society.

4

Rights

Do the Californian anaesthesiologists discussed in the last chapter have a moral right to refuse en masse to oversee state executions by lethal injection? Does a civil registrar have a moral right to refuse to officiate at same-sex partnership ceremonies? Having examined the nature of conscience and conviction, I want to consider now whether either conscience or conviction gives us defeasible moral protections—moral rights—against interference by other people. In particular, I want to consider whether either of them generates a moral right to disobey the law.

In what follows, I show that conscience generates a moral right that protects our ability to honour our special moral responsibilities (Section 2). This moral right of conscience is essentially a claim-right that others not interfere with our carrying out our responsibilities. As such, the right protects those acts of disobedience that are conscience-driven and responsibility-prioritizing.

I then show that conscientious moral conviction generates two moral rights. The first protects the cognitive pre-conditions for moral conviction. It is a moral right to have a certain control over the inner domain of our own minds including a right to free thought. I show that this moral right to inner control and free thought is more limited than we might suppose. It is limited by the fact that we have no general right in many contexts to think as we wish: we have no general right to control our attention and no general right against manipulation (Section 3). The second right is a moral right to expression of thought including a limited right to act in ways expressive of our moral convictions, ie a moral right of conscientious action (Section 4). Although standard liberal views in the spirit of John Stuart Mill tend to run freedom of thought and freedom of expression together, maintaining that there is no free thought worth the name without free expression, nevertheless I show that the right to inner control and free thought is independent of the right to expression. There is important non-instrumental value in free thought as thought, part of which lies in its constitutive contribution to conscience. By contrast, the right to expression is not independent of the right to free thought.

Both of the moral rights arising from moral conviction are rooted in the principle of humanism outlined in the Introduction to this book, a principle that respects our deep moral convictions. This principle acknowledges that society and the law place overly burdensome pressure on us when they coerce us always to privilege conformity with law above our deep convictions. In light of the communicative principle of conscientiousness specified in Chapter 1,[1] the limited moral right of conscientious action applies more readily to civil disobedience than to personal disobedience even in reasonably good societies (Section 4). This humanistic case for the moral right to civil disobedience can be supplemented by an observation about the double harmony between campaigners' and society's interests in the stabilizing, democracy-promoting benefits of civil disobedience.

To set the scene, let me begin by distinguishing moral rights from legal rights and by challenging the commonly accepted view that if something is a moral right, then there is a presumption in favour of establishing it as a legal right.

1. Moral Rights versus Legal Rights

A moral right is a justified claim to protection rooted in an interest of the right-holder that is sufficiently weighty to ground duties in other persons.[2] As such, to quote Raymond Frey, though he was an avowed sceptic of moral rights, a moral right is,

---

[1] Recall that the communicative principle of conscientiousness says that, when we judge some conduct to be seriously wrong we must not only 1) avoid such conduct ourselves to the best extent that we are able, and 2) judge such conduct in others to be wrong as well, but also, other things being equal, 3) be willing to bear the risks of honouring our conviction, and 4) be willing to communicate our conviction to others. Unlike personal disobedients, civil disobedients demonstrate their conscientiousness through their willingness to bear the risks of trying to communicate their concerns to others.

[2] Cf Raz, Joseph (1986) *The Morality of Freedom*. Oxford: Clarendon Press.

a right which is not the product of community legislation or social practice, which persists even in the face of contrary legislation or practice, and which prescribes the boundary beyond which neither individuals nor the community may go in pursuit of their overall ends.[3]

Some moral rights are protected entitlements to positive benefits in the form of services and/or negative benefits in the form of non-injuries. Other moral rights are protected options for action, that is, rights of conduct.[4] Rights of conduct, which are my focus in what follows, outline and protect a sphere of autonomy and liberty of action for us with which interference by others is justifiably restricted and of which positive protection by others may justifiably be expected. That protected sphere secures a space for us to act unencumbered in ways that may be objectionable, though it does not immunize us from criticism.

One merit of this Razian account of moral rights is that it accommodates grounds of rights that go beyond what is good just for us as the right-holder to include the services that a right secures for people other than us the right-holder. For example, a journalist's right to protect her sources and her expansive rights of expression serve the journalist's own interests. But, those rights would not have the same weight and importance that they have if protecting her interests did not also serve the public interest in the circulation of information.[5] There is a double harmony here. Although the journalist's interests must be

---

[3] Frey, Raymond (1980) *Interests and Rights: The Case Against Animals*. Oxford: Clarendon Press, 7. Cited in Feinberg, Joel (1992) 'In Defence of Moral Rights' in *Oxford Journal of Legal Studies* 12: 2, 149–69.

[4] Rights of conduct, as protected options for action, are not to be confused with liberty-rights in the Hohfeldian sense. Given their Hohfeldian baggage, the terms *privilege* and *liberty* are ill-suited to characterize moral rights of conduct. At the same time, it is necessary to avoid Robert P. George's contention that many rights of conduct are weaker, 'shadow' rights of the duties that government, society, or individuals have, on grounds other than the agent's rights, not to interfere with her possibly objectionable conduct. Possible grounds for non-interference with a person's performance of reprehensible acts, George says, are that the interference may be self-defeating or counterproductive, or may prevent persons from fulfilling more compelling obligations, or may put either the interferer or a third-party at risk, etc. George, Robert P. (1993) *Making Men Moral: Civil Liberties and Public Morality*. Oxford: Clarendon Press, 117–18.

[5] Raz (1986), 247–8. Raz goes on to say a few pages later: '... aspects of freedom of speech cannot be explained at all except as protecting collective goods, i.e., preserving the character of the community as an open society. The freedom of the press illustrates the point. In most liberal democracies the press enjoys privileges not extended to ordinary individuals. Those include protection against action for libel or breach of privacy, access to information, priority in access to the courts or to Parliamentary sessions, special governmental briefings, and so on. They are sometimes enshrined in law, sometimes left to conventions. The justification of the

served for these rights to exist, the weight and indeed the justification of these rights does not reduce to the interests of the right-holding journalist alone.[6] In the same vein, Joseph Raz observes with regard to dissenters that '... while political theorists often highlight the protection for the individual dissident which [a right to dissent] provides, in practice its primary role has been to provide a collective good, to protect the democratic character of the society'.[7] Although Raz would not endorse my extending his argument to a general moral right to civil disobedience, nevertheless I argue later that a similar double harmony does exist between civil disobedients' moral right to engage in suitably constrained communicative breaches of law and society's interests in the enhancement of democratic deliberation.

Moral rights differ from legal rights, first, in terms of institutional recognition, and second, in the justness of their protected claims. Moral rights lack both an institutional pedigree and institutional recognition, but identify a justified moral claim that gives an exclusionary moral reason to protect certain interests. Legal rights, by contrast, have both an institutional pedigree and institutional recognition, but do not necessarily protect important interests.

A further, oft-cited, though mistaken distinction between moral rights and legal rights concerns their enforceability.[8] Legal rights are said to be enforceable and moral rights not to be.[9] But, of course, some legal rights are not practically enforceable such as ancient rights that are still on the books, and many moral rights are both enforceable and enforced through convention and social censure. The actual difference here between moral and legal rights lies not in enforceability, but in the mechanisms for enforcement.

The salient issue for my purposes is how moral rights interact with legal rights. A common liberal view is the so-called legal-right presumption that when we have a moral right there is, as Raz puts it,

---

special rights and privileges of the press are in its service to the community at large.' Raz (1986), 253.

[6] Raz's notion of *double harmony* may be understood to speak either to the weight of the right only or to both the weight and the justification for the right. Although I am inclined to adopt the latter interpretation given Raz's comment that the *justification* of the journalist's right does not reduce to her interests alone, nevertheless I appreciate that many readers of Raz would favour the former interpretation.

[7] Raz (1986), 253–4.

[8] For an extended discussion of enforceability, see Reiff, Mark (2005) *Punishment, Compensation, and Law: A Theory of Enforceability*. Cambridge: Cambridge University Press.

[9] Cf Cranston, Maurice (1983) 'Are There any Human Rights?' in *Daedalus* 112: 4, 1–17.

'a presumption for giving that right legal recognition'.[10] (To the extent that Raz endorses this presumption, this is where he and I part company on the theory of rights.) A stronger version of the legal-right presumption is what Feinberg calls the 'there ought to be a law' theory of moral rights, according to which the claim that person A has a moral right to do, have, or be x is to be understood, insofar as it makes any sense at all, to be saying that A ought to have a legal right to x.[11] I take the thrust of the thought to be that when we have a moral right not only is it possible, in principle, to codify it as a legal right, but there is a *pro tanto* moral reason to do so.

In my view, there are grounds to be sceptical about both the conceptual part of this claim—that it is true of all moral rights that they could be translated into legal rights and duly enacted into law— and the evaluative part of this claim—that there is invariably a *pro tanto* moral reason to make such a translation assuming it's possible. I shall highlight these grounds for scepticism partly to undermine one argument against a moral right to civil disobedience, that it cannot be translated into a legal right. If I am right that the legal-right presumption is mistaken, then this argument against a moral right to civil disobedience misses its mark.

Concerning the conceptual part of the legal-right presumption, there are at least two conceptually intelligible categories of moral rights that, by nature, cannot be translated into legal rights. (Whether these conceptually intelligible moral rights I am about to mention ultimately turn out to be moral rights is another matter; the point here is that the concept of a *moral right* can, in principle, accommodate categories of rights that the concept of a *legal right* cannot.) The first is a moral right to have certain spheres of our lives, whatever they may be, not subject to the regulation of law. They are spheres on which the law remains silent. Codifying such a moral claim into law would undermine that very claim because the law would then be speaking about what it purportedly is silent about.

The second is the moral right to engage in (certain) deliberate breaches of law. The law cannot recognize a legal right *deliberately* to break the law. Were the law to say it recognized such a right, then the act in question would not be in breach of law. Saying the law could recognize a legal right deliberately to break the law is like specifying the

---

[10] Cf Raz, Joseph (1979) *The Authority of Law*. Oxford: Oxford University Press, 262.
[11] See Feinberg (1992).

truth-value of 'This sentence is false'. It is paradoxical.[12] By contrast, the concept of a *moral right* does not exclude the possibility of a moral right deliberately to break the law. It does not rule out either incidental breaches of law such as personal disobedience or deliberate breaches of law such as civil disobedience and rebellion against a tyrannical government. In this spirit, Feinberg, for one, notes that the ultimate human right to resist oppression and to apply force against ruinous injustice must be acknowledged side by side with the impossibility of institutional reflection of that right.[13]

Thinkers such as Jeremy Bentham, who maintain that the notion of moral rights is nonsense upon stilts, or Raymond Frey, who maintain that moral rights talk is a confused and indirect way of referring to legal rights, must either reject these two categories of moral right as being unintelligible or square the circle of specifying how they could be legal rights.

Now a critic might raise two objections. The first is that the law is not as internally coherent and determinate as my claims need it to be to sustain the thought that it is paradoxical to speak of a legal right to break the law. Often the law is indeterminate or inconsistent. There are conflicting laws on the books. Therefore, the law cannot be held to a standard of internal coherence that would give rise to the paradox that prevents law from recognizing a right to break it. In reply, where the law is indeterminate or inconsistent, it is not possible to specify what the legal right would be in these cases, but it is possible to specify what the moral right would be.

The second objection is that my analysis is unimaginative, as there are at least two possible rights to break the law that the law can recognize. The first is the very right to resist oppression that Feinberg calls the ultimate human right. In German Basic Law, there is a constitutional right of resistance: 'All Germans shall have the right to resist any person seeking to abolish this constitutional order, if no other remedy is available.'[14] The second is jury nullification (otherwise called

---

[12] I put aside here the various proposed solutions to the liar's paradox in the philosophy of language and logic.

[13] In saying this, Feinberg quotes Robert Cover's analysis of the writings of Justice Joseph Story, a US Supreme Court Justice during the 1840s. Feinberg (1992).

[14] The four sections of Article 20 are: (1) The Federal Republic of Germany is a democratic and social federal state; (2) All state authority is derived from the people. It shall be exercised by the people through elections and other votes and through specific legislative, executive and judicial bodies; (3) The legislature shall be bound by the constitutional order,

jury equity), which is the legal right or power of a jury to acquit a defendant that it would declare guilty if it followed the court's legal instructions.[15]

But, in my view, neither of these acts is a breach of law. The German constitutional right of resistance in cases of necessity is not an act of non-conformity with formal expectations. It is rather a built-in check on expected conformity with other laws. And, it is framed as a right to resist 'any person', not a right to resist the legal order. Jury nullification is admittedly an act of non-conformity with formal expectations literally understood as the judge's instructions, but that kind of non-conformity is not in breach of law when juries have the legal power to make determinations against legal instructions.

Let me now turn to the evaluative part of the legal-right presumption, which says that there is invariably a *pro tanto* moral reason to translate a moral right into a legal right assuming that that translation is possible. Undoubtedly, there is a strong moral reason to ensure the protection of some moral rights in law, such as women's right to vote or women's right not to be subjected to genital mutilation. But, there is no moral reason to favour legal codification of other moral rights even though that codification is conceptually possible, such as a spouse's right not to be lied to about polygamous behaviour. Between these two extremes, there are domains that favour some legal codification of moral rights, but only in broad terms. A case in point might be former Canadian Prime Minister Pierre Trudeau's sound-bite that 'the state has no business in the bedrooms of the nation'. The law may properly specify a condition of 'amongst consenting adults', but beyond that, it may be that it should not regulate in this area of people's lives. Finally, there are domains in which, in principle, there are *pro tanto* moral reasons to favour translating moral rights into legal rights, but in practice this is likely to result in abuses of the protection, such as rights to filibuster. In short, there is no *pro tanto* reason to codify moral rights in domains where the law ought not to tread or would serve no valid purpose.

In general, the legal-right presumption implies a dismissive view of moral rights. It sees them as rights that ultimately are fit to be legal rights.

---

the executive and the judiciary by law and justice; (4) All Germans shall have the right to resist any person seeking to abolish this constitutional order, if no other remedy is available.

[15] Cf Brooks, Thom (2004) 'A Defence of Jury Nullification' in *Res Publica* 10: 4, 401–23. 'Juries are said to "nullify" the law insofar as they depart from the law when rendering a verdict.'

As Feinberg notes, such a view cannot be reconciled with familiar uses of the language of moral rights, such as the language of people exercising their moral rights prior to those rights being recognized in law (as in the case of demonstrators arrested for illegal picketing) or the language of *condemning* practices such as female genital mutilation in societies where that practice is lawful; 'what we condemn here and now is not merely that the law does not prohibit it, but that it is done at all'.[16]

In sum, some moral rights cannot be translated into legal rights and some moral rights have no moral reason to be translated into legal rights. Despite this, moral rights as moral rights can and often should have a bearing on how upholders of the law operate. I return to this point in my discussions in Part II of this book on the demands-of-conviction defence, necessity defence, and punishment. My reasons for highlighting the erroneousness of the legal-right presumption are not only to put aside one argument against a moral right to civil disobedience, but also more generally to set the stage for my defence of both the moral right of conscience and the moral right of conscientious action, neither of which can generate a *pro tanto* moral reason to establish an equivalent legal right with the same content. By contrast, the moral right to inner control and free thought can and does generate a *pro tanto* reason for establishing an equivalent legal right on the assumption that the legitimate parameters of the law will not intrude on the sphere that this right protects. This assumption is based on the thought that *ceteris paribus* the law should not be in the business of regulating our thoughts, but should be in the business of regulating the extent to which other people may try to mess with our thoughts.

2. A Moral Right of Conscience

As discussed in Chapters 2 and 3, conscience enables us to become responsive to our special moral responsibilities. It enables us to recognize that often the only morally acceptable way to honour them is to disobey formal norms. The moral right of conscience protects us in honouring the responsibilities that society sometimes cannot recognize as morally acceptable. In other words, the right is a claim against

---

[16] Feinberg (1992).

interference by others with our carrying out our moral responsibilities.[17] It is in essence a duty-based right.

At first glance, such a right may seem mysterious since it looks like a right to act well, and we do not need a right to protect us in acting well. The function of rights of conduct is to give us protection in a certain sphere to choose to act wrongly.[18]

But, the right of conscience is not mysterious. It protects a justified moral claim founded on a sufficiently weighty interest in being able to fulfil our moral responsibilities even when competing considerations make fulfilling those responsibilities morally problematic. For instance, if our society has to go to war in self-defence, we may act wrongly when we insist that we stay home to care for our parents. But, if called to account for this, we can invoke our moral right to honour our responsibility to do so.[19] Similarly, environmentalists may act wrongly by damaging coal companies' property in an effort to delay environmental degradation. But, if called to account, they can invoke their moral right to honour their responsibilities to protect human beings, animals, and the planet.[20] And, anti-war activists such as Sisters Carol Gilbert, Ardeth Platte, and Jackie Marie Hudson may act wrongly by trespassing onto a US military base to protest against US military policy.[21] But, they can, and did, invoke their basic rights in a free society to expose non-violently and symbolically their government's threat, or commission, of war crimes. The nuns claimed they acted out of both their religious faith and their responsibilities under the principles of the Nuremberg Charter to act against government policies that violate international law.[22]

---

[17] For an interesting discussion of the relation between rights and duties, which asks why duties are not rights (though they can be protected by rights), see Cruft, Rowan (2006) 'What Aren't Duties Rights?' in *The Philosophical Quarterly* 56: 223, 175–92.

[18] Cf Raz (1979), chs 14 and 15; Waldron, Jeremy (1981) 'A Right to do Wrong' *Ethics* 92: 1, 21–39.

[19] Cf Sartre, Jean Paul (1946) 'Existentialism is a Humanism' (various edns).

[20] I discuss this case in Chapter 6.

[21] The nuns protested against US military policy by cutting through a chain-link fence in northeastern Colorado to gain access to a nuclear missile silo. Wearing suits labelled 'Citizens Weapons Inspection Team', the nuns pounded with hammers on the concrete cover of the silo and drew crosses with their own blood. They then sang hymns and prayed until they were arrested. The nuns offered numerous reasons for their civil disobedience, some of which pertain to the protection of basic rights, others to nuclear disarmament, and others to US policy in Afghanistan, Iraq, Sudan, and more generally. Cada, Chryss 'Three Nuns and a Test for Civil Disobedience' in the *Boston Globe* 27 May 2003.

[22] I discuss this case in Chapter 5.

Of course, our invocation of a moral right of conscience may not be decisive. We might be wrong when we invoke it. Or we might have hefty competing moral responsibilities that weaken our invocation of it. Or, even if we are correct to invoke it, our right of conscience is not absolute and it may not carry the day with those to whom we invoke it.[23] In Chapter 6, I examine the mixed success that campaigners have had before the law in appealing to their moral responsibilities to argue for the necessity of their disobedience. For now, I conclude that the moral right of conscience undoubtedly protects *some* disobedience, including some civil disobedience, such as Rosa Parks' refusal to give up her bus seat in 1955. But, it does not protect civil disobedience in general. For that we must look beyond the moral right of conscience, to the two moral rights of conviction: the moral right of inner control and free thought (Section 3) and the moral right of conscientious action (Section 4).

3. A Moral Right to Inner Control and Free Thought

3.1 *The nature of the right*

We might think that, if any right is wholly unconstrained, it must be the right to inner control, free thought, and belief.[24] Such a right is not straightforwardly a right of conduct, though it is a right to do things with our minds. It is also not a duty-based right like the right of conscience. This right is, if anything, a right to independence from external constraints and influences on our minds. This independence applies both to the *process* of thinking and to the *products* of thinking.

---

[23] The right of conscience is also complex given the multiplicity of our moral roles. A person can be both a parent and a doctor, a judge and a spouse. What acts of disobedience does the moral right of conscience protect? Would it protect the judge who acquits her own guilty child (putting conflicts of interest aside)? Would it protect the doctor who gives priority to treating her own child? The legal side will be explored in later chapters; but, the short moral answer is yes, provided that the acts in question are ones to which conscience would be responsive. If so, then the acts are morally acceptable, and hence are protected under the moral right of conscience.

[24] I have stipulated that a moral right to inner control and free thought is a pre-condition for having genuine moral convictions. Note that the right to free thought captures a much wider range of things than convictions. As outlined in Chapter 1, unlike free thought, *conviction* is constrained by conditions of internal consistency and minimal evidentiary satisfactoriness.

Concerning the process of thinking, it is a right to carry out our thinking freely and independently from external pressures by other people as well as we can. In its most expansive, ideal form, such a freedom of thinking would be a moral right to have absolute control over the 'inward domain of our consciousness', to use Mill's phrase.[25]

Concerning the products of thinking, the ideal would be comprised of free thoughts whose content is not influenced by, or shaped in reaction to, external pressures from others. In these rich, ideal terms, *free thought* is, as John Skorupski puts it, 'thought ruled by its own principles and by nothing else; in other words by principles of thinking that it discovers by reflecting on its own activity'.[26]

As ideals, free thinking and free thoughts feed into a broader ideal of independent-mindedness as the sustained capacity to think in meaningful ways not principally shaped by others' thoughts and behaviour.[27] This ideal would protect our thinking whatever thought we wish to think at any given moment irrespective of whether that thought was formed independently of others' influence. The capacities necessary for an ideal of independent-mindedness would be those capacities that comprise the cognitive part of an ideal of conscience. They are the capacities to reflect independently on the moral quality of our own and others' conduct, motives, intentions, emotions, dispositions, character, and ideals.

This ideal of unconstrained inner control and free thought is just that—an ideal. Despite its intuitive appeal, it is not plausible as the content of a practicable moral right of inner control and free thought.

---

[25] Mill, John Stuart (1859) *On Liberty*, ch 1. 'This, then, is the appropriate region of human liberty. It comprises, first, the inward domain of consciousness; demanding liberty of conscience, in the most comprehensive sense; liberty of thought and feeling; absolute freedom of opinion and sentiment on all subjects, practical or speculative, scientific, moral, or theological.'

[26] Skorupski, John (2006) *Why Read Mill Today?* London: Routledge, 6–7. Skorupski notes that this characterization supports either of two interpretations: either free thought is thought that is unconstrained by external pressures including, but not limited to, authoritarian pressures or it is thought that is radically presuppositionless. I shall put the second of these aside, as it takes us away from the evaluative tasks of moral and political philosophy.

[27] As an aside, is dissent an example of independent-mindedness or of reactivity? On the one hand, Archibald MacLeish says that, '... the dissenter is every human being at those moments of his life when he resigns momentarily from the herd and thinks for himself'. MacLeish, A (1956) 'In Praise of Dissent' in *The New York Times*, 16 December. On the other hand, while a dissenting thought might be the product of a *process* of free thinking, the *product* is not free from that against which it is a reaction. Dissent may offer a beginning for the development of free thoughts. But, it may also offer a beginning for conformism within the circles in which it is accepted.

The kind of moral right that could be practicable is much more modest. Here are three arguments why that is so: 1) the attention argument, 2) the valuable hierarchical relationships argument, and 3) the mental limitations argument.

3.2 The attention argument

The attention argument pertains to the process of thinking. A wholly unconstrained right to free thought would protect not only our choices of opinions, thoughts, feelings, and sentiments on all matters, but also our choices of how to direct our attention. In other words, a wholly unconstrained moral right of free thought would include a claim against intrusions on our attention.

Yet, commonsensically, we do not behave as though, nor do we believe that, we have any claim, let alone an *unconstrained* claim, against intrusions on our attention. Typically, we breezily intrude on each other's attention confident in the assumption that we have no *pro tanto* moral duty not to do so outside libraries, churches, operating theatres, bedrooms, and bathrooms, and even in those places our respect is sloppy.[28] Although the ubiquity of our intrusions on each other's

---

[28] In *A Room of One's Own* (1929), Virginia Woolf describes perfectly the experience of interrupted meditation in her account of daydreaming by the river on the grounds of a Cambridge men's college. She says: 'There one might have sat the clock round lost in thought. Thought—to call it by a prouder name than it deserved—had let its line down into the stream. It swayed, minute after minute, hither and thither among the reflections and the weeds, letting the water lift it and sink it until—you know the little tug—the sudden conglomeration of an idea at the end of one's line: and then the cautious hauling of it in, and the careful laying of it out? Alas, laid on the grass how small, how insignificant this thought of mine looked; the sort of fish that a good fisherman puts back into the water so that it may grow fatter and be one day worth cooking and eating. I will not trouble you with that thought now, though if you look carefully you may find it for yourselves in the course of what I am going to say. But however small it was, it had, nevertheless, the mysterious property of its kind—put back into the mind, it became at once very exciting, and important; and as it darted and sank, and flashed hither and thither, set up such a wash and tumult of ideas that it was impossible to sit still. It was thus that I found myself walking with extreme rapidity across a grass plot. Instantly a man's figure rose to intercept me. Nor did I at first understand that the gesticulations of a curious-looking object, in a cut-away coat and evening shirt, were aimed at me. His face expressed horror and indignation. Instinct rather than reason came to my help, he was a Beadle; I was a woman. This was the turf; there was the path. Only the Fellows and Scholars are allowed here; the gravel is the place for me. Such thoughts were the work of a moment. As I regained the path the arms of the Beadle sank, his face assumed its usual repose, and though turf is better walking than gravel, no very great harm was done. The only charge I could bring against the Fellows and Scholars of whatever the college might happen to be was that in protection of their turf, which has been rolled for 300 years in succession they had sent my little fish into hiding.'

attention is a modern phenomenon, such intrusions have always occurred, and presumably are inescapable, which belies the possibility, let alone the general acceptability, of a wholly unconstrained right to free thought. Now, of course, commonsense morality may be mistaken. But, on this point about attention, I think it is correct. We may well have a largely unconstrained moral right to *try* to direct our attention as we wish, but we have no unconstrained moral right to succeed.

That said, there are other types of deliberate intrusions on our minds against which we do have a moral right, most notably pernicious intrusions that seek to target not our attention, but our capacity to perceive without attention, as so many corporate, commercial, and political campaigns seek to do for dubious reasons. Such deliberate subliminal intrusions fall afoul of the principle of humanism that respects our capacity for reasoning and conviction. Respecting each other's thoughts and beliefs does not begin with protecting a space for expression. Instead, it begins with not seeking surreptitiously to inculcate new thoughts and beliefs in each other and not trying to manipulate our thoughts and beliefs subliminally for nefarious or self-serving purposes. It begins in not taking advantage of our 'predictably irrational' susceptibilities to framing devices and default positions as well as our tendency to have negativity bias, loss aversion, and status quo bias.[29] Therefore, although the right to free thought includes no claim to have full control over our own attention, it does include a claim against devious intrusions that capitalize on the ways our minds typically work.[30]

Of course, devious intrusions must not be confused with all forms of manipulation. Not all forms of manipulation are rights-intruding, as my valuable hierarchical relationship argument will make clear. This means that there is no general moral right *ceteris paribus* against manipulation. Let me begin with a non-hierarchical example. Suppose that my briefly manipulating an unimportant thought of yours will achieve a great good. Suppose that my subliminally making you believe for a

---

[29] For an overview of the psychology literature on our susceptibilities, see Ariely, Daniel (2008) *Predictably Irrational: The Hidden Forces that Shape our Decisions*. London: HarperCollins.

[30] The medium matters. There is a difference between the use of rhetoric in writing and the use of subliminal messaging in video ads. There is usually the possibility to reflect critically on written communications while we are reading them. There is usually little possibility to reflect on visual messages while we are watching them, and they may affect our thinking in such a way that we are then less able to reflect on them afterwards.

moment that I am Pat and not Mike is coincidentally the only way for me to save a village from destruction in a war. Do you really have a right to free thought that extends to the protection of such trivial thoughts, which I infringe upon (or violate) with my manipulation?[31] I doubt it. But, if we say that you do have a right here, then we must distinguish this case from a case in which I *distract* your attention for a moment in order to save the village. Since you have no right *ceteris paribus* not to be briefly distracted by me, why should we think you have a right not to be briefly and trivially manipulated by me? Perhaps, there is more at stake in the manipulation case since there is the worry that my manipulating you could lead you to engage in wrongful actions, which is not as much of a worry when I distract you. But, that worry is really a worry about a slippery slope to non-trivial forms of manipulation. It is not a worry about this trivial manipulation itself. And, the slippery slope worry could apply to non-trivial distractions as well.

3.3. *The valuable relationship argument*

This leads me to the second argument for the limited nature of the right to free thought, which is the valuable hierarchical relationship argument. It pertains to both the process and the product of thinking. A wholly unconstrained right to free thought would necessarily be insensitive to content and context. But, in valuable hierarchical relationships, such as those between parent and child, teacher and disciple, spiritual guide and novice, there is no presumption in favour of unconstrained free thought. Indeed, there is often a strong presumption against it.[32] Typically, parents do not manipulate their children in rights-intruding ways when they inculcate in them specific values, norms, beliefs, and cultural habits. Nor, typically, do they manipulate them in rights-intruding ways when they cajole, bribe, or threaten them into behaving well. Commonsensically, it is only when this inculcation process renders a child either likely to lead a terrible life

---

[31] Such a case is not improbable. Cary Grant made diverting use of manipulating Audrey Hepburn's beliefs about his identity in the 1963 film *Charade*. Spoiler alert: the second to last line of the film, uttered by Hepburn, nicely sums it up: 'Oh, I love you Adam, Alex, Peter, Brian, whatever your name is! . . . I hope we have a lot of boys and we can name them all after you.'

[32] Indeed, within the parent-child relationship and the teacher-student relationship, the senior party has a duty *to* influence the junior party's mind, not a duty not to do so.

or fit for only one way of life that it is rights-intruding.[33] It is typically the effects on the child's present and future that make some parental manipulations rights-intrusions.[34]

Now, one might think that, although the conventions of valuable hierarchical relationships dictate that the junior party defer and outwardly emulate the senior party, nevertheless the junior party retains a full freedom to hold what convictions she likes within the privacy of her mind. But, in reply, unless the junior party has an iron will and an impervious spirit, that freedom is no freedom worth the name in the face of the senior party's concerted, expert efforts to rewire her mind. The fact that the parent or teacher cannot reach inside the pupil's head does not mean that his efforts to inculcate beliefs in her will be any less effective. If we think otherwise and assume that only interferences with our bodies can meaningfully circumscribe our freedoms, then we take an overly physicalist view of freedom that, amongst other things, is callously dismissive of the effects of psychological abuse. In sum, in valuable hierarchical relationships, parents' or teachers' intrusions with thought are typically not rights-affecting even though they can be manipulative. In contrast, the manipulative intrusions of many media messages *are* rights-affecting because, amongst other things, they are not legitimated by a valuable hierarchical relationship; they cannot be easily avoided since they are ubiquitous and often subliminal; and they are often poorly motivated.

As an aside, it is worthwhile to consider the relation between free thought and free emotion. Philosophers think a lot about free expression and a bit about free thought, but very little about free emotion. Can we think of freedom of thought without thinking about freedom of emotion or vice versa? Probably not. Protection of emotional freedom is an important issue because, for one thing, rhetoric and manipulation tend to get at our thoughts by getting at our emotions. What is interesting is that, typically, we think this is far more troubling

---

[33] Joel Feinberg observes that 'an education that renders a child fit for only one way of life forecloses irrevocably his other options'. Feinberg, Joel (1994a) *Freedom and Fulfilment*. Princeton: Princeton University Press, 82.

[34] The inculcation that we experience as children points to another argument against the possibility of wholly unconstrained free thought: the very first thoughts we have when we begin to think as young babies and children are heavily influenced by the people who are raising us and by our general environment. The modes and patterns of thinking that we acquire as children are not freely formed. Indeed, there is an inescapable tension between providing us with the stimulation needed to cultivate thought at all and protecting us from influences, as they undermine the potential for wholly unconstrained free thought.

than the reverse. Typically, we do not think it troubling that reasoned discussion can get at our emotions and intuitions by getting at our capacity for logical reasoning. But, that should trouble us since cold reason can lead us away from the best of the human heart. These are all ideas for another day.

3.4 The mental limitations argument

My third argument pertains to both the process and products of thinking. A wholly unconstrained right to inner control and free thought is not securable in principle for all people. It is not securable for irremediably psychologically ill people, clinically depressed people, or cognitively impaired people whose thoughts can be debilitating in the absence of, or even in the presence of, medical intervention. For these people, free thought is an ideal that, in all probability, will continue to elude them. If there were a wholly unconstrained moral right to free thought, then these people would have a legitimate grievance and a claim to be recompensed for not having their right to free thought actualized.

One objection to this argument is that we are all 'cognitively impaired' to some extent since we are all unable to engage in fully unencumbered free thinking to produce free thoughts, and hence there is no issue of compensating some for an unrealizable ideal.

In reply, the parameters of what counts as fully free thought undoubtedly must be set with reference to the thinking capacities of human beings. But, even within those parameters there will be a rich notion of cognitive potential that can be called 'fully unconstrained free thought' below which some persons will markedly fall.

This reply gives rise to another objection, which is that the incapacity of some to exercise a right does not set the parameters for what counts as a right. There are people who cannot walk, but we do not then think there is no right to walk. So, the fact that some people cannot exercise free thought does not entail that there is no unconstrained right to free thought.

In reply, for the people who cannot walk, we build ramps and elevators. The reason we do this is that there are rights of movement and we adjust our structures to enable people who cannot walk to realize their rights of movement. In the case of a right to free thought, we can adjust things to some extent to enable some people who are otherwise incapable of free thought to think more freely, but such persons would have no claim to compensation for being unable to have fully unconstrained free thought.

The rather surprising conclusion that follows from the attention argument, valuable hierarchical relationship argument, and mental limitations argument is that our moral right to inner control and free thought is quite limited. We cannot have a wholly unencumbered right here even though it is a fundamental right of the mind. That said, my arguments have focused on the circumstances of thinking and our capacities to think. I have not focused on the content of thoughts. There is one sense in which the right to inner control and free thought is expansive in a way that my discussion has not highlighted, and that is as a negative liberty to think any thought. This does not mean that we have a right to think any given thought at any given time. Rather, it means that there is no thought that anyone could tell us we have no right to think *ever*.[35]

Now, despite its conceptual and practical limits, the right to inner control and free thought is an intuitively plausible right for many reasons. One is the centrality of thought, belief, and reasoning for autonomy and dignity. Another often cited reason, which I reject, turns on the relation between free thought and expression of thought. I will show that the right to free thought is meaningful not only in relation to expression of thought, but also independent of it.

3.5 The value of free thought

J. B. Bury takes the view that a right to free thought is only meaningful to the extent that it includes free expression of thought. Bury argues that, on its own, freedom of private thinking is of little value and of considerable disvalue to a person: 'It is unsatisfactory and even painful to the thinker himself, if he is not permitted to communicate his

---

[35] I thank Carl Fox for highlighting this point. Matthew Clayton has pressed me in conversation to explain why we have a moral right to think racist or sexist thoughts since there is no value in such thoughts. If we could give people a drug that prevented them from thinking bigoted thoughts, would there be any right-of-thought-based reason not to give it to them? My answer is yes. One reason is that the value of protecting such thoughts lies in their educative potential. By examining such thoughts, we can learn to see their flaws and more generally cultivate our reflective abilities. But, of course, that potential is contingent on our remembering that we have thought the thought. A second reason focuses on what it means to have a protected sphere in which to think. It means having the space to think poorly and meanly, not just the space to think well. For the right to inner control and free thought to be any right worth the name, it has to protect us in thinking the nasty thoughts as well as the nice ones.

thoughts to others, and it is obviously of no value to his neighbours.'[36] Bury continues:

it is extremely difficult to hide thoughts that have any power over the mind. If a [person's] thinking leads him to call in question ideas and customs which regulate the behaviour of those about him, to reject beliefs which they hold, to see better ways of life than those they follow, it is almost impossible for him, if he is convinced of the truth of his own reasoning, not to betray by silence, chance words, or general attitude that he is different from them and does not share their opinions. Some have preferred, like Socrates, some would prefer to-day, to face death rather than conceal their thoughts. Thus freedom of thought, in any valuable sense, includes freedom of speech.

Mill seems to take a similar position when he states that it is impossible to separate Liberty of Thought from the cognate liberties of speaking and of writing.[37]

This view, that any meaningful right of free thought must include a right of free expression, is mistaken. I agree that part of the meaning and value of free thought seems to be tied to expression of thought for two reasons. First, expression of thought serves individual and collective interests in the collision of opinions, which in turn enhances our capacity to think. Second, as Bury notes, concealing our thoughts can be difficult and psychologically damaging.

But, not all of the meaning and value of free thought is tied to expression (as I outline shortly). And, indeed, that part of the value of free thought that is tied to expression may be only contingently tied to it. Here are two reasons to think so.

First, consider the value of expression for improving understanding through the collision of opinions. Suppose that we live in a society called Consensus Land whose members, including ourselves, all reflectively and comprehendingly hold roughly the same beliefs on important issues and those beliefs are broadly stable, true, and justifiable. Would it be in our interests for the teachers of our society to manufacture some

---

[36] Bury, J. B. (1913) A *History of Freedom of Thought*. Accessed from Project Gutenberg: <http://www.gutenberg.org/files/10684/10684-h/10684-h.htm>.

[37] Mill (1859), ch 1. Mill gives a more refined statement of his position in Chapter 2: 'The liberty of expressing and publishing opinions may seem to fall under a different principle, since it belongs to that part of the conduct of an individual which concerns other people; but, being almost of as much importance as the liberty of thought itself, and resting in great part on the same reasons, is practically inseparable from it.'

false disagreement so as to keep the truth alive in our minds, as Mill would say?[38] It seems not, since there is no instability, general complacency, or uncomprehending prejudice about our beliefs in our society to which false disagreement might be a useful antidote. Hence, we in Consensus Land do not need there to be free expression of false views in order to keep our minds alive to the truth. Our reflection about the truth is not improved by the expression of (false) thought.

A critic might object that Consensus Land rules out Mill's view by hypothesis since it assumes not only that we hold roughly the same beliefs, but that these are factually correct and justifiable, ie that we have access to the truth, and hence there is no point in preserving expression of conflicting opinions.[39]

In reply, the point of Consensus Land is not about our access to the truth, because in Mill's imagined society as well people have arrived at the truth. The issue is rather whether expression (of false views) is necessary either for us to maintain a 'lively apprehension' of that truth or for us to gain an increasingly skilled and thoughtful attitude towards the truth. Consensus Land shows that, under conditions of stability and reflection, expression is not necessary to enhance the quality of our understanding of the truth. It is only when the truth is unstably recognized owing to our complacency and dull-mindedness that expression may be necessary to keep us alive to the truth. Of course, in most cases, instability, complacency, and falsity are likely to reign and, therefore, much can be said for the way that free expression can further intelligent and living apprehension of truth.

Second, consider the value of free thought to the person whose freedom it is. I do not deny that having freedom of thought without freedom of expression can be psychologically painful. Forced self-censorship can undoubtedly be traumatic. Indeed, my communicative principle of conscientiousness is a recognition of the inextricable link between having a sincere moral conviction and being willing to communicate that conviction. But, the psychological harms of self-

---

[38] Mill argues that 'The loss of so important an aid to the intelligent and living apprehension of a truth, as is afforded by the necessity of explaining it to, or defending it against, opponents, though not sufficient to outweigh, is no trifling drawback from, the benefit of its universal recognition. Where this advantage can no longer be had, I confess I should like to see the teachers of mankind endeavouring to provide a substitute for it; some contrivance for making the difficulties of the question as present to the learner's consciousness, as if they were pressed upon him by a dissentient champion, eager for his conversion.' Mill (1859), ch 2.

[39] I thank an anonymous referee for OUP for highlighting this objection.

censorship are distinct from, and possibly less serious than, the psychological harms of being denied a right to free thought as such. The harms (and wrongs) of denying our right to free thought are those of psychological abuse including brainwashing, subjugation, intimidation, and subliminal influencing. Protection from such abuse has both instrumental and non-instrumental value independent of expression.

The instrumental value of being protected from psychological abuse is obvious. For one thing, our lives go better. So too do the lives of the people with whom we have contact. Our emotional well-being, our capacity to live a meaningful life, and our ability to contribute positively to society are immeasurably greater when we are not subject to psychological abuse. And these benefits arise irrespective of whether we have a right to free expression. Thus, Bury and, possibly, Mill are mistaken when they tie the value of free thought strictly to free expression. For another thing, the instrumental value of having a protected life of the mind includes all the pleasures that private reflection can bring. A nice ally for this point is the poet William Wordsworth, who closes his famous poem on daffodils with the following lines: . . . I gazed—and gazed—but little thought/ What wealth the show to me had brought:/ For oft, when on my couch I lie/In vacant or in pensive mood,/They flash upon that inward eye/Which is the bliss of solitude;/And then my heart with pleasure fills,/And dances with the daffodils.

The non-instrumental value of free thought lies in its contributions to personal autonomy and to morality. In brief, having the freedom to undertake inner reflection is fundamentally important for developing autonomous judgement and for the kind of inner awareness that is crucial for conscience. In being necessary for conscience, free thought is necessary for personal morality. The capacity to be morally responsive is the fruit of the practices of attention, reflection, and self-awareness, which cannot be cultivated if there is no protection of free thought.

In more detail, even when other conditions for personal autonomy go unmet, the preservation of free thought has value. It can be the last refuge for the silenced, the suppressed, and the enslaved, for whom free thought without expression, while painful, can be self-preserving. Prisoners consigned to solitary confinement tend to take solace in the life of the mind for as long as possible, replaying conversations, recalling poems and films, and reliving memories.[40]

---

[40] Cf Gawande, A. (2009) 'Hellhole: The United States holds tens of thousands of inmates in long-term solitary confinement. Is this torture?' *The New Yorker*, 30 March 2009.

Indeed, the point can be put more strongly. Suppose that we were unable to express ourselves. Suppose we were fully paralyzed. Does the life of our mind lose all its value when we cannot express its happenings? Surely not. A nice example is journalist Jean-Dominique Bauby, who was paralyzed after a severe stroke to the brainstem that left him able only to flutter his left eyelid. In his autobiography, *The Diving Bell and the Butterfly*, Bauby shares his rich inner life through his small flickering avenue of expression.[41] It is filled with memories and imaginings, great feasts, and loves. And, that rich inner life would not have been any less rich or real were his left eyelid to have failed him.

In sum, a meaningful right to inner control and free thought exists independently of a right to free expression. To respect this right, it is necessary to ensure that we each have minimally adequate access to stimulation and information, and are protected from certain intrusions on our minds. One benefit of showing that the right to free thought is independent of free expression is that it opens up conceptual space to consider afresh what it means to respect each other's moral convictions, which is my main focus. It allows us to argue that respect for each other's moral convictions begins with not trying to influence those convictions for ill-motivated or ill-directed purposes. It does not begin with allowing everyone to act expressively on their convictions, even though many religious people would insist that their beliefs are not being respected when they are not given full rein to act expressively on them.

Although free thought is independent of free expression, free expression is not independent of free thought. There is no right to free expression worth the name without a right to free thought. The reasons are clear. Unless we are guaranteed some control over the inner workings of our own minds, the freedom to express ourselves is an empty gesture that gives us a forum in which to parrot back like happy slaves the propaganda that has penetrated us most effectively. I do not wish to belittle the right to expression, which will be my topic in the next section, but simply to note that it is dependent on the protection of more fundamental rights of the mind, constrained though they may be.

---

[41] Bauby's assistant would recite the alphabet to him and he would blink at each letter he wished to use. Bauby, Jean Dominic (1997) *The Diving Bell and the Butterfly*. London: Fourth Estate.

4. A Moral Right of Conscientious Action

4.1 Free expression

Expression is the manifestation of thought, emotion, and opinion. It can take innumerable forms. It can be verbal or non-verbal. It can be intentional or unintentional (eg facial expressions). It can be direct or mediated. It can be musical. It can be visual, such as in a display of symbols or a failure to display. It can be collective or individual. It can be peaceful or violent. It can be harmful or helpful. Expression encompasses both speech and action since much, if not most, action is expressive. The moral right to free expression is as much a right to expressive action as it is a right to verbal expression.

What expression is not is communication. The right to free expression is not a right to *communicate* that expression to others. Conceptually, this is because expression is not, by nature, an other-directed activity. We can express ourselves alone and in isolation from others and in forms that are unintelligible to others. By contrast, communication is, by nature, an other-directed activity. It involves an interaction between at least two parties—a 'communicator' and a 'receiver'—and their interaction is distinguished by its success. Through communication, we successfully transmit some data to our receiver either intentionally or unintentionally. And, the success of it depends on certain things being true of our receiver. She must not only possess adequate cognitive abilities of comprehension and reasoning, but also exercise those abilities appropriately to interpret correctly what we impart.[42] Evaluatively, the moral right of expression does not entail a right of communication because that would imply an implausibly demanding right to succeed that required relevantly placed people to attend and somehow comprehend whatever we impart.[43] The right of expression includes, at most, a right to *try* to communicate.

The moral right of expression also includes whatever right there is to engage in conscientious action since *conscientious* action is action expressive of deep moral conviction. However, a right of conscientious

---

[42] The fact that audiences must comprehend in order for communication to occur places minimal content-sensitive constraints on *intentional* efforts to communicate. In order for our efforts to count as genuine communicative efforts, we must aim to satisfy minimal standards of accessibility and intelligibility. (I return to these conditions for communication in Chapter 7.)

[43] See O'Neill, Onora (2009) 'Ethics for Communication' in *European Journal of Philosophy* 17: 2, 167–80.

action is a *limited* right to act in ways that honour and reflect our moral convictions. Its limits are drawn by humanistic principles of respect for others' moral rights. Its limits are not drawn by the conceptual criteria for *conscientiousness*. And, its limits are not drawn by the boundaries of the law even in a reasonably good society. In principle, therefore, a limited moral right of conscientious action includes a limited moral right of conscientious *disobedience*. In what follows, I argue that, given the communicative principle of conscientiousness, the moral right of conscientious action more readily applies to civil disobedience than to personal disobedience.

4.2 Civil disobedience

Most philosophers who have discussed civil disobedience defend a *limited* moral right, not a general moral right, to engage in this practice. But they disagree markedly over its central elements including the grounds for the right, its scope, and the kinds of regimes in which it exists. John Rawls, for example, maintains that, in his nearly just society, we may be supposed to have a right to engage in civil disobedience only when three conditions are met. The disobedience must be undertaken 1) in response to an instance of substantial and clear injustice, 2) as a last resort, and 3) in coordination with other minority groups.[44] Rawls' approach has been rightly criticized both for not clearly distinguishing his account of *justified* civil disobedience from an account of the disobedience that we have a *right* to take, and for not explaining whether his account can be extrapolated to non-ideal societies.

In contrast with Rawls, Raz notes that, to say there is a moral right to civil disobedience is to allow the legitimacy of resorting to this form of political action to our political opponents. It is to allow that the legitimacy of civil disobedience does not depend on the rightness of our cause or on other supposed conditions of justifiability such as last resort or coordination with other minorities. In Raz's view, the right to civil disobedience is derivative of a right to participate in the political decision-making process. In consequence, he argues that, although there may well be a moral right to civil disobedience in illiberal regimes to reclaim that part of our participation rights that are not adequately respected by the law, there is no such moral right in liberal regimes

---

[44] Rawls, John (1971) *A Theory of Justice*. Cambridge: Harvard University Press, 371–6.

because in those regimes there is adequate protection for ordinary forms of political participation. Consequently, liberal societies can only be expected to tolerate those acts of civil disobedience that are genuinely justifiable or obligatory.[45]

Ronald Dworkin grounds the right to civil disobedience in our equal status as beings worthy of concern and respect. The right is not just founded on our right to political participation, but on all of the rights that we have against our government. We may be supposed to have a fundamental right against our government, such as a right to freedom of expression, when that right is important to our dignity, to our standing as persons equally entitled to concern and respect, or to some other personal value of consequence. We have a right to disobey a law, Dworkin says, whenever that law wrongly invades our rights against the government. Thus, the moral right to breach the law is not a separate right additional to other rights against the government. It is that part of our rights against the government which the government fails to honour.[46]

Despite the disagreements over the nature and scope of the moral right to civil disobedience, political philosophers have tended to treat the case for it separately from that for a moral right to personal disobedience ('conscientious' objection) on the grounds that these practices are sufficiently disparate that, if they are protected by moral rights, they must be protected by different moral rights. Whereas the civil disobedient ostensibly asserts her right to participate politically, the personal disobedient asserts her immunity from certain norms of the society.

It is a by-product of this forced separation that we get the dubious proposal from Raz (noted just now) that the moral right to civil disobedience is regime-sensitive and that, although there may well be a moral right to civil disobedience in illiberal regimes, there is no moral right to civil disobedience in liberal regimes where there is, by stipulation, fair and

---

[45] Raz states: 'Given that the illiberal state violates its members' right to political participation, individuals whose rights are violated are entitled, other things being equal, to disregard the offending laws and exercise their moral right as if it were recognised by law... [M]embers of the illiberal state do have a right to civil disobedience which is roughly that part of their moral right to political participation which is not recognised in law.' By contrast, in a liberal state, Raz argues, a person's right to political activity is, by hypothesis, adequately protected by law. Therefore, in such a regime, the right to political participation cannot ground a right to civil disobedience. Raz (1979), ch 15. See also Green, Leslie (2003), 'Civil Disobedience and Academic Freedom' in *Osgoode Hall Law Journal*, 41 (2–3), 381–405.

[46] Dworkin, Ronald (1977) *Taking Rights Seriously*. London: Duckworth, 192.

adequate access to participation. The reason that fair access to participation rules out a moral right to civil disobedience, in his view, is the following:

Every claim that one's right to political participation entitles one to take a certain action in support of one's political aims (be they what they may), even though it is against the law, is *ipso facto* a criticism of the law for outlawing this action. For if one has a right to perform it its performance should not be civil disobedience but a lawful political act. Since by hypothesis no such criticism can be directed against the liberal state there can be no right to civil disobedience in it.[47]

One preliminary response to Raz is that, even in liberal regimes, persistent and vulnerable minorities are less able than majorities are to make their views heard before decisions are taken and laws are enacted.[48] Therefore, Raz's stipulation that, in liberal regimes, no credible criticism can be directed against the law for outlawing a certain action is a much weightier one than he acknowledges.

A second, related response given by David Lefkowitz is that, if we appeal to political participation rights to defend our disobedience, we do not necessarily criticize the law for outlawing our action. This is because the members of minorities can appreciate that democratic discussions often must be cut short so that decisions may be taken, and therefore they may view current policy as the best compromise between the need to act and the need to accommodate continued debate. Nonetheless they can point out that, with greater resources or further time for debate, their view might have held sway.

The implication of both of these responses is that there is a comparative unfairness in the nearly inescapable imbalance of political power between majorities and vulnerable minorities, which codified participatory rules cannot eliminate, and therefore, the scope of legitimate participation should accommodate at least some suitably constrained civil disobedience by vulnerable minorities (irrespective of the merits of their causes) since this rectifies somewhat the imbalance in participatory

---

[47] Raz (1979), 273.
[48] Bertrand Russell notes that often it is difficult to make the most salient facts in a dispute known through conventional channels of participation, partly because the controllers of mainstream media tend to grant defenders of unpopular views limited space to advance their causes. Russell, Bertrand (1998) *Autobiography*. London, Routledge, 635.

power.[49] As Lefkowitz puts it, this reduces as much as possible the impact that luck has on the popularity of a view.

Although I am attracted to this 'bad luck' argument, there are at least three problems with it. The first is that the argument does not necessarily entail a right to civil disobedience. If there are other viable ways to redress participatory power imbalances between majorities and vulnerable minorities, then our society could legitimately opt for those ways rather than for allowing some civil disobedience. It is only if civil disobedience is the only way, or undeniably the best way, to redress unjust imbalances in participatory power and affirm a commitment to political equality that the bad luck argument entails a moral right to civil disobedience.

The second problem is that the bad luck argument sails perilously close to the mistaken claim that minorities have a moral right to *communicate*, that is, a moral right to be heard, and not just a moral right to express themselves in the hope of shaping the debate. Briefly, the minorities' argument that they should be allowed to step outside the law to participate, because were there more time for debate or were they better resourced their view might have triumphed, implies that they have a claim to compensation or reparation for not being attended to by those shaping the debate.

The third problem is that, if the bad luck argument does entail a moral right to civil disobedience, then that right is a right only for the members of vulnerable minorities. The bad luck argument does not give us a general moral right to civil disobedience. This will seem unproblematic to thinkers who root the right to civil disobedience in political participation rights, but it is problematic in the eyes of those like myself who believe that the most compelling grounds for a right to civil disobedience lie, first, in a principle of humanistic respect for deep moral conviction, and second, in an acknowledgment of the overly burdensome pressure that society and the law place on us when they coerce us always to privilege the law before our deeply held moral convictions.[50] In contrast with Lefkowitz, I maintain that the moral

---

[49] Lefkowitz, David (2007) 'On a Moral Right to Civil Disobedience' in *Ethics* 117 (January), 202–33. For discussions of the issues related to differential treatment of minority groups acting in breach of law, see Calder, Gideon and Emauela Ceva (eds.) (2010) *Diversity in Europe: Dilemmas of Differential Treatment in Theory and Practice*. London: Routledge.

[50] *Overly burdensome pressure* is to be understood here in terms of undue burdensomeness rather than unfeasible burdensomeness. *Undue burdens* are unreasonable burdens that may or may not be feasible to secure. Requiring you to devote your days off to some cause of mine

right to civil disobedience is a general right, not just a right of vulnerable minorities. And, its foundation lies not in participatory rights but in the principle of humanism and hence in society's duty to honour human dignity however popular or unpopular our moral convictions may be. Since, in my view, this is the foundation for any credible moral right to civil disobedience, we should consider civil disobedience together with personal disobedience in our analysis of moral rights. Both make assertions of conscientiousness, and therefore both are most fruitfully considered in relation to a single proposed right to conscientious disobedience to determine which has the best case for protection as a right.

As I noted in Chapter 1, the standard view is that a humanistic principle gives modest protection for private personal disobedience, but not for civil disobedience.[51] For example, in the context of war, Raz argues that the killing and subjugation of other peoples must never be viewed lightly, even in unfortunate cases when such acts are necessary and justified. 'Whatever the justification, undeniably the readiness to kill or to participate in oppression have profound significance for the one who carries out such acts. Hence, the right to conscientious objection to such acts takes precedence over the legal obligation to take part in them....'[52] The same kind of reasoning is invoked in less extreme contexts to excuse professionals, such as doctors, nurses, pharmacists, and judges, from carrying out some of the functions of their office that would be psychologically burdensome for them.

But, as my defence of the communicative principle of conscientiousness made clear, not all objectors are made equal. In the case of war, a draft dodger is most plausibly protected by a right of conscientious disobedience not when he seeks to evade detection or keep his own hands clean, but when he is willing to be seen to dissociate himself from the order to go to war, and to bear the risks of communicating

---

would be unreasonable, but feasible. *Unfeasible burdens* are presently impossible burdens that may nonetheless be reasonable in principle. Asking you to get me to the hospital when I am gravely injured and this would be at little cost to yourself is reasonable, but unfeasible when you don't drive and are otherwise unable to assist me. Unfeasible burdens intersect with undue burdens at the point where the resource-costs of an otherwise reasonable burden place excessive pressure on would-be duty-bearers or third-parties.

[51] Raz (1979), 286; Horder, Jeremy (2004) *Excusing Crime*. Oxford: Oxford University Press.

[52] Raz, Joseph (2003a) 'Bound by their Conscience' in *Haaretz* 31 December 2003.

that decision. Unlike the soldier who evades detection and the soldier who is indifferent to the war, the civilly disobedient soldier is willing to risk being held to account. His act does not raise the spectre of doubt about his sincerity that is raised by the secretive, self-preserving acts of the private objector. The private objector's evasion raises the worry that his conviction is too shaky to bear the risks of communication.

This humanistic case for the moral right to civil disobedience can be supplemented by an appeal to the double harmony between civil disobedients' interests in having this right of conscientious action protected and society's interests in the deliberation-enhancing effects of this kind of constrained breach of law. For example, the civilly disobedient soldier may serve his society's interests in addition to his own. There is a double harmony between his interests in the right to civil disobedience grounded in the principle of humanism, on the one hand, and society's interests in hearing his concerns about the war, on the other. His efforts to communicate may expose his society to a view not presented by the mainstream media.[53] And, this may empower society to hold government more accountable and thereby reinvigorate general discussion about the merits of the war. It may force the champions of dominant opinion to defend their views. And, his disobedience can perform at least some of these services even when he is mistaken about either the facts or his principles.[54] And, when his cause is well-founded, he may serve society not only by questioning, but by inhibiting a moral wrong or rectifying a moral wrong, thereby acting as a stabilizing force within society.[55]

One implication of my account is worth noting. In contrast with standard takes on civil disobedience, I hold that the moral right to civil disobedience includes a moral right against lawful punishment. Briefly, a standard, pre-theoretical view is that to be civilly disobedient at all we have to be punished for our breach of law. My view is that, to be civilly disobedient, we must accept the *risk* of being punished, which flows

---

[53] CNN president Walter Isaacson is said to have authorized his news service to provide two different versions of their coverage of the Iraq War, a more critical one for global audiences and a watered down one for Americans. See Lovell, Jarrett (2009) *Crimes of Dissent*. New York: New York University Press.

[54] As Raz himself observes, 'while political theorists often highlight the protection for the individual dissident which [a right to dissent] provides, in practice its primary role has been to provide a collective good, to protect the democratic character of the society'. Raz (1986), 253–4.

[55] Cf Rawls (1971), 383.

from our conscientious communicative efforts, but we need not actually be punished, and we need not turn ourselves in so that we can be punished. This is consistent with my account of a moral right to civil disobedience as a right that does not generate grounds for a legal right (Section 1). Hence, a moral right against punishment for civil disobedience does not generate grounds for a *legal* right against punishment. I defend this position in Chapter 8.

4.3 *Objections against the moral right to civil disobedience*

Now, a critic might argue that, even though civil disobedients often act from deep moral conviction and may incidentally benefit society through their protest, their motives are at least partly political and strategic, and hence their conduct is not fully conscientious and therefore it falls outside the scope of the humanistic principle of respect for autonomy and dignity. By contrast, the *personal* disobedient does not choose for purely strategic reasons the laws to be disobeyed, and therefore, her act is conscientious and can, in principle, claim protection under a moral right rooted in respect for autonomy and dignity.[56]

I respond to this strategic-action problem at length in the next chapter. For now, I simply note that the strategic-action objection misrepresents the motivational differences between communicative disobedience and personal disobedience. First, paradigmatically, civil disobedience involves principled disobedience undertaken by persons who appreciate the importance for integrity of communicating their views. In cases of *direct* disobedience at least, there is no question of strategy that arises. Second, politics and strategy can figure in personal disobedience, especially in cases of evasive personal disobedience. Breaches of law carried out in secret with the aim of remaining secret are strategic acts, especially when the acts are chosen with calculation to preserve liberty from legal interference. For these reasons, civil disobedience should not be ruled out from the humanistic principle on the basis of motivation, and 'conscientious' objection should not necessarily be ruled in (as I elaborate later on).

More generally, a critic might worry that, since I do not constrain the kinds of causes that a moral right to civil disobedience might protect, I have brought the rats in the house with the cats, and have

---

[56] Horder (2004), 224.

given bigots, racists, and xenophobes of all stripes a moral right to break the law in defence of their causes.

In principle, I have done this. However, I have also argued for *process*-related constraints on what counts as civil disobedience (Chapter 1). As conscientious, communicative actors, civil disobedients are sincere and serious in their desire to bring about a *lasting* change in policy, which means that they appreciate the reasons they have not to be overly radical in their communication. That is, they appreciate the reasons they have to seek rationally to persuade others of their view rather than to force them to make changes. They know that the appeal of their communication may be lost if it is drowned out by coercive or intimidatory tactics.[57] And, they know that their appeal rests on treating their audience as interlocutors with whom they can engage in a moral discussion. And, they are sensitive to the fact that they may be mistaken, while still believing as conscientious agents that their cause is sufficiently credible that it can be given a reasoned defence to other people. Consequently, although the bigot may find shelter for her cause under the right to civil disobedience on the grounds of the humanistic principle, the acts that she may take in defence of her cause are radically restricted by the conscientiousness that makes her acts ones of civil disobedience.[58]

---

[57] As noted in Chapter 1, violence is not, by definition, at odds with the conscientious communication and persuasive aims of civil disobedience. Nor is it, by definition, a poor mode of communication. That said, violence is not in itself a feature exemplified in paradigmatic civil disobedience; it is merely compatible with the key features which distinguish this practice from more extreme forms of protest. Attention must be given to the kind of violence employed and the ramifications of employing it. Only in cases where the violence does not seriously breach the rights of others or have seriously untoward consequences for the society can such conduct fall within the right to civil disobedience.

[58] Even civil disobedience undertaken in pursuit of a valuable objective falls outside the right when disobedients employ poor modes of communication. For example, vigorous communicative disobedience undertaken during a time of peace and security has different ramifications from disobedience undertaken during a national crisis. In the latter case, even if this vigorous dissent were taken in defence of well-founded goals and used means that otherwise would be acceptable, it would cause or risk great harm in this state of emergency and could not reasonably be described as persuasive since the extremity of the situation would rule out the possibility for deliberative discussion between government and citizenry. In brief, disobedience that accords with the paradigm action this right is meant to protect may be impossible in these circumstances. Nevertheless, the disobedient could have strong reasons to take this action, that is, reasons of duty, moral consistency, or respect for others. Suppose the government handles the emergency badly or makes rapid decisions that have long-term implications. Depending on the nature of the emergency, civil disobedience, however inappropriate its use, may be defensible (worthy of protection) in these circumstances because the disobedient ensures that, when the community is disrupted by the shock of crisis, an

4.4 Personal disobedience

As my analysis suggests, it is less easy to accommodate personal disobedience under the moral right of conscientious action because it does not satisfy the communicative principle of conscientiousness. This claim must be tempered in relation to different kinds of personal disobedience since there is an evaluative difference between the evasive disobedient and the non-evasive disobedient. The non-evasive disobedient does not strategize about how to keep her disobedience secret, and so, to that extent, she is willing to be seen to disobey. An example could be Sikhs wearing turbans while motorcycling where riding without a helmet is illegal. That act cannot be done in secret, though it may well be done with no communicative aims other than to assert immunity from the laws requiring helmets. When that is true, such agents do not satisfy the communicative principle of conscientiousness because what they communicate (incidentally) is only that they are serious about asserting their immunity from community norms, not that they are serious about the cause that has prompted them to manifest this assertion of immunity. Unless their 'cause' actually *is* their assertion of immunity from certain community norms (in which case their conduct may be better construed as civil disobedience), their non-evasive acts lack the correct orientation to satisfy the communicative principle of conscientiousness.

But, surely, some acts—including some *evasive* acts—that do not satisfy the communicative principle of conscientiousness are protected by a right of conscientious action since the communicative principle is particularly onerous for persons who have unpopular views. Surely, the humanistic principle must be sensitive to the onerousness not only of rule-adherence, but also of the risks of self-exposure.

This I do not wish to deny. However, the humanistic principle is an egalitarian principle that cannot accommodate assertions of rights that either violate the dignity of others or threaten their basic needs. Concrete examples will, of course, invite nothing but controversy, but the acts I have in mind are the parent's refusal to take her child with curable diabetes to see a doctor; the fire-fighter's refusal to assist the homosexual couple whose house is burning; the town registrar's refusal to marry homosexual couples; and the doctor's refusal to

---

attempt is made to hold authorities accountable for their decisions. What such cases show (with a nod to Raz) is that circumstances are relevant to whether a disobedient's action falls under the right to civil disobedience.

provide urgent medical services when no other doctor is available. There is no moral right of conscientious action in these cases.

Two possible challenges to my view are the following. First, a critic might object that if a person's refusal does not prevent a service from being available, then that refusal does not threaten the interests of other persons. A doctor who refuses to perform abortions can be replaced by another doctor who is willing to do so, and therefore, the humanistic principle of equal respect for dignity is not breached.

In reply, there are two problems with this proposal. First, for the equal dignity of all to be respected, important services must be provided in a non-discriminatory fashion. When persons have certain public services under their control, this limits their moral right to refuse to distribute those services in a non-discriminatory fashion. Second, if the doctor who recuses herself appeals to others' willingness to provide the service that she opposes, she may be engaging in a form of morally-inconsistent free-riding. There may be an inconsistency between her judgement that the procedure is wrong and her desire that others do it so that she doesn't have to refuse directly. By free-riding on the willingness of others to do what she finds objectionable so that she may escape social pressure, she fails to respect the dignity and interests of those seeking to provide the service in a non-discriminatory way.

The second possible challenge to my view is that I have allowed people to do things under the banner of a right to civil disobedience that I have forbidden them to do under the banner of a right to personal disobedience. Suppose that a religious mother *openly* refuses to take her sick child to a doctor and does it with an eye to communicating her position to others and bearing the risks that go with that. It seems that, in my view, she has a moral right to act, even though her act falls afoul of the humanistic principle of respect for others' dignity and rights.

In reply, the mother does not have a right to act because her act is neither civil disobedience nor assistive disobedience. Recall from Chapter 1 that there are some acts that are not conscientious if they are done *for the purpose of* communicating disapprobation for a law. These include acts that directly affect the interests of another being and that, if conscientious, would be done for the sake of that being and not for the sake of communicating a position. If the mother is serious about engaging in *civil* disobedience, then the *process*-related constraints of civil disobedience will inform the kinds of communicatively conscientious acts available to her. In all likelihood, she will have to engage in indirect civil disobedience for several reasons. First, direct disobedience of childcare laws would be unlikely to secure a receptive response from a diverse audience. Second, direct disobedience of childcare laws would belie her supposed appreciation that she may be mistaken about her view. Third, there is a reasonable presumption that the risks of communication will be sufficiently great that they might prompt her to think carefully before deciding how to act. There is a greater probability that a communicative act will be intercepted and neutralized, if necessary, than a clandestine one will be; she would show her conscientiousness by accepting this risk.

Conclusion

In this chapter, I defended three moral rights: 1) a moral right of conscience, 2) a moral right to inner control and free thought, and 3) a moral right of conscientious action. I began by challenging the legal-right presumption which says that all genuine moral rights are translatable into legal rights and that there is always a *pro tanto* reason to make that translation. This thesis is mistaken both conceptually and evaluatively. Two moral rights that cannot give rise to equivalent legal rights are the duty-based moral right of conscience, which protects us in honouring our moral responsibilities, and the conviction-based moral right of conscientious action, which includes a moral right to civil disobedience, but does not (generally) include a moral right to personal disobedience. The moral right of conscientious action is derivative of the moral right to free thought, which I have shown is surprisingly more constrained than we might suppose.

Although two of the three moral rights examined in this chapter cannot be translated into legal rights, they inform the analysis of how the law ought to respond to the disobedience that they protect. It is to that analysis that I turn in Part II. Briefly, my focus in Part II shifts from moral theory to legal theory. I make use of the conceptual and normative ground built up in Part I. In this Part, I have shown, among other things, that there are reasons to be sceptical about the conscientiousness of many personal disobedients (private 'conscientious' objectors), especially when they disobey the law in secret or in determined non-engagement with their community. I have also shown that there are reasons to be sanguine about the conscientiousness of civil disobedients since their act is a constrained, communicative one that bears the risks that go with seeking to persuade others that there are good reasons for the disobedience. My purpose in Part II is to explore what this reversal of the standard liberal picture of civil disobedience and personal disobedience means for how the law should respond to these practices.

PART II
Law

5

Demands-of-Conviction Defence

The quiet depth of conviction with which she spoke.

—George Elliot[1]

Civil disobedients have had a chequered experience before the law. Sometimes they are treated well by police, praised in court, and acquitted.[2] Sometimes charges against them are dropped. Other times, they are treated like ordinary offenders. And, other times they are demonized as threats to social order. This chequered experience reflects the strong disagreement amongst judges (and juries) about the seriousness of civil disobedience. The *seriousness* of a wrong is understood as the combination of 1) its degree of harm, risk of harm, or rights-intrusion, and 2) the offender's degree of culpability.[3] Standardly, the greater that the harm and/or culpability is, the greater the justification for punishment. In recent judicial decisions, three contrasting positions on civil disobedience can be found. The first is that civil disobedience is indistinguishable from ordinary offending. The second is that civil

---

[1] Eliot, George (*1859*) *Adam Bede*, I. i. ii. 43.
[2] For an interesting discussion of the norms of the pre-arrest treatment of civil disobedients, see Smith, William (2012) 'Policing Civil Disobedience' in *Political Studies*, doi: 10.1111/j.1467-9248.2011.00937.x.
[3] The only offenders who are culpable are those who are reasoning and capable, in principle, of taking responsibility for their conduct. Only they are the proper interlocutors with the state about their offending. For a critical discussion of the standard idea that the severity of punishment should be proportionate to the moral seriousness or 'moral gravity' of the crime, see Reiff, Mark (2005) *Punishment, Compensation, and Law: A Theory of Enforceability*. Cambridge: Cambridge University Press, 125ff.

disobedience is more serious than ordinary offending. The third is that civil disobedience is less serious than ordinary offending.

One advocate of the first position is former British Columbia Court of Appeal Chief Justice Allan McEachern. The case was that of Kenneth Loylet Bridges who in 1988 engaged with others in picketing and intimidating the users and operators of the Everywoman's Health Centre Society abortion clinic. CJ McEachern stated in *R v Bridges* (1991) that:

Civil disobedience is a philosophical, not a legal principle... Even philosophers agree that those who disobey any law, by civil disobedience or otherwise, must expect to be punished according to law. Civil disobedience is not a defence to any wilful breach of the law.[4]

In this view, civil disobedience is irrelevant and disobedients deserve the same punishment as ordinary offenders. There are reasons we might think this view is credible. One reason pertains to norms of proportionality, generality, and uniformity in the application of law. Since trespass is prohibited, persons who breach trespass laws in protest of those laws or other laws may seem to be equally liable as persons who breach trespass laws for private purposes. A second, related point noted by Kent Greenawalt is that any principle that says legal officials may permit morally justified illegal acts to go unpunished will result in some failures to punish unjustified acts, for which the purposes of punishment would be better served. 'Even when officials make correct judgements about which acts to excuse, citizens may draw mistaken inferences, and restraints of deterrence and norm acceptance may be weakened for unjustified acts that resemble the justified ones.'[5] Therefore, so the argument goes, all such violations should be treated alike. We might call this point the slippery slope argument (I address it in the next chapter).

The former point about generality and proportionality is erroneous since it disregards the motivational differences between civil disobedients and ordinary offenders as well as the differences in self-restraint in their choice of action. Civil disobedience should be seen in the eyes of the law as a different kind of disobedience from ordinary offending,

---

[4] CJ McEachern, *R v Bridges* (1991) 62 C.C.C. (3d) 455 at 458 (B.C.C.A.).
[5] Greenawalt, Kent (1987) *Conflicts of Law and Morality*. Oxford: Clarendon Press, 273.

which leaves two options. Either civil disobedience is more serious or it is less serious than ordinary offending.

The most common arguments for the view that civil disobedience is more serious are democratic ones and instrumental ones. The thought is that civil disobedients improperly arrogate to themselves licence to disregard laws by which others hold themselves to be bound, which generates risks for society.[6] Consider the case I noted in Chapter 4 of the three nuns, Sisters Carol Gilbert, Ardeth Platte, and Jackie Marie Hudson, who sought through their trespass and vandalism to raise awareness in northeastern Colorado about weapons of mass destruction and to focus attention on US atrocities abroad. The nuns were found guilty of injury to, interference with, and obstruction of the national defence of the US as well as causing $1000 in damage to government property. They were sentenced to 41 months, 33 months, and 30 months' imprisonment respectively, including three years of supervised release.[7] Justice Harris L. Hartz, speaking on behalf of the US 10th Circuit Court of Appeal, argues in *US v Platte et al* (2005) that:

Civil disobedience can be an act of great religious and moral courage and society may ultimately benefit. But if the law being violated is constitutional, the worthiness of one's motives cannot excuse the violation in the . . . eyes of the law. History has not been short of evidence of the risks, the evils, that can attend subordinating the requirements of law to one's personal view of morality.[8]

One such 'evil' is showing disrespect for other citizens who have exercised their judgement in making the laws in a fair, deliberative, and democratic way. Assuming that democratic law is an epistemic authority, a second 'evil' is disobedients' willingness to risk that they are privileging a worse judgement about how to act over a better one.

---

[6] One might ask how disobedients differ from ordinary offenders in this respect. Do not ordinary offenders improperly arrogate to themselves licence to disregard laws that others are following? The answer is 'yes', they do. But they do so in a different way from that ostensibly done by civil disobedients. Ordinary offenders do not seek to use their offence to serve a policy-forming agenda. The worry about civil disobedients' 'improper arrogation' is that they seek to hijack the deliberative process.

[7] The nuns' previous political offences were cited by the prosecution to substantiate the call for stiff sentences. In 2000, the nuns illegally entered the Colorado Springs Air Force Base, struck a parked Marine fighter jet with a hammer, and poured their blood on its landing gear. Charges were dropped.

[8] *United States of America v Platte et al* (2005), 401 F.3d 1176 (10th Cir.).

Both of these 'evils' of failing to subordinate to law apply to personal disobedience as well to civil disobedience. But that point tends not to be highlighted.

There are other 'evils' that pertain to civil disobedience alone given its communicative aspects and its tendency to attract publicity. The main risk is that disobedience done 'in the presence of authority' can create insecurity in various ways. One way is by leading law-abiding people to believe that the laws will not be adhered to when someone judges them to be wrong. A second, knock-on way is by pushing officials to respond more forcefully to disobedience to prevent law-abiding citizens from feeling insecurity about enforcement.[9] Another risk relates to violence. Those who see civil disobedience as more serious than ordinary offending might argue that any use of violence aggravates civil disobedience particularly when it increases the harm of the offence or directly incites further and unjustified instances of violence.

In my view, most of these 'evils' are overstated or mistaken. They rely on unduly narrow notions of *democratic deliberation* and *respect* as well as an overly optimistic view of law's epistemic authority and an overly pessimistic view of the effects of civil disobedience on security. Moreover, I allayed worries about violence in Chapter 1 and will say more on this in Chapter 6. I grant, however, that, in practical terms, violence does seem to change the tone of the discussion. Although it may eloquently communicate a dissenter's seriousness and frustration, it pushes authorities to respond in ways consonant with their stance on violence, which may well be harsher than those they would otherwise wish to use towards civil disobedience, especially when it is taken in defence of values they can appreciate. I address these points in Sections 3 and 4.

The third position on civil disobedience sees it as less serious than ordinary offending. Judges who see civil disobedience in this more favourable light include Maine Superior Court Judge Allen Hunter who heard the case of Iraq war protesters Nancy Galland and Richard Stander. Galland and Stander were found guilty of criminal trespass during a protest against the US invasion of Iraq at the Bangor, Maine, Federal Building in March 2003. Hunter rejected the prosecution's call

---

[9] Greenawalt (1987), 351–2. Of course, Rawls has argued contrarily that the very publicity of civil disobedience is a mark of its civility and of campaigners' willingness to deal fairly with authorities. I explore these issues later on in my response to the democracy problem.

for heavy fines and chose instead to sentence the two to 20 hours of community service: At the trial, Hunter argued (2004):

I remember that in the 1960s there were actions of civil disobedience that, eventually, made our life better... We all have derived benefits from acts of civil disobedience like the Boston Tea Party. That act of civil disobedience has played an extremely important and vital political role in our history... From time to time in our history, we see events that involve civil disobedience that make us all uncomfortable. I'm not sure that's a bad thing. Those of us who prefer the comfort of a status quo are made to feel uncomfortable when we have people engaging in actions which violate the norm.[10]

In this view, civil disobedients are recognized as conscientiously motivated campaigners whose protests often serve the interests of society by forcing a desirable re-examination of moral boundaries even when the cause that the campaigners champion may be questioned. This is the view I endorse. I maintain that, irrespective of a dissenter's cause, civil disobedience is generally less serious than ordinary offending. In consequence, it should be treated more leniently than ordinary offending. But, even if civil disobedience is less serious than ordinary offending, that does not mean that punishment is never warranted (see Chapters 7 and 8).

In this chapter and the next, I examine two putative legal defences for principled disobedience: a demands-of-conviction defence (Chapter 5) and a necessity defence (Chapter 6). Both of these are controversial, though only the latter has received much attention. The demands-of-conviction defence is an excusatory defence that tracks conscientious moral conviction. The necessity defence is, in this context, a justificatory defence of needs-responsiveness that tracks conscience. After arguing for the general plausibility of both defences, I show that, within a liberal democracy, each defence applies more readily to civil disobedience than to personal disobedience.

In the course of arguing for these defences, I address four possible objections: 1) the strategic action problem; 2) the democracy problem;

---

[10] Williams, Lynne (2004), 'Restraining Dissent is Harmful' in *Bangor Daily News* 10 September. See also Galland, Nancy and Stander, Richard (2003), 'Bangor Judge, Too, Recognizes Importance of Civil Disobedience' in *Peace Talk*. Retained in author's files.

3) the competition of values problem; and 4) the proportionality problem. The latter two pertain principally to the necessity defence. My responses to these objections turn on, first, the communicative principle of conscientiousness that I outlined in Chapter 1, and second, the under-acknowledged capacity of democratic law to recognize the importance of values other than conformity with law. This second element I call the modesty of law thesis.

Before proceeding, let me briefly review what it means to have a conscientious moral conviction. It means having a sincere and serious though possibly mistaken moral commitment. To have such a commitment, we must satisfy the four core conditions of the communicative principle of conscientiousness, discussed in Chapter 1. These are the consistency condition, the universality condition, the non-evasion condition, and the dialogic condition. The non-evasion condition requires that we not evade the consequences of our convictions merely for reasons of self-protection. This condition can accommodate some anonymous acts and temporarily clandestine acts provided that the reasons for our secrecy are not to avoid the personal costs of detection, but rather, for example, temporarily to ensure success. To succeed in releasing animals from research laboratories or vandalizing military property, for example, it is necessary to avoid advance publicity. Such disobedience nonetheless may be regarded as 'open' or 'non-evasive' when followed by an acknowledgment of the act and the reasons for acting. The dialogic condition requires that we be willing to communicate our judgement that a perceived injustice warrants our opposition. This condition is not satisfied by personal disobedience of either the non-evasive or the evasive variety since such acts are not done either *in order to* engage others or *because* the act will engage others in deliberation about the merits of the cause.

Before I explore the demands-of-conviction defence, let me briefly comment on the complex conceptual territory of *justifications* and *excuses*. For my purposes, it is appropriate to endorse John Gardner's account of *justification* and *excuse*, though I shall raise a few questions about that account concerning degrees of defensibility and mixed motivations.[11]

---

[11] The material in the next section elaborates some ideas in Brownlee, Kimberley (2009), 'Review of Gardner, Offences and Defences' in *Ethics* 119: 3, 561–6.

1. Justifications and Excuses

Gardner argues that if we adopt an Aristotelian conception of the *person* as a being that strives for rational excellence, then what matters for us as persons is that we can give a good account of ourselves by being able to offer reasons for why we acted as we did. Our basic responsibility, as Gardner calls it, does not involve our seeking to avoid the bad consequences of any wrong we do by denying responsibility, which we would seek to do on a Hobbesian conception of the *person*. Rather, it involves our asserting that, despite everything, we are responsible adults.[12] It is reasonable to assume that we not only would want to assert our basic responsibility if we take ourselves seriously, but have an interest in asserting it as reasoning beings. This account of basic responsibility chimes with my defence of the moral roles thesis in Chapter 3 and with my defence of the duty-based moral right of conscience in Chapter 4.

According to this Aristotelian picture, if we can, we give a justificatory explanation for any wrong we do. What it means to be justified has evolved both in law and in legal and moral theorizing. In the past, *justification* was understood in more stringent, unqualified terms than it tends to be now. The traditional legal understanding of *justification* tracks what Gardner calls the 'closure' view (or the monistic view) of wrongdoing arising from the Kantian and Benthamite traditions, which takes justified actions to be unqualifiedly right or good actions. In these monistic traditions, an action is wrong if, and only if, it is unjustified. For Kant, there can be no moral reason for performing an action if there are moral reasons against performing that action since it is always morally wrong to fail to do what we have a moral reason to do. Similarly, for utilitarians such as R. B. Brandt, '... an act is *morally wrong* if it would be properly disapproved of... in the *absence* of an excuse or justification. An act is *morally right* if it is not morally wrong'.[13] Thus, on the closure view, any wrong is an unjustified wrong since the reasons that might have been used to justify it have

---

[12] Gardner, John (2003), 'The Mark of Responsibility' in *Oxford Journal of Legal Studies* 23: 21, 157–71. Since all rational beings want to assert their basic responsibility, all else being equal they cannot but welcome whatever contributes to that assertion. Accepting punishment, for example, contributes to that assertion if it expresses their basic responsibility, if that is the public meaning of a punitive act.

[13] Brandt R. B. (1989) 'Morality and its Critics' in *The American Philosophical Quarterly* 1989, 26: 2. Cited in Gardner (2007).

already been taken into consideration in settling that it is wrong.[14] In short, to offer a justification essentially is to deny that we did wrong.

By contrast, the more contemporary view of *justification*, which aligns with the classical views of ancient Greek philosophy, does not see talk of 'justified wrongdoing' as oxymoronic. When we commit a wrong by violating a requirement it may be possible nevertheless to show that our conduct is vindicated by undefeated reasons. Such conduct is not unqualifiedly 'right' or 'good'. Rather, it is tolerable or permissible or acceptable, all things considered. In this more nuanced view, when we give a justification, we show that our action was performed for undefeated reasons, which are neither overridden nor excluded by other reasons. When we can show that we act for an undefeated reason, Gardner reminds us, we need not then give attention to the other reasons for or against our action. It is sufficient that the reason we act for is undefeated.[15]

This nuanced view of wrongdoing pays tribute to an important aspect of what it means to be human, which is being able to have goals, projects, and values, to make choices and decisions, to feel regret when those choices conflict with other values, and to give an account for why those goals, values, and choices were pursued. Although, to an extent, the closure view also can make room for this part of human life, it nonetheless denies that those actions that conflict with what we have moral reason to do can have moral worth. Talk of justification, Gardner observes, highlights a striking asymmetry in human thought and experience between the pursuit of positive value and the avoidance of negative value. This asymmetry is brought to the surface by claims about justification, he says, only because such claims implicate both reasons for and reasons against an action.[16] Whereas an accusation of wrongdoing points to the presence of certain reasons against an action, an assertion of justification points to the presence of certain reasons for that action.

If we cannot give a justificatory explanation for our action, then we can hopefully give an excusatory explanation that our action was performed for reasons that we had for *believing* that we were justified in

---

[14] Gardner, John (2007) *Offences and Defences*. Oxford: Oxford University Press, 77.
[15] Gardner, John (1996) 'Justifications and Reasons' in *Harm and Culpability*. A. P. Simester and A. T. H. Smiths (eds.), Oxford: Clarendon Press, 112–13.
[16] Gardner (2007), 97.

acting.[17] This is a narrow conception of *excuse*, but since my project focuses on *deliberate* breaches of law (ie civil disobedience) and intentional acts that are incidentally in breach of law (ie personal disobedience), I shall put aside the issue of whether to embrace a broader conception of *excuse* that includes denials of responsibility.

In Gardner's words, 'Excuses point to features of [our] situation that do not militate in favour of the action [we] took, but nevertheless do militate in favour of the beliefs or emotions or attitudes (etc) on the strength of which [we] took that action'.[18] In such cases, we have an undefeated reason for thinking that our action is justified, but the considerations that could be reasons for our action together are insufficient to justify the action because they are defeated reasons.[19] According to Gardner and Timothy Macklem,

> the paradigm excuse is that one had a justified belief in justification. This excusatory case is sometimes known to lawyers as a case of 'putative' or 'perspectival' justification. The qualifications 'putative' and 'perspectival' show that something less than a real justification for the action is involved. This means, to our minds, that something less than a real reason for the action is involved. Instead it is a real reason for belief that there is a reason for action.[20]

In cases where there is only one reason at issue and we are mistaken to believe that it favours our action, then we have in fact no reason, let alone an undefeated reason, to take the action. If we have an undefeated reason to believe we have reason to act, then our excused action is, to an extent, vindicated by reason because when called on to explain our conduct, it is possible to point to the reason we had for believing that we had reason to act as we did.

---

[17] Not all excuses are belief-based. Some are emotion-based. Anger and fear can lead one to think that one's action is justified when it is not. Cf Gardner, John and Macklem, Timothy (2002) 'Reasons' in *The Oxford Handbook of Jurisprudence and Philosophy of Law*. Jules Coleman and Scott Shapiro (eds.), Oxford: Oxford University Press. This conception of *excuse* differs from the more traditional definition from John Austin that when we give an excuse we admit that the action was bad but we do not accept full or even any responsibility for it. Cited in Husak, Douglas (2005) 'On the Supposed Priority of Justification to Excuse' in *Law and Philosophy* 24: 557–94.

[18] Gardner (2007), ch 4.

[19] The reasons against an action do not disappear when they are defeated. They retain their force and may be cause for great regret on the part of the agent that her action violates them. See Gardner (1996).

[20] Gardner and Macklem (2002), 444.

1.1 Complicated cases

This picture of wrongdoing, justification, and excuse raises some interesting questions. One question concerns what Gardner calls 'complicated cases' in which it is difficult to separate a denial of wrongdoing from an assertion of justification. Such cases frequently arise in the realm of criminal law, he says, where the difference between offences and defences often can be unclear. If we kill for reasons of self-defence, for example, it could be said either that we have acted wrongly but with justification or that we have not acted wrongly *because* we acted with justification:

To say that the defendant committed a criminal wrong but was justified comes to the same thing, in the end, as saying that she committed no criminal wrong... Regarding some arguments available to criminal defendants it is admittedly unclear, morally as well as legally, whether they are to be regarded as denials of wrongdoing, or rather as concessions of wrongdoing coupled with assertions of justification. That is because, morally as well as legally, some wrongs... do admittedly anticipate, in their very definitions, various arguments that would otherwise count as justificatory.[21]

One might think that the accommodation of complicated cases like self-defence causes the nuanced, pluralistic view of wrongdoing to collapse into the monistic, 'closure' view of wrongdoing. But, it does not. The merit of the pluralistic view lies in its recognition that a denial of wrongdoing and an assertion of justification can be pulled apart, a phenomenon that the closure view cannot accommodate. The pluralistic view need not be committed to the claim that denial of wrongdoing and assertion of justification never coincide. Instead, it can incorporate the idea that, in special cases, the justification for an action makes that action *alright* all things considered. In the self-defence case, for example, it is because certain reasons for making a lethal attack are present and acted on (we act for the reason of saving our own life) that other reasons against lethal attack are absent.[22]

---

[21] Gardner (2007), 79–80.
[22] As an aside, two reasons to favour building justification into the very definition of 'self-defence' are that, first, this acknowledges that the reasons for which we act often shape the very nature of our action, and second, this retains the valuable distinction between a denial of wrongdoing and an assertion of justification.

1.2 Degrees of justification and excuse

Another interesting question is whether the pluralistic view, which can accommodate degrees of wrongdoing, can also accommodate degrees of justification and excuse. Since, in this conceptual framework, *justification* is conceived of in terms of a binary distinction between undefeated and defeated reasons, it seems at first glance that justifications at least cannot come in degrees. However, commonsensically, both excuses and justifications admit degrees. For instance, excuses can sometimes be supplemented by partially justificatory elements. If we have otherwise good, but *defeated* reasons for some act, we may offer something more than a mere excuse for our conduct. We may offer a partial justification by showing that the reasons against our action are countered by at least ordinary, but no less real reasons in favour of that action.

Similarly, sometimes our actions can be only partially excused, such as when we have a partially justified belief that there are reasons to take that action. Such a belief would be one that we have reasons to hold, though those reasons would be outweighed by the reasons against holding that belief. Although an action that is only partially excused gains little by way of defence, such an action is nonetheless vindicated by reasons. There are real reasons behind our belief that we should take this action, and we may point to these albeit inconclusive reasons when called on to explain our conduct. (Sometimes, we can offer even less than that, namely, we can offer only our perception that there were reasons to believe that there were reasons to act.)

As explanations that admit degrees, justifications and excuses align well with a pluralist ethical framework. Just as an action may be morally acceptable or obligatory to the extent that it serves one moral value and morally wrong to the extent that it contravenes another moral value, so too an action may be justified to the extent that it is done for a particular reason and not justified to the extent that it is not done for that reason.

The fact that justifications and excuses admit degrees is noteworthy for my purposes in two respects. The first concerns the status of the demands-of-conviction defence. This defence is, I shall argue, an excusatory defence, but one might think it could have partially justificatory elements since the 'value' that the offender seeks to protect through her disobedience is not just whatever cause she believes gives her undefeated reason to act. The 'value' also includes the genuine value of her autonomy, agency, and capacity for persistent commitments, which together may seem to lend a justificatory gloss to what would otherwise have to be an assertion of mere excusability.

It is important, however, not to misconstrue the value of autonomy when our choices are bad choices. Otherwise the justificatory gloss of autonomous choice would be present even when we commit murder. One option is to say that the value of autonomy is restricted to valuable acts. Another option is to bite the bullet and say that the value of autonomy is present even in an autonomous act of murder, but that value is wholly outweighed by the gross disvalue of the act. Another option is to say that the value of autonomy is restricted not to valuable acts, but to acts that do not interfere with the autonomy of others. These are weighty issues in the complex conceptual territory of *justification* and *excuse*, which I shall have to put aside to focus on the demands-of-conviction defence as an excusatory defence.

The second issue concerns cases where the reasons that otherwise would offer a successful justificatory defence are coloured by negative factors such as mixed motivations. This is most relevant for the necessity defence, which I take up in the next chapter. Briefly, consider the person who acts on the basis of two considerations only one of which is an undefeated reason. Suppose a bored police officer decides that today she will arrest all and only speeding drivers who have beards.[23] When she next arrests a bearded speeder, she acts not only for the undefeated reason that the person is speeding, but also for what she takes mistakenly to be a reason, namely, that the person is bearded. It is clear that the police officer's action is not alright all things considered even though an undefeated reason is operative in her decision to act. Similarly, suppose a disobedient rescues animals from laboratories in which they are being tortured, and she does it not for the reason of protecting the animals from suffering but for the reason of bringing publicity to her environmental cause (recall Chapter 1 on respect). Her act is not fully justified, although she acts in a way that could be fully justified, because the reason for which she acts is not undefeated even though the act it leads her to take is one that has undefeated reasons in its favour.

The conceptual territory of justifications and excuses is a treacherous one, but the Gardnerian account that I broadly endorse is robust, in

---

[23] This example is drawn from Nathanson, Stephen (1985) 'Does it Matter if the Death Penalty is Arbitrarily Administered?' in *Philosophy and Public Affairs*, 14, 157.

keeping with the kind of pluralistic moral outlook that frames my discussion, and credible for the purposes of exploring the practices of civil disobedience and personal disobedience.

2. The Demands-of-Conviction Defence

Let me now consider to what extent conscientious moral conviction can support a legal excuse for disobedience of the law.[24] I take as my starting point Jeremy Horder's account of what he calls the demands-of-*conscience* defence, which he says is an excusatory defence little recognized in law premised on the requirement to treat people with equal respect as autonomous beings.[25] Although I agree with Horder that such a defence—which I call a demands-of-*conviction* defence—is credible, I supplement his autonomy-based account of it with a further, two-part ground for the defence based on psychological costliness and akrasia. I then part company with him in my analysis of the acts that this proposed defence protects. Whereas Horder denies that the defence extends to civil disobedience, I argue that it applies most readily to civil disobedience.

2.1 *Grounds for the defence*

There are at least three putative grounds for a demands-of-conviction defence: 1) respect for autonomy, 2) psychological costliness and akrasia, and 3) compulsion. I will show that only the first two of these are compelling.

The first ground is respect for our autonomy as beings who are part authors of our own lives. Horder argues rightly that, to insist that we should always sacrifice our commitments in order to comply with legal demands, however trivial those demands may be, is to place disproportionate emphasis on the importance of law-abidingness. And, this unduly affects our prospects for realizing full personal autonomy, the value of which is key in a liberal democracy. This is the political

---

[24] The defence at issue here follows the narrow, technical sense of 'defence' in criminal law, that is, as any part of a defendant's case which 1) if advanced successfully would warrant acquittal, and 2) is compatible with the defendant conceding that the offence charged had indeed been committed. Cf Gardner (2007), 141.

[25] Horder, Jeremy (2004) *Excusing Crime*. Oxford: Oxford University Press, ch 5.

expression of the humanistic principle that I discussed in the last chapter.

This autonomy ground is an assertion of our basic responsibility, that our disobedience was an autonomous act taken on the strength of commitments that we may point to when asked to account for our action. It is an assertion that, when pressed, it is possible for us to give reasons (or partial reasons) for our believing we had undefeated reason to act. In other words, it is possible for us to give an excuse or partial excuse to those who do not share our view of what is most important.

The second ground for the demands-of-conviction defence is, I argue, psychological costliness and akrasia. This ground has a non-instrumental side and an instrumental side. In non-instrumental terms, the demands-of-conviction defence recognizes the psychological importance, distinct from autonomy, of our not always having to give priority to literal adherence with the law over our own beliefs and commitments. The defence recognizes the psychological risks of self-alienation, incongruity, and akrasia that dog absolute expectations that we adhere to formal norms. In valuing autonomy, it is necessary to value also the conditions for autonomy, one of which is an integrated mind and the capacity for practical reasoning (as discussed in Chapters 2 and 3). This ground reflects the Aristotelian interest in, and desire for, responsibility. It highlights that, unless we are given opportunities to cultivate the skills of practical reasoning, good judgement, and will, we will be less able and less motivated to take responsibility for our conduct.

In instrumental terms, the psychological-costliness ground shows that it is in the interests of a liberal democracy that legal dictates not assert absolute priority either in principle or in practice since this can cause weakness of will (or akrasia) and, consequently, can risk leading to a general decline in law-abidance. If the law asks us always to give priority to literal compliance, then we may find it more difficult generally to follow the law, even the good laws, than we would do if the law's expectations were not absolute and unyielding. In short, the psychological-costliness ground recognizes that it is important for a well-functioning liberal democracy that its members maintain the will, commitment, and capacity for general law-abidance.[26] The defence

---

[26] For a discussion of the value of law-abidance, see Edmundson, William A. (2006) 'The Virtue of Law-Abidance' in *Philosophers' Imprint* 6: 4, 1–21. Edmundson uses a narrower conception of *law-abidance* than I use here.

acknowledges the threat to this posed by absolutist expectations that limit our opportunities to cultivate the skills of practical judgement.

Consider an analogy with physical integrity. Laws that either intrude on our physical integrity or place overly demanding burdens on us physically run afoul of humanistic respect for persons.[27] For example, laws that *require* us to vote, to pay our taxes in person, to take our kids to school in person, and to walk everywhere rather than drive (for environmental reasons) may well *each* be acceptably burdensome, but are overly burdensome in aggregation. The same is true for psychological integrity. The psychological burdensomeness of following any particular law may be acceptable, but the aggregative burdensomeness of absolutely binding law is overly demanding.

A third putative ground for the demands-of-conviction defence, which I reject, is compulsion.[28] The thought here is that we are compelled, or our will is so overborne, by our convictions that the only act we could take is the breach of law we took. This notion of *compulsion* differs from the legal notion of *moral involuntariness*, according to which our act is morally involuntary if we really had no other choice but to commit the offence because, say, we face a threat to our life or limb. (I explore the legal notion of *moral involuntariness* in the next chapter on necessity.) The compulsion ground is problematic for several reasons.

To begin with, it is unclear whether such 'compulsion' amounts to an assertion of responsibility or a denial of responsibility. On the one hand, 'conviction'-based compulsion would have to differ from physical compulsion since only in the latter case are we not agents. In cases of physical compulsion, there is no *actus reus*. The innocent person that the evil aggressor hurls down a well at a man trapped at the bottom is subject to physical compulsion. There is no act that is the innocent threat's act. She is simply used as a tool by the aggressor to do wrong. As Ian Dennis notes, when we are so used, we do not will the act.[29] But, when we act on the basis of conviction we *do* will our acts even if we say we 'could not do otherwise'. However, on the other hand, if we are *compelled* to will our act, then, although we wish to be seen to

---

[27] See Chapter 4 for a specification of over-burdensomeness in terms of undue or unreasonable burdens.
[28] Cf Fletcher, George (1978) *Rethinking Criminal Law*. Boston: Little, Brown & Co.
[29] Dennis, Ian Howard (2009) 'On Necessity as a Defence to Crime: Possibilities, Problems and the Limits of Justification and Excuse' in *Criminal Law and Philosophy* 3, 29–49.

will it, we could not will otherwise and, hence, are not responsible for our willing. Neither the assertion of responsibility nor the denial of responsibility gives an intuitive picture of such 'compulsion'. That said, the denial of responsibility is the more problematic of the two. Here are two reasons why.

For one thing, a denial of responsibility for a supposedly conviction-driven act is in tension with the Aristotelian conception of us as persons who wish to show that we have reasons for acting as we do. Denying responsibility for our convictions and conduct reflects the Hobbesian conception of the person under which we seek to avoid the consequences of our conduct rather than show that, despite everything, we can give reasons for why we thought we should act as we did. It sits entirely at odds with both the non-evasion condition for conscientiousness and our interests in taking responsibility for our conduct.

For another thing, unless supplemented by other elements, the compulsion ground gives a false portrait of conscientiousness as a brute, passionate, unthinking, if not slightly deranged obsession by whose force we are spellbound and rendered less autonomous. The kinds of commitments with which such blind compulsion would most readily align are those least likely to satisfy the minimal conditions of logical coherence and evidential satisfactoriness (see Chapter 1). Examples include the parents who believe that as a matter of honour they must kill their daughter who has been raped, or the parents who instruct their daughter who has become pregnant to kill her pet dog in punishment, or the parents who refuse to take their child with curable diabetes to see a doctor, or the zealous animal liberationist who poisons factory animals' feed. A demands-of-conviction defence premised on compulsion would most likely protect the capricious passions and proclivities of the least reasonable rather than the sincere, serious, reflective moral commitments of the more reasonable. Hence, I reject it.

2.2 *The nature and scope of the defence*

With the autonomy ground and the psychological-costliness ground for this defence in hand, we may ask: To which kinds of acts does the defence apply? And how strong a defence does it give?[30] The answer to

---

[30] The fact that excusability comes both in degrees and in complex, hybrid forms has a particular bearing on the analysis of conviction-driven disobedience since some disobedience

the second question turns largely on the answer to the first. What are the limits to the kinds of acts that we could claim are excused on grounds of conviction? What kinds of harms could we do? What kinds of wrongs could we do?

Horder argues that the demands-of-conviction defence (as I call it) applies only to a limited range of acts of personal disobedience, such as a refusal to have a blood transfusion, a failure to complete our part of a double-suicide pact, or a refusal to withdraw treatment on request from a terminally ill patient to whom we are attached (though he has doubts about this last example). In these cases where the defence could apply, Horder says that some accommodation must be made for our moral commitments and non-moral goals and projects constitutive of our identity. When these commitments clash with the demands of the law, we can show that we had reason to believe we had undefeated reasons to act.

In a broadly similar vein, Joseph Raz holds that, although granting a general legal right to private (conscientious) objection would be problematic since it would entail allowing us to disobey the law for reasons of personal conviction even when by doing so we act egregiously,[31] nevertheless there should be limited protection from being coerced to act against conviction.[32] Operating in the background is the idea that, in at least some (private) contexts, we should not be held liable for breach of law if the breach is committed because we think the law is morally objectionable. This arises, Raz argues, from the principle of humanism, which acknowledges society's duty to honour human

---

may not be animated by either ordinary reasons for action (let alone by undefeated reasons for action) or good reasons for believing there are reasons for action. Rather it is animated at best by weak reasons for believing there are reasons to act, reasons such as the apparent epistemic authority of their religious leaders or of their community's traditions and norms. Such disobedience differs from the disobedience that is not animated by a coherent set of beliefs at all and which as such is not conviction-driven. The latter can be easily dismissed, but the former cannot. Whether they may claim a partial excuse for their act depends in part on the act they take.

[31] In many US states, the law includes a religious exemption for child abuse and neglect that allows parents to appeal to religion or faith-based rituals as a legal defence for such abuse. I noted in Chapter 1 the 2008 Wisconsin case where this defence of exemption was not available to a couple, as they were charged with second-degree reckless homicide, not child abuse and neglect, after allowing their 11-year-old daughter to slip into a coma and die due to curable juvenile diabetes while the family stood around her and prayed. The parents could have faced 25 years in prison, but were sentenced to six months' imprisonment respectively (one month per year for six years) and 10 years' probation.

[32] Raz, Joseph (1979) *The Authority of Law*. Oxford: Oxford University Press, 286.

dignity and personal autonomy. It entails amongst other things respecting that we can have deep convictions, and that the law places overly burdensome pressure on us when it coerces us to privilege the law above our convictions in all cases.

Both Raz and Horder argue that this modest legal protection does *not* extend to civil disobedience. The reasons, which I anticipated in the last chapter, concern 1) the ostensibly political and strategic nature of civil disobedience, and 2) the problems for democracy posed by legitimating a practice like civil disobedience. In essence, the thought is that, although civil disobedience is often animated by deep moral conviction, the motives for it are at least partly political and strategic. When we civilly disobey in a liberal democracy, we deliberately breach the law so as to challenge the legitimacy of democratically enacted laws (the strategic action problem). In so doing, we challenge the democratic legislature's supreme right to take strategic decisions for the whole community even though the legislature is better placed than we are to account for all of the reasons that bear on the right guidance to follow (the democracy problem).[33] Hence, our conduct falls outside the scope of the humanistic principle that underlies the demands-of-conviction defence. By contrast, if we engage in personal disobedience, we do not seek to challenge the state's right, through law, to take decisions on behalf of the entire community. That is, we do not choose for purely strategic reasons the laws to be disobeyed.[34]

I anticipated my responses to these objections in the last chapter where I showed that a genuine humanistic principle of respect appreciates that conviction is communicative and non-evasive. At a minimum, Raz and Horder's qualified humanism-inspired protection of personal disobedience is insufficient, if not entirely misplaced. Let me respond to the strategic action problem and democracy problem in turn.

3. The Strategic Action Problem

The fact that civil disobedience is undertaken *for the purpose of* communicating both condemnation of a policy and a desire for change might

---

[33] Horder (2004), 224.
[34] Horder (2004), 224.

seem to fuel the charge that it is strategic and hence falls outside an appropriate interpretation of humanism. But, this relies on an overly simplistic view of the operative reasons that drive such disobedience.[35]

First, it is true that, if we engage in *indirect* civil disobedience, we breach a law that we do not oppose and to that extent we act strategically. But, sometimes it is not so much strategy as necessity that forces dissenters to engage in indirect civil disobedience. Sometimes indirect disobedience is the only action available. A civilian cannot directly refuse to follow lawful orders from the military. A person on the street cannot refuse to perform contracted experiments on animals. Also, sometimes, indirect disobedience can be more justifiable than direct disobedience is when it causes less harm or, in addition, is a more efficacious way to redress perceived injustices. Police officers would cause less harm by breaching their uniform codes than by engaging in an illegal strike.

Second, if we engage in *direct* civil disobedience, the strategic action objection is not forceful at all. This is due to the communicative principle of conscientiousness. Direct civil disobedience involves conscientiously communicative disobedience of the very law opposed. The operative reason for communicating condemnation includes *dissociating* from the law opposed through a conscientious refusal to follow it. Rosa Parks' refusal to give up her seat and the ensuing bus boycott were communicative acts of dissociation from a bigoted policy. That dissociation was not strategic. It was founded on a moral judgement.

A further reply to the strategic action problem focuses on personal disobedience. It is mistaken to suppose that politics and strategy do not figure in at least some personal disobedience, specifically, evasive personal disobedience. Breaches of law carried out in secret with the aim of remaining secret are strategic acts. Breaches of law chosen with calculation to preserve liberty from coercive interference from the law are strategic acts. As such, excepting cases of existential threat such as the historical threat to Jews, personal disobedience has no greater claim and often a lesser claim than civil disobedience has to protection under a humanistic principle of respect for conscientiousness.

The strategic-action problem might be re-presented as a concern that modest protection of civil disobedience would provide a strategic

---

[35] This section elaborates some ideas in Brownlee, Kimberley (2012a) 'Conscientious Objection and Civil Disobedience' in *The Routledge Companion to Philosophy of Law*. Andrei Marmor (ed.), London: Routledge, 537–8.

reason for other would-be protesters, whether or not like-minded, to break the law to further their political aims. This would ostensibly undermine the legal defensibility of civil disobedience. And it could give rise to further unwelcome follow-on threats to common goods, such as a greater willingness amongst protest movements to forego a preference for law-abiding protest in favour of rights violations.[36]

In reply, when we engage in suitably constrained civil disobedience, we have not necessarily foregone a preference for law-abiding protest in favour of rights violations because it is not inevitable that civil disobedience violates rights. Moreover, the worry that a legal defence for civil disobedience would create a strategic reason for other would-be protesters to break the law rests on a mistaken slippery slope. The legal defence would not be available for more radical forms of illegal protest. And, burdening us when we are civil disobedient in order to deter non-civil dissent uses us as a means to prevent other types of conduct, which, unlike our own, are not constrained and conscientiously motivated. Punishing civil disobedience in order to restore deterrence levels disrespects us as autonomous persons who contribute to collective decision-making in tolerable ways.

Undoubtedly, it is difficult to show that an act of disobedience was not opportunistic. But, one possible test is whether our *disobedience itself* benefits us personally. If it does not, then there is little reason to think it is opportunistic. The overall cause of a protest—such as equal rights for women—may well benefit us, but that is different from our *disobedience itself* benefiting us.

4. The Democracy Problem

The democracy problem has three forms: 1) an epistemic argument; 2) an anti-paternalist argument; and 3) a procedural fairness argument. The epistemic argument says that civil disobedience challenges the democratic legislature's supreme right to take strategic decisions for the whole community even though the legislature is better placed than individual citizens are to account for all of the reasons that bear on the right guidance to follow. The anti-paternalist argument says that it is disrespectful to engage in civil disobedience because, in doing so, we

---

[36] Horder (2004), 224.

assume we know better than other members of our community. That is, we insult our fellow citizens by privileging our own judgement above that of the democratic process. The procedural fairness argument says that, even if we do know better than others which policy to adopt, we act unfairly by disregarding the procedural democratic mechanisms that the society has adopted for resolving disagreements and moving forward to a decision.

Each of these forms of the democracy problem could be said to animate the judgment, mentioned on page 157, by the US Court of Appeals for the 10th Circuit on the three nuns. After emphasizing the risks and evils that can attend subordinating the requirements of law to our own view of morality, Justice Hartz, speaking for the court, then quotes Judge Stevens from *United States v Cullen*:

One who elects to serve mankind by taking the law into his own hands thereby demonstrates his conviction that his own ability to determine policy is superior to democratic decision making. [Defendants'] professed unselfish motivation, rather than a justification, actually identifies a form of arrogance which organized society cannot tolerate. A simple rule, reiterated by a peaceloving scholar, amply refutes [Defendants'] arrogant theory of defense: 'No man or group is above the law.'[37]

In highlighting the risks that attend 'subordinating the requirements of law' to our own moral outlook, Justice Hartz maintains that civil disobedience shows the offender to be one who places herself above the law and the democratic decision-making process.

There are at least three possible replies to the epistemic form of the democracy problem, some of which I anticipated in Chapter 3. First, as a general objection, this argument is dubious on empirical grounds. It is doubtful that legislatures are *invariably* better placed epistemically than, say, environmentalists or soldiers are to account for all of the reasons related to whether and how to protect the environment or to go to war, especially since legislatures must contend with innumerable pressures that are likely to diminish their attentiveness to all salient reasons. These include time-pressures, media, opposing parties, party ideology, political capital, and well-funded lobbyists with profit-driven agendas. In view of these pressures, legislatures will sometimes be *less* well placed

---

[37] *United States of America v Cullen* (1971), 454 F.2d 386, 392 (7th Cir.). Cited from *United States v Platte et al* (2005).

than on-the-ground experts are to assess the relevant reasons. At other times, they will be comparably placed or differently placed than on-the-ground experts are to assess relevant reasons. Only rarely, if ever, will they be undisputed epistemic authorities for the society.

Second, how well-placed a party is to account for the reasons for or against a policy is a matter not only of epistemic access to relevant facts, but also of motivation to acknowledge those facts. Both the pressures that well-funded lobbies and media can exert and the threat of losing power are strong incentives for legislators to ignore reasons running counter to their electoral self-interest.

Third, even if the legislature were best placed to assess the relevant reasons for and against a policy, its members could still benefit from pointed minority opposition to ensure that they remain alive to all of the salient reasons, given the competing pressures they face.

Let me turn to the anti-paternalist form of the democracy problem. In reply, if we engage in civil disobedience, we do not necessarily put ourselves above the law and disrespect our fellow citizens who follow the ordinary procedures for democratic participation. First, our efforts need not be seen as a challenge to the democratic process because democracy is a work in progress. It is never the case that the votes are counted, the decisions taken, and then everyone goes home. Democracy is an ongoing process of giving and taking, discussing and competing, and prioritizing and adapting. Defeated parties may continue to challenge the majority position and their doing so, far from being anti-democratic, reflects the true spirit of democracy as a system that accommodates diverse positions and is sensitive to shifts in perspectives. Moreover, on a sufficiently nuanced understanding of democratic deliberation and citizen obligation, civil disobedience can make a distinctive contribution. When breakdowns in the mechanisms for engagement occur, civil disobedience is one comparatively modest way to rectify these democratic deficits by focusing attention on neglected issues.[38] In performing such services, our civil disobedience is consistent with, and supportive of, democracy. This argument is not intended to lend a justificatory gloss to the excusatory demands-of-conviction defence. Rather, it shows that civil disobedience is not paternalistic and anti-democratic. Consequently, paternalistic worries need not be raised against the demands-of-conviction defence.

[38] Markovits, Daniel (2005) 'Democratic Disobedience' in *Yale Law Journal* 114, 1897–952.

Second, when we civilly disobey, we willingly expose ourselves to the *risk* of punishment in order both to act in ways consistent with our deeply help commitments and to communicate our concerns to society. Think of the nuns who communicatively breached the law out of a sincere commitment to certain beliefs, however misguided. They acted from the strength of their conscientious conviction and not from a desire to place themselves above the law.

Let me turn finally to the procedural fairness form of the democracy problem. My reply here echoes the arguments noted in Chapter 4 that there is inescapable comparative unfairness between majorities and vulnerable minorities both in their capacity to get their concerns onto the public table for discussion and in their ability to influence policy before decisions are taken. Given this comparative unfairness, there must be some leeway in how such persons are permitted to participate. Putting the point bluntly, it is not unfair to grant such persons some space outside the bounds of the law to communicate their convictions; it is unfair to *deny* it to them. My use of this argument is more modest than the use I described in Chapter 4. I am not using this argument to defend a right to civil disobedience. I am using it to advance an excusatory defence for civil disobedience.

At first glance, my reply to the procedural fairness problem seems to give us only a defence for minorities' resort to civil disobedience. However, my reply may be more powerful than it first appears. This is because what it means to be a comparatively disempowered minority is context-sensitive. Members of society who are comparatively empowered in relation to most others can be comparatively disempowered in contexts where their power is insufficient. For instance, the members of the legislature who form either the opposition party or a third or fourth party are not comparatively disempowered in relation to most members of society, but they are comparatively disempowered in relation to the governing party. Hence, a breach of formal norms, such as a walkout, may be the only effective way for them to influence policy formation.

Finally, a general reply to all three forms of the democracy problem is the following. Within a liberal society, as Horder himself acknowledges, the state's strategic concern to maintain authority over the use and threat of force by displacing people's inclination to retaliate against wrongdoers with the criminal law, is bound up with and tempered by the requirements that 1) people not expect all wrongdoing to be controlled solely or largely through the *state's* authority to punish, and that 2) wrongdoers' dignity and needs be acknowledged.[39] This nuanced view of the liberal state's strategic aims is compatible with a generous set of excusing conditions that acknowledge wrongdoers' humanity. Thus, there is nothing, in principle, about the demands-of-conviction defence as an excusatory defence that need trouble a liberal commitment to democratic rule of law.

Conclusion

In this chapter, I outlined the first of two legal defences for civil disobedience. This demands-of-conviction defence is an excusatory defence premised on 1) personal autonomy and 2) psychological integrity. There are both instrumental and non-instrumental psychological costs in imposing absolute, unyielding legal expectations on people. I distinguished my account of the demands-of-conviction defence from Jeremy Horder's account, which denies its applicability to civil disobedience. I argued, contra Horder, that this defence applies more readily to civil disobedience than to personal disobedience in virtue of the greater conscientiousness of the former practice. I then responded to two interrelated objections: the strategic action problem and the democracy problem. I showed that civil disobedience is neither necessarily strategic nor necessarily anti-democratic. These lines of objection will be explored again in the next chapter on the necessity defence.

---

[39] Horder (2004), 196.

6

Necessity Defence

> Actually, we who in engage in nonviolent direct action are not the creators of tension. We merely bring to the surface the hidden tension that is already alive.
>
> —Martin Luther King Jr[1]

In 2008, six Greenpeace activists were acquitted by a jury in Maidstone, UK, for occupying and criminally damaging the Kingsnorth power station to the tune of £30,000.[2] In 2011, 20 environmentalists were convicted by a jury in Nottingham, UK, for *planning* to do similar things at the Ratcliffe power station.[3] Both groups made pleas rooted in appeals to necessity. The first group argued that they had a 'lawful excuse' in that their act was taken to prevent the greater evil of immediate harm to human lives and property caused by climate change. The second group straightforwardly argued the 'necessity' of their act to prevent death and serious injury caused by CO2 emissions and climate change. The first defence worked, the second didn't.

---

[1] King, Martin Luther Jr (1963) 'Letter from Birmingham City Jail'. Reprinted in Bedau, Hugo (ed.) (1991) *Civil Disobedience in Focus*. London: Routledge, 68–84.

[2] Vidal, John (2008), 'Climb Every Chimney...' *The Guardian*, 12 September 2008.

[3] In this case, it appears that the judge stepped up when the jury did not. Judge Jonathan Teare spared 18 of the activists from jail sentences and instead imposed lenient sentences ranging from 18 months' conditional discharge to 90 hours' unpaid work. Judge Teare noted that the public might consider his sentencing 'impossibly lenient', but he had been put in a highly unique position given the moral standing of the campaigners. He said: 'You are all decent men and women with a genuine concern for others, and in particular for the survival of planet Earth in something resembling its present form.' Cited from Lewis, Paul and Prakash, Nidhi (2011) 'Ratcliffe coal protesters spared jail sentences' *The Guardian*, 5 January.

Although juries are sometimes inclined, like the Maidstone jury was, to acquit people for acts of civil disobedience, generally disobedients have had a notoriously difficult time arguing necessity as a defence for breach of law.[4] Trial judges and particularly appeal court judges have tended to dismiss a necessity defence for civil disobedience, though they sometimes mete out lenient, non-custodial punishments to campaigners. In this chapter, I explore the philosophical respectability of appealing to necessity as a defence for civil disobedience. I do not seek to be faithful to any existing legal system or set of legal doctrines, though I engage with some of the recent legal theory debates about necessity in the UK. Instead, I seek to offer some philosophical reflections on the nature of *necessity*, and to show that a case can be made, in principle, for the applicability of a necessity defence to (some) civil disobedience.

In particular, I take a pluralistic approach to necessity that highlights, in the context of civil disobedience, the centrality of non-contingent basic needs. I argue that a defence of necessity applies, in principle, to acts of civil disobedience that are responsive to non-contingent basic needs and rights including brute survival needs and the equally fundamental humanistic needs of basic political recognition, social inclusion, and respect. I address two main objections to my view, which are the competition of values problem and the proportionality problem. The first says that the law (rightly) cannot accommodate competition from other values, such as the values we prioritize before the law when we appeal to necessity for civil disobedience. The second says that, in a liberal democracy, civil disobedience is never the 'only reasonable means' by which to redress abuses of basic needs or rights because, amongst other things, adequate ordinary opportunities for meaningful political participation are available to all citizens in a spirit of democratic engagement and collective self-restraint. In reply, amongst other things, I advance a modesty of law thesis according to which liberal democratic law has an under-acknowledged capacity to recognize the legitimacy and importance of values other than literal conformity with the law. This is evidenced, first, by the viability of the demands-of-

---

[4] As crown prosecutors and corporations know, campaigners who use non-violent action to challenge the law are often acquitted by juries. John Vidal notes: 'In the past decade, prosecutions of protesters against GM crops, incinerators, new roads and nuclear, chemical and arms trade companies have all collapsed after defendants argued that they had acted according to their consciences and that they were trying to prevent a greater crime.' Vidal (2008).

conviction defence discussed in Chapter 5, second, by the extent to which necessity is incorporated into law in different guises, and third, more generally, by the underlying commitment to humanism that animates liberal democracies.

1. The Nature of Necessity

1.1 Competing principles of necessity

In common law jurisdictions, the lack of success that civil disobedients have had in advancing a defence of necessity may be due less to anything special about civil disobedience than to an apparent rejection by common law judges of a general principle of necessity. Ian Howard Dennis observes that necessity has always been problematic as a defence for criminal liability partly because of 'the historic reluctance of the common law to recognise any general principle that the defendant can be exculpated where his act is necessary... to "promote some value higher than the value of literal compliance with the law"'.[5] I do not challenge judges' reluctance to recognize a *general* principle of necessity since I endorse a pluralistic approach to necessity, but I will challenge the underlying assumption behind this reluctance, that the law cannot readily recognize values other than literal adherence to the law.

Legal and moral philosophers have advanced different rationales for a general principle of necessity, such as a 'lesser of two evils' rationale and a 'moral involuntariness' or 'compelled will' rationale.[6] In its simplest form, the lesser evil rationale is a harm-based rationale that the necessary act taken does less harm than the harm threatened. For example, if I can prevent you from assaulting an elderly person by tripping you, then I may trip you, and indeed should trip you, as this does less harm than the harm you threaten to do. By contrast, the compelled will rationale is a culpability-based rationale that we are exculpated in cases of necessity because our will is overborne by the necessity. This kind of 'moral' involuntariness does not mean that we are (or feel) compelled

---

[5] Dennis, Ian Howard (2009) 'On Necessity as a Defence to Crime: Possibilities, Problems and the Limits of Justification and Excuse' in *Criminal Law and Philosophy* 3, 29–49. In this passage, Dennis quotes Williams, G. (1961) *Criminal Law the General Part* (2nd edn). London: Stevens & Sons, 728.

[6] Cf Fletcher, G. (1978) *Rethinking Criminal Law*. Boston: Little, Brown & Co. Cited in Dennis (2009).

by our religious or moral beliefs to act in certain ways, which was the kind of 'compulsion' I dismissed in the last chapter. Rather, 'moral involuntariness' means that we are not morally blameworthy for the wrong we do because that *wrong* was involuntary or compelled. For example, if you threaten to blow up Parliament unless I assault the next passer-by, my will not to assault someone is overborne by the necessity of doing so to prevent your killing many people.

Both of these putative rationales are problematic. The harm-based lesser-evil rationale is implausibly under-inclusive, as Dennis notes, since it cannot accommodate the necessity of perpetuating a harm that is equal to or greater than the threatened harm, such as killing in self-defence or using force to effect an arrest.[7] Moreover, it is simplistically utilitarian, and hence normatively doubtful as a rationale to apply to morally complex cases involving peoples' lives, needs, and rights. A more nuanced version of the lesser evil rationale, adopted by Jeff McMahan and David Rodin, focuses not on minimizing overall aggregate harm, but on avoiding the greater injustice by committing a lesser injustice.[8] This more sophisticated rationale avoids the problems of simplistic utilitarianism, but may still be under-inclusive if it cannot accommodate the necessity of perpetuating a comparably serious injustice or a graver injustice than that threatened where doing so is morally justified by some value other than justice, such as mercy or benevolence.

The moral involuntariness rationale is problematic, first, because it is conceptually and evaluatively ambiguous. It sits on the fence between a denial of responsibility because our will is overborne and an assertion of responsibility because, unlike physical compulsion, we will the act we take: I will my act of assaulting the passer-by or of tripping you because of the crisis I face.[9] The problem here is not that, in such cases, we may be only partially excused or partially justified because we are only partially responsible owing to diminished capacity, duress, etc. The problem is that it is unclear whether the 'moral involuntariness' defence tries to honour an Aristotelian picture of us as persons who seek to take responsibility for our conduct, or whether it instead falls back on a

---

[7] Dennis states: 'there is no requirement in the law of private or public defence that the defendant's use of force should be the lesser of the evils. A potentially lethal attack may be met by the use of deadly force, and deadly force may even be permissible if it is the only reasonable means of effecting a lawful arrest in certain circumstances.' Dennis (2009).

[8] McMahan, Jeff (2009) *Killing in War*. Oxford: Oxford University Press, ch 1.

[9] For a brief commentary on this ambiguity, see Dennis (2009).

Hobbesian picture of us as ones who seek in self-interest to deny responsibility and escape judgment.

Second, the moral involuntariness rationale is also implausibly under-inclusive, as Dennis notes. It seems unable to accommodate measured exercises of judgement in response to danger, such as a doctor's weighing the merits of a certain medical procedure for a patient unable to consent.[10] If doctors take a decision to separate conjoined babies so that the healthier of the twins may live, it would be odd to say that the doctors' wills were *overborne* even though they act under pressure and are responding to a crisis.

This under-inclusiveness stems from the search for monism that all necessity defences must appeal in the end to the same basic value. Hence, these rationales disregard the many varied yet linguistically intuitive concepts of *necessity* that we have, which cannot all be accommodated within the inner logic of either 'lesser evil' or 'moral involuntariness'. These include the concepts of: 1) external force, pressure, compulsion, and determinism; 2) logical entailment and conceptual rigour; 3) desperate need, poverty, and misery; 4) the essentials for life and for continued existence; and 5) morally necessary duties that cannot properly or reasonably be left undone. This range of concepts can be accommodated within a pluralistic account that says that necessity defences can ultimately be grounded in appeals to different, competing values.

Many of these commonsense notions of *necessity* have found recognition in the law, but not in the form of a single unified defence called 'necessity'. Rather, different dimensions of necessity have been incorporated into a variety of defences with different nomenclature and different rationales such as self-defence, third-party intervention, duress by threats, duress by circumstances, and (more recently) medical necessity.[11] These defences may be taken to aim to track, be it well or poorly, the conceptual and evaluative differences amongst various kinds of necessary acts, the reasons that could be given for those acts,

---

[10] Cf *Re A (Children) (Conjoined Twins: Medical Treatment) (No. 1)* [2001] Fam 147 (CA (Civ Div)).
[11] See Clarkson, C. M. V. (2004) 'Necessary Action: A New Defence' in *Criminal Law Review*, February, 81–95. Dennis notes that 'It is perhaps the judges' intuition that different moral principles were involved that may help to explain the very different historical development of necessity at common law from self-defence and duress by threats.' Dennis (2009).

the standards of reasonableness that would have to be met, the relevance or irrelevance of past actions, and the degree of proportionality or self-restraint that would be required. Of course, the philosophical respectability of the legal distinctions built up from such material can be questioned or in need of refinement. The point is simply that, distinct values are operative in these diverse contexts, and yet, each context can be framed by a plausible notion of *necessity*.

1.2 A pluralistic approach to necessity

Given the variety of commonsense notions of *necessity* and the evaluative distinctions pertinent to them, there is reason to approach necessity in pluralistic terms, and not as a single type of appeal. I agree with Dennis that we should properly speak of a family of necessity defences rather than of *a single* necessity defence. However, I disagree with how Dennis then specifies the parameters of this family. He says that this family, like all families, shares certain features. In his view, the shared features of necessity defences are the following:

1. all necessity defences are exculpatory in the sense that they provide grounds for the non-imposition of criminal liability that do not deny the voluntariness of the defendant's act or *mens rea*;
2. they are all not offence-specific defences, but have claims to generality;
3. they all require examination of the defendant's reasons for action; the defendant's act must be intended to be the instrument for the avoidance of some undesirable event or danger;
4. they all require the defendant's act to have been necessary, in the sense that it was the only reasonable means open to the defendant to avoid the event or danger;[12] and
5. they all require some relationship of proportionality between the avoiding act (which would otherwise incur criminal liability) and the event or danger to be avoided.[13]

---

[12] Although this condition is framed in objective language, I take it that Dennis intends it to be interpreted in different ways according to the context. In some cases, objective standards of reasonableness will apply, in others subjective standards will apply. In some, the defendant's beliefs will be what matter, in others the objective facts of the case will be what matter.

[13] It is unclear whether Dennis presents these conditions as a description of the key common features of existing necessity defences in UK law, or as a normative account of the criteria for anything to be a genuine necessity defence. He offers no arguments other than existing law to support these conditions, but rather summarizes the features that he takes to be common at a very general level amongst defences that appeal to necessary action.

At a *very* general level, Dennis' approach may be unproblematic because, at that very general level, we might agree with C. M. V. Clarkson that what unites necessary acts such as self-defence, duress, and medical necessity is more important than what separates them: in all of them, a defendant commits what would otherwise be a crime to avoid some sort of crisis to protect herself and/or others. And, the real issues are how the law should respond and in what circumstances it should afford a defence.[14]

But, beyond that very general level, we do want an account that can be responsive to the complexities of practical reality, to differences in motivation and action, and to the pluralism of moral experience. A genuinely pluralistic account can do these things much more adroitly than a monistic account can. But, it's not at all clear that Dennis' account can do these things. There are three interrelated problems with Dennis' account that together suggest that, far from being a context-sensitive, pluralistic account of necessity, his account collapses into a general monistic account.

The first problem is that Dennis specifies the above list as a set of *necessary* conditions and not as a set of overlapping key features that highlight family resemblances. This makes for an unduly restrictive classification. At least one of the above conditions is not necessary. That is condition 2. Why could not a defence on the basis of necessity be offence-specific? A genuinely pluralistic approach to necessity would accommodate this possibility.

The second problem is that some of Dennis' conditions that may indeed be necessary are overly narrow. For instance, conditions 4 and 5 state that the necessary act must be not only 'proportional', but the 'only' reasonable means to respond to the threat or danger. But, suppose there are at least two otherwise criminal acts that we could take that would be reasonable and proportional responses to the crisis. Suppose that in the earlier Parliament case I could reasonably rob the passer-by rather than assault her to prevent you killing many people. Do I have no defence for my assault because there was at least one other otherwise criminal act that I could have reasonably taken? Surely not. Or suppose it is not possible to rank fully the reasonableness of one response over another. Robbing may be more reasonable along one dimension than assaulting is and less reasonable along another, or the

---

[14] Clarkson (2004).

two acts may not be comparable at all in this case. Do I have no defence because there is no single breach that could be deemed 'most reasonable' or the 'only reasonable means' amongst the breaches available? Surely not.

Related to this, it is strange in one sense to speak of 'proportionality' in relation to necessity because *proportionality* connotes balancing, equalizing, and neutralizing. A proportional response is neither too severe nor too lenient. This is a key concept in punishment theory, particularly desert theory, according to which the severity of punishment should be *proportional* to the seriousness of the crime (or crimes) committed: neither too sweet nor too sour; a pound of flesh and neither one ounce more nor less. The principle of proportionality takes both *ordinal* and *cardinal* forms. *Ordinal proportionality* speaks to the relative severity of the punishment; it should be proportional to that meted out for other crimes of comparable seriousness, and reflect the relative reprehensibility of the offence determined by both the harm it does or risks and the offender's degree of culpability.[15] Jaywalking should be punished less severely than robbery, and robbery less severely than murder. *Cardinal proportionality* speaks to the absolute severity of the punishment. Robbery should not be punished with either a life sentence or a modest fine. But it could be punished in either of those ways under a principle of mere ordinal proportionality provided that less serious offences such as jaywalking receive milder punishments than robbery does, and more serious offences such as murder receive harsher ones such as death.[16] As all this implies, in desert theory, a punitive response is out of proportion, and hence unjustified, when it is too mild as much as when it is too harsh.

By contrast, in cases of necessity, the milder the response we need to take to avert the crisis the better. It is, therefore, more appropriate to speak of *parsimonious* responses to necessity than of proportionate responses to necessity. A parsimonious response is no more severe than what is needed for us reasonably to avoid the threat or crisis. There are two kinds of non-excessiveness built into parsimony. First, the act must be no more severe than what is needed to avert the threat. Second, of the acts that would avert the threat (if there are any), the act

---

[15] Cf Ashworth, Andrew (1998) 'Desert' in *Principled Sentencing: Readings on Theory and Policy* (2nd edn). Andrew Ashworth and Andrew von Hirsch (eds.), Oxford: Hart Publishing, 143.

[16] See Tasioulas, John (2006) 'Punishment and Repentance' in *Philosophy* 81, 279–322.

must be no more severe (or not significantly more severe) than the severity of the threat. Thus, parsimony is sensitive both to the relative severity of our options in a crisis and to the relative severity of the crisis itself.

The second condition just noted is highlighted in the following case.[17] Suppose that you threaten to sprain my finger for purely malicious reasons, and there are only two physically possible ways for me to avert this assault. I can either kill you or render you a quadriplegic. Although my rendering you a quadriplegic satisfies the first condition for parsimony since it is no more severe than what is needed to avoid the threat to my finger, it does not satisfy the second condition since my rendering you a quadriplegic would be significantly more severe than your threat to my finger. Given the second condition, there is no parsimonious response available to me here, in which case a parsimonious attempt, such as kicking you, might be defensible even though it will be unsuccessful in averting the attack.[18]

The notion of *parsimony* does not raise under-inclusiveness worries in the way that the harm-based 'lesser of two evils' rationale does because a parsimonious response in, say, a case of self-defence may well do equal or greater harm than that threatened. It also does not raise worries about having to rank responses according to their degree of parsimony because parsimonious responses need not be unique. In an incomplete ranking, more than one response will be available to us. The parsimony of a response will depend on several factors including the context and the identity of the person facing the crisis. Concerning the context, it may well be reasonable and parsimonious for us to kill an aggressor to save our own life, but, outside extreme society-threatening emergencies such as the Parliament case, it may well not be reasonable and parsimonious for us to kill an innocent person under duress. Concerning the person facing the crisis, it may well be reasonable and parsimonious for a weak person to stop a strong aggressor by

---

[17] I thank Jonathan Quong for drawing my attention to this second dimension, and for providing the following example.

[18] Suppose though that I have a third option. Instead of killing you or rendering you a quadriplegic, I could prevent your spraining my finger by my spraining Jane's finger. Of the options available, this act would be the least severe one needed to avert the threat, and in a simple sense it would not be more severe than the threat to me. Hence it would seem to be parsimonious. But the simple assessment of the severity of my act is probably mistaken. It would be unreasonable of me to impose a comparable harm on Jane to avoid the same threat to me.

killing him, but not for a strong person to stop a weak aggressor by killing her when knocking her out would be sufficient to abort the attack.

A third and final problem with Dennis' account also relates to its narrowness. The problem comes in his interpretation of the scope of the application of necessity defences. He restricts the kinds of 'undesirable events or dangers' that could exculpate necessary action to cases of emergencies and conflicts of duty where a danger of death or serious injury is present. With my use of the language of 'crisis', I may have given the impression that I too think necessity cases are limited to emergencies or threats of death or serious injury. But, I do not. The language of 'crisis' does not imply *emergency* as the cases of medical necessity demonstrate. When doctors make difficult decisions on behalf of patients who cannot consent, they face a crisis but not inevitably an emergency. In my view, the language of 'crisis' and 'threats' implies fundamental importance.[19] Although I agree with Dennis that any development of necessity as a defence should be restricted, I do not agree that emergencies and conflicts of duty involving a danger of death or serious injury are 'the most serious harms in any principled ordering of harms', the threat of which actuates the instinct for self-preservation in an emergency or the altruistic impulse to save someone else to whom we owe a duty of care. In saying that these are the most serious concerns, Dennis invokes a conception of our most fundamental needs that jars with a humanistic understanding of such needs and the moral demands they generate. Let me outline a few features of needs to make this point clear.

Needs come in two flavours: contingent and non-contingent. Soran Reader and Gillian Brock note that the way to distinguish the two is to ask the question 'What for?' because it is part of the grammar of the word 'need' that it has an end for which the need is a necessary condition. Contingent needs are requirements for contingent ends, which the needing being might or might not have. For example, 'I need 60 pence.' 'What for?' 'I can't make a phone call without it.' By contrast, non-contingent needs are necessary conditions for non-contingent ends that the needing being could not but have. For example, 'I need water.' 'What for?' 'I can't live without it.' The mark of the unique, moral importance of non-contingent needs, Reader and

---

[19] See Clarkson (2004).

Brock point out, is that the being whose needs are at issue simply cannot go on unless its need is met: 'the very existence of the needing being as we know it is at stake'. For this reason, non-contingent needs are uniquely grave and urgent moral demands for support lest the needing being cease to exist.[20]

The relevant kind of existence is not simply existence, but continued existence or persistence for that being as the *kind* of being it is. For example, a person who is put in long-term solitary confinement and who becomes semi-catatonic as a result, may well continue to exist in a brute sense, but she does not continue to persist as a reasoning being capable of forming and maintaining meaningful, interdependent relations with others, making autonomous choices, and undertaking worthwhile projects. The violation of her non-contingent need for minimally adequate social inclusion has undermined her existence as a social being.[21] That said, the qualifier 'as the kind of being it is' should not be interpreted too broadly, as this could generate either overly burdensome duties for others to maintain a being's select way of being or perverse duties for others to maintain a being's morally intolerable way of being.[22]

Within the category of non-contingent needs there are basic needs and non-basic needs. Basic needs pick out the *minimal* needs for continued survival as the kind of being it is. Non-basic needs go beyond this moral minimum. Specifying the difference more fully is difficult. Reader and Brock say that the difference tracks a distinction between the normativity of public morality and the normativity of private morality. They say that, in public morality, not all non-contingent needs count as moral demands because needs-based public policy for a constituency, such as the constituency of women, children, humans, or non-human animals, is *general*, and hence must take as

---

[20] Reader, Soran and Brock, Gillian (2004) 'Needs, Moral Demands, and Moral Theory' in *Utilitas* 16: 3, 251–66.

[21] For a discussion of the human right against forced social deprivation in punishment, see Brownlee, Kimberley (2012b) 'Social Deprivation and Criminal Justice' in *Rethinking Criminal Law Theory: Canadian Perspectives on the Philosophy of Criminal Law*. François Tanguay-Renaud and James Stribopoulos (eds.), Oxford: Hart.

[22] Reader and Brock make an important point in noting that sometimes continued existence of a being as the kind of being it is does not generate moral demands for moral agents. A child abuser may need all sorts of help in order to carry on as a child abuser, but moral agents connected to him may reasonably not take these needs to be morally demanding. Reader and Brock (2004).

normative only those non-contingent needs that are shared by the whole constituency.

This way of specifying the difference between basic and non-basic needs is unattractive for several reasons. First, it relies on an overly sharp distinction between public and private morality, which I challenged in Chapter 3. Briefly, Reader and Brock take an inflexible view of the implications of law's generality. They do not acknowledge that a given need does not fall outside the scope of society's interest simply because public policy is too blunt a tool to accommodate it. Second, Reader and Brock employ an unnecessarily strict condition of universal need within a constituency. Not all women can bear children, but women as a constituency have non-contingent basic needs of reproductive choice, protection, and care. Third, in relation to needs, the notion of a *constituency* itself is contentious. Does ethnicity pick out a constituency? Does cognitive impairment pick out a constituency? Does economic position pick out a constituency? If so, what is the existence as the 'kind of being it is' that we would seek to protect within these constituencies? Finally, in consequence, Brock and Reader fail to appreciate that both non-universal needs and needs that go beyond the *minimum* required for continued existence can fall within the purview of society.

My own proposal is to adopt a range principle, according to which protection of the minimal needs for survival of a certain kind of being is informed by the ranges of needs of the beings of that kind. The shape and size of fundamental needs will vary across the beings of a certain kind. But, those variations will fall within certain ranges that may be taken as basic for that kind of being even though they are not universal amongst the beings of that kind. From this, broad categories of basic need can be specified. For example, I take it that the categories of non-contingent basic need for persons include, first, the necessities for brute survival such as water, food, shelter, security, and companionship; second, basic skills and protections such as education; and third, protection of reasoning capacity, expressive agency, a *degree* of autonomy, social inclusion, respect, and recognition.[23] A comparable set of basic needs can be fleshed out for children, for women, for elderly people, and so on. The set of non-contingent basic needs for persons does not obviously include all avoidance of serious harm or injury since such

---

[23] The non-contingent *non-basic* needs of reasoning persons go beyond this minimum to include things like access to meaningful relationships and projects.

harm may prevent loss of life or may be the price for other basic needs, or may be the price for commitments on which we may reasonably place greater value, such as the life and health of another.[24]

As a frame for the most fundamentally important concerns that could trigger necessity cases, the notion of *non-contingent basic needs* is richer and more plausible than Dennis' notion of 'danger of death or serious injury'. In making non-contingent basic needs our focus, we do not resurrect the simplistic harm-based analysis of necessity that Dennis rightly eschews, but which his own notion seems to invoke. Rather, we recognize that a varied set of fundamental moral demands could credibly prompt us to take necessary action.

Moreover, non-contingent basic needs drive our sense of which duties and responsibilities cannot reasonably be left undone. These are the urgent duties to attend to others' and our own most important needs as the conditions for our continued existence as the kinds of beings we are. Since such needs are not restricted to physical threats or loss of life, they open up logical space for the defence of complex and distinctly human needs such as recognition, social inclusion, respect, and autonomy as well as the defence of the needs of beings who cannot defend themselves, such as animals and other animate beings. For these reasons, the notion of *non-contingent need* fits well within a pluralistic approach to necessity.

In general, there are four merits of a genuinely pluralistic, context-sensitive approach to necessity. First, it is more accommodating of both the pluralistic nature of morality and the complexities of practical realities than is a monistic, undifferentiated principle of necessity. Second, it is more faithful to our diverse linguistic intuitions about the concept of *necessity*. Third, it can recognize that different standards can be applied to different people in relation to their different moral roles and responsibilities. This is in keeping with both the account of moral responsibility that I developed in Chapter 3 and the account of a duty-based moral right of conscience that I developed in Chapter 4. For example,

---

[24] See Reader and Brock for a brief bibliography of different accounts of non-contingent human needs. Reader and Brock include inanimate objects in the category of 'beings' that can have non-contingent needs. I do not regard such objects as 'beings'. A *being* is a thing that is or was alive. In my view, the notion of 'need' is used in a metaphorical sense when it is applied to such objects as paintings, buildings, processes, and ideas. Restricting the subjects of genuine needs to animate things is consistent with the etymology of the word 'need', which is a cognate of *nē-*, *nēo-* meaning 'distress' or 'death'. Cf *Oxford English Dictionary* (current online edition).

the standards for reasonableness and parsimony for police officers, soldiers, and medical personnel can be informed by the training, experience, and formal powers that these parties have.[25] Finally, a pluralistic account is, in principle, a more accommodating framework within which to consider the credibility of a necessity defence for civil disobedience because it does not require civil disobedients to satisfy a cookie-cutter threshold of parsimony or reasonableness.

Dennis does not see a context-sensitive, pluralistic approach as being friendly, in principle, to civil disobedience, and given how he understands this approach that is not surprising. He summarily rejects the applicability of a necessity defence to civil disobedience, but does not flesh out his reasons. Those reasons seem to include the democracy problem and the strategic-action problem addressed in the last chapter as well as the competition of values problem and the proportionality problem (better described as the parsimony problem) that I will address in what follows.[26] After responding to these problems and articulating the modesty of law thesis, I shall respond to two further objections concerning the avoidance of punishment and slippery slopes.

2. The Competition of Values Problem

2.1 Modesty of law

The competition of values problem concerns the regulation of competing values. It says that the law (rightly) cannot accommodate competition from other values. That is, it cannot recognize that there could be a value higher than that of adhering to the law, which, as noted on page 181, is one reason that necessity is a fraught territory in common law. Hence, there can be no defence of necessity for civil disobedience (let alone for much else).

In reply, I offer the modesty of law thesis that the law is better able to recognize the legitimacy of competing values than the competition of

---

[25] Cf Clarkson (2004).

[26] Dennis states: 'It is...clear that the principle suggested here would not permit the use of necessity as a possible justification for direct action for political purposes, as [Simon] Gardner has proposed. It is easy to see that, for example, allowing necessity in answer to a charge of disclosing secret information on the basis that D wished to draw attention to the shortcomings of the security services and improve their performance, would raise acute problems about competitions of value, proportionality, and the respective roles of the courts and the legislature.' Dennis (2009).

values problem suggests. Support for this thesis can be found in the demands-of-conviction defence discussed in the last chapter.

For one thing, the demands-of-conviction defence, like necessity defences, is a formal acknowledgment by the law of the possibility of value-competition, ie that there can be values other than the law to which people are legitimately attached as reasoning and feeling beings, and that those values should not, in all cases, be displaced or undermined by an insistence on adherence to the law.

For another thing, more substantively, the demands-of-conviction defence implies that the law can acknowledge the importance of both the particular value of autonomy and the mental conditions for autonomy such as psychological integrity, practical reason, and motivation to act well. In consequence, the law can also acknowledge the legitimacy of competition between autonomy and adherence to law. This in turn implies that the law can acknowledge the value of specific categories of relationship, project, commitment, and belief that are necessary conditions for cultivating a minimally autonomous life. This includes close personal relationships (as sources of social inclusion, education, and identity), social acceptance, meaningful work, duties of care, community membership, and civil and political rights.

From this we can glean further substantive elements of the law's ability to acknowledge the legitimacy of (potentially) competing values. These are elements that can differentiate between justifiable and non-justifiable acts of civil disobedience. Acts of civil disobedience that are consistent with and animated by respect for non-contingent basic needs and rights, are ones that the law can, in principle, acknowledge as legitimate because they are in keeping with the principle of humanism that tempers law's own insistence on the priority of adherence to law. And, acts of civil disobedience that either disregard or oppose non-contingent basic needs and rights can make no appeal to a defence of necessity since they run afoul of the underlying principle of humanism.

This last constraint on civil disobedience—that, to be necessary, it cannot disregard or oppose other people's basic needs and rights—does not apply to other acts of necessity, such as my diverting a runaway trolley from my child to an innocent stranger which disregards the latter's right not to be killed. This constraint of respect applies to civil disobedience because the grounds for its necessity, when it is necessary, lie in humanism. That is, the grounds lie in the reasonableness and parsimony of resorting to certain constrained breaches of law to highlight abuse of basic needs and rights. Such acts of necessity may intrude only on contingent needs and non-basic rights.

In needs-responsive civil disobedience lies one application of conscience as self-conscious moral responsiveness (discussed in Chapters 2 and 3). Acting on the basis of a well-functioning conscience means, first, being sensitive to the claims that basic needs and rights have on our attention as grave and urgent moral demands, and second, when necessary, privileging those needs and rights over other considerations such as the (instrumental) value of adherence to law. This position echoes Martin Luther King Jr's Letter from Birmingham Jail, which I quoted at the outset of this chapter. He continues his statement by saying: 'We bring [the tension] out in the open, where it can be seen and dealt with. Like a boil that can never be cured so long as it is covered up but must be opened with all its ugliness to the natural medicines of air and light, injustice must be exposed, with all the tension its exposure creates, to the light of human conscience and the air of national opinion before it can be cured.'[27]

2.2 Liberal democracies

Now a sceptic might say that crises of the non-contingent-basic-need variety that could, in principle, justify civil disobedience simply do not arise in liberal democracies. The sceptic could certainly make this the case by defining *liberal democracy* so that liberal democratic governments would not engage in or tolerate the kinds of abuses that could make civil disobedience necessary. But such a definition would be a non-standard one, and would set such a society at a distance from existing societies and likely societies.

Certainly, liberal democracies are not, or should not be, political tyrannies where 'the voice of protest, of warning, of appeal is never more needed' and 'more than ever, it is the duty of the good citizen not to be silent'.[28] But, even in liberal democracies, tyrannies arise. As Mill

---

[27] King (1963).
[28] The full quotation from Charles Eliot Norton's 1898 speech to the Men's Club of the Prospect Street Congregational Church in Cambridge, Massachusetts, is: 'The voice of protest, of warning, of appeal is never more needed than when the clamor of fife and drum, echoed by the press and too often by the pulpit, is bidding all men fall in step and obey in silence the tyrannous word of command. Then, more than ever, it is the duty of the good citizen not to be silent.' Reprinted in Norton, Sara and DeWolfe, M. A. (eds.), (1913) *Letters of Charles Eliot Norton*. Boston: Houghton Mifflin.

notes, social tyranny can often be more pressing and more effective than legal or political tyranny.

[Society] practises a social tyranny more formidable than many kinds of political oppression, since, though not usually upheld by such extreme penalties, it leaves fewer means of escape, penetrating much more deeply into the details of life, and enslaving the soul itself. Protection, therefore, against the tyranny of the magistrate is not enough; there needs protection also against the tyranny of the prevailing opinion and feeling; against the tendency of society to impose, by other means than civil penalties, its own ideas and practices as rules of conduct on those who dissent from them; to fetter the development, and, if possible, prevent the formation, of any individuality not in harmony with its ways, and compel all characters to fashion themselves upon the model of its own.[29]

And, liberal democracies are by no means free of such conformist pressures. Let us then acknowledge not only that liberal democratic governments can engage in rights-abuses, but also that liberal societies can be guilty of needs-neglect resulting from (though not only from) conformist pressures, influences, and biases. Let us also remember, as argued in the previous chapter, that the expression of commitments other than literal conformity with law has instrumental value for democratic law itself. Autonomy is good for democratic law. Deliberation and discussion are good for democratic law. And, constrained protest and breach of law are, on balance, good for democratic law.

At this point, some examples of needs-responsive civil disobedience are in order. One example is the climate change cases noted at the outset of this chapter, about which I say more in Section 3.1. A second example concerns personal decision-making. If the law were to ban certain morally objectionable acts such as adultery, it could be justifiable on grounds of necessity to engage in civil disobedience against that law even though adultery is something that people morally ought not to do. The law should not be legislating against it, and we would be justified in challenging laws that did.

A third example concerns the treatment of convicted offenders in prison. Data on the US and other western liberal democracies show that tens of thousands of offenders are held in extremely brutal,

---

[29] Mill, John Stuart (1859) *On Liberty*, ch 1 (various edns).

degrading, cruel, and socially privative conditions.[30] Prisoners are often denied the ordinary kinds of supportive social interaction that make for a minimally decent human life. And, many prisoners are put in long-term solitary confinement, which the empirical evidence shows tends to cause acute psychological and physical deterioration.[31] No doubt factors other than the solitude could account for some of a persons' deterioration in solitary confinement, but there is a commonality amongst persons' recollections of long-term solitary confinement, namely, that they report it to be as agonizing as torture.[32] And, for many, their psychological and emotional deterioration continues to affect them long after their release.[33] One recent case of solitary confinement in Canada is that of James Bacon who was held in near total isolation for several months at the Surrey, British Columbia, pre-trial detention centre. In this case, the isolation was not imposed as a punishment since it preceded Bacon's trial for gun offences. In June 2010, Bacon successfully argued that his pre-trial detention in solitary

---

[30] For an examination of abuse in US prisons, see *The Report of the Commission on Safety and Abuse in America's Prisons* (2006), online: <http://www.vera.org/project/commission-safety-and-abuse-americas-prisons>. For an examination of the use of segregation and isolation in Canadian federal penitentiaries, see Jackson, M. (2002) *Justice Behind the Walls*. Vancouver: Douglas & McIntyre. For a general critique of the use of 'special, maximum-security' prisons in the United States, see Lippke, R. (2004) 'Against Supermax' in *The Journal of Applied Philosophy* 21, 109–24. See also, Lippke, R. (2007) *Rethinking Imprisonment*. Oxford: Oxford University Press.

[31] Prisoners of war and long-term incarcerated offenders often report on their release that they initially experience solitary confinement with despondency and depression, but over time begin to feel themselves disintegrating. They sleep over 12 hours a day, forget facts and memories, and lack the energy to read, eat, or move. Some begin to hallucinate, have panic attacks, and mutilate themselves. Some go into a semi-catatonic state and become unable to respond to basic instructions. In his memoir, journalist Terry Anderson reports on his solitary confinement in prison: 'The mind is a blank. Jesus, I always thought I was smart. Where are all the things I learned, the books I read, the poems I memorized? There's nothing there, just a formless, gray-black misery. My mind's gone dead. God, help me.' Cited from Gawande, A. (2009) 'Hellhole: The United States holds tens of thousands of inmates in long-term solitary confinement. Is this torture?' *The New Yorker*, 30 March. For extensive references linking acute loneliness to acute mental and physical deterioration, see Cacioppo, J. Research Summary (Faculty of Psychology, University of Chicago) online: <psychology.uchicago.edu/people/faculty/cacioppo/index.shtml>.

[32] According to Gawande (2009), a US military study of a 140 naval aviators imprisoned in Vietnam reported that 'they found social isolation to be as torturous and agonizing as any physical abuse they suffered'.

[33] For a defence of the human right against social deprivation, which distinguishes *social deprivation* from *voluntary self-isolation,* see Brownlee, Kimberley 'A Human Right against Social Deprivation' (in progress).

confinement breached his rights under the Canadian Charter of Rights and Freedoms.[34]

The treatment of prisoners is an important and neglected concern in liberal democracies. Prisoners differ from other persistent and vulnerable minorities because, for them, the methods of civil disobedience are largely unavailable and certainly inadvisable. This is because the most effective way that a prisoner demonstrates he is ready to reintegrate into society is by being as compliant and obedient as possible, though this is a sad mockery of the reflective, engaged, independent-minded citizen that he is told to aspire to be. Given that prisoners have little or no voice in many liberal democracies, particularly when they are denied the right to vote, to have a say over their conditions, or to engage in work that is meaningful as an expression of an effort to repent and reform, the task of raising awareness about their abysmal conditions and their needs-neglect rests with others. Given the urgency and the disregard of this issue, civil disobedience is a reasonable and parsimonious way to raise awareness about it.

Against this, a critic would undoubtedly raise the democracy problem and/or the proportionality problem. But, the former has been discredited in the previous chapter and the latter will be discredited now.

3. The Proportionality Problem

3.1 *The scope of the defence for civil disobedience*

The proportionality problem, or parsimony problem, states that, within a liberal democracy, civil disobedience, even needs-responsive civil disobedience, is never a reasonable and parsimonious means through which to redress serious needs-neglect or injustice because adequate ordinary opportunities for meaningful political participation are available to all citizens.

A preliminary answer to this problem lies in the earlier reply to the competition of values problem, which highlighted the alignment

---

[34] Bolan, K. (2010) 'Judge rules Jamie Bacon's rights violated by treatment in jail' *Vancouver Sun*, 10 June. Mark McEwan J of the BC Supreme Court stated that BC Corrections breached James Bacon's Charter rights on several fronts 'by creating circumstances and maintaining the petitioner in circumstances that manifestly threaten the security of his person (which includes both a physical and a psychological dimension) by the unlawful deprivation of his rights for an unlawful purpose'.

between needs-responsive civil disobedience, humanism, and necessity. In cases where civil disobedience is supportive of non-contingent basic needs and rights that the government is neglecting or abusing, and where ordinary efforts to highlight this injustice would be ineffective (which they most likely will be when defended by a persistent and vulnerable minority) then resort to constrained acts of civil disobedience can be justified on grounds of necessity.

That said, civil disobedience is a deliberate breach of law that can and often does cause damage or harm. And, civil disobedience comes in different forms: 1) violent and non-violent; 2) direct and indirect; 3) as a last resort and as a first resort; 4) likely to succeed and unlikely to succeed; and 5) purely motivated and multiply or impurely motivated. As a consequence, not all civil disobedience could be, even in principle, a reasonable and parsimonious response to crises of basic needs and rights.

Being animated by basic needs and rights places constraints on the cognitive, affective, and conative features of the civil disobedience that could be a necessary act. But, what are those constraints? What standards must a disobedient's act meet to be a reasonable and parsimonious response to a crisis? Within a liberal democracy, should a necessity defence ever be available, in principle, for violent civil disobedience, indirect civil disobedience, or disobedience that is unlikely to succeed? Should it be available for disobedience taken on the basis of mixed motives, such as that done as much to raise our standing in our fellows' eyes as to redress injustices? Should it be available for disobedience grounded in an unfounded belief that the action is truly necessary? In keeping with the pluralistic, context-sensitive approach that I endorse, none of these types of civil disobedience is ruled out a priori. The devils and the deities are in the details.

First, concerning violence, as I noted in previous chapters, violence is not, by nature, at odds with either civility or respect for rights because, although the word *violence* has negative connotations, it includes a wide range of acts and events, major and minor, intended and unintended, that sometimes cause, but other times only *risk* damage or injury. It is implausible to say that every modest, non-injurious act of violence in the course of disobedience is, by definition, uncivil and at odds with respect for basic needs and rights. Focusing on modest instances of violence draws attention away from the more salient issues of harm, abuse, and neglect of persons' needs, which tend to impact more severely on persons' interests than do modestly violent breaches of law.[35] Moreover, as Raz observes, sometimes the wrong or harm done by a law or policy is so iniquitous that it may be legitimate to use violence to root it out; such violence may be necessary to re-establish the rights that coercive practices seek to suspend.[36] Of course, as I discussed in Chapter 1, non-violent dissent is generally preferable because it does not encourage other acts of violence, does not carry the same risk of antagonizing potential allies, does not (necessarily) risk cementing opponents' antipathy, does not distract the public's attention, and does not give authorities an excuse to use harsh countermeasures against disobedients.

Second, concerning direct and indirect disobedience, it is not invariably the case that the former is preferable or reasonable and parsimonious. As I noted in the last chapter, in cases of indirect disobedience, we breach a law that we do not oppose and to that extent we do act strategically. But, our strategic act may be reasonable and parsimonious when neither direct disobedience nor ordinary participation is open to us. For example, it is difficult if not impossible for ordinary citizens to engage in direct disobedience against military policy. Indirect disobedience, such as refusing to pay taxes or trespassing onto military bases to engage in minor acts of vandalism, may be the closest that ordinary citizens can get to direct disobedience. Indeed, indirect disobedience is the only form of civil disobedience open to us in any context where what we oppose is that the law permits certain conduct and yet we are ourselves not involved in that conduct. For example, where the law permits animal testing, clear-cut logging, or segregation of schools, we can only directly civilly disobey if we are agents in those institutions. If we are not agents in those institutions, then only indirect civil disobedience is open to us.[37] In such contexts, indirect disobedience may be reasonable and parsimonious. Moreover, even where direct civil disobedience is an option, indirect disobedience may be reasonable and parsimonious when it would do far less harm or wrong. For example, suppose that the punishment for sexual assault is death. It would be indefensible to protest against this overly harsh punishment by engaging in sexual assault. It would be immeasurably better to engage

---

[35] As I mentioned in Chapter 1, Joseph Raz's example is that of a legal strike by ambulance workers, which will in all likelihood do far greater harm than, say, a minor act of vandalism. Raz, Joseph (1979) *The Authority of Law*. Oxford: Oxford University Press, 267.
[36] Raz (1979), 267.
[37] I thank Steve Cooke for highlighting this general point.

in constrained forms of indirect disobedience that would do far less harm or wrong and would, most likely, be a more efficacious way to redress this injustice.

Third, concerning last resort, John Rawls himself acknowledges that the 'last resort' criterion is a presumption: 'Some cases may be so extreme that there may be no duty to use first only legal means of political opposition.'[38] That said, to avail ourselves of a necessity defence, a modified, context-sensitive Rawlsian constraint of last resort may be credible. The constraint says that needs-responsive civil disobedience may be justifiable as a matter of necessity only when lawful efforts have repeatedly shown the majority to be immovable or apathetic to this legitimate cause.[39] It is difficult to specify when the point of 'last resort' has been reached. But, in the case of persistent and vulnerable minorities, who may be impotent in their use of ordinary channels of participation, that point may be reached fairly quickly even in liberal democracies given the near-inescapable imbalance in participatory power.

Fourth, concerning likelihood of success, an act need not be effective to be reasonable and parsimonious. If we strike out in self-defence, we need not prevent all harm to ourselves in order to defend our use of force.[40] Similarly, intuitively, civil disobedience is most justifiable when dissenters are a persistent and vulnerable minority whose situation is desperate and whose government refuses to attend to their more conventional forms of protest. Nobel Peace Prize Laureate Elie Wiesel puts it nicely in saying, 'There may be times when we are powerless to prevent injustice, but there must never be a time when we fail to protest.'[41] And, even when immediate or direct success seems unlikely,

---

[38] Rawls (1971), 373.

[39] See Rawls (1971), 371–7.

[40] There appears to be a consensus amongst philosophers writing on defensive harm that at least a reasonable prospect of success is a condition for permissible defensive force in extreme cases. However, there are at least three reasons to doubt this condition. First, there is expressive value in endeavouring to protect either our own life or that of another who is under (unjust) threat, even if that effort is unlikely to succeed. For a discussion of this topic, see Statman, Daniel (2008) 'On the Success Condition for Legitimate Self-Defense' in *Ethics* 118, 659–86. Second, an effort that is unlikely to succeed nonetheless may succeed; any credible boundary of 'reasonable prospect for success' must be context-sensitive and person-sensitive. Third, the condition of likely success, or reasonable prospect of success, is comparatively unjust towards weaker victims since weaker victims are both relatively less likely to succeed, and absolutely less likely to succeed, in fending off attackers than are stronger victims. I thank Jon Quong for comments on these points.

[41] Wiesel, Elie (1986) 'Hope, Despair, and Memory: Nobel Lecture' 11 December 1986. Retrieved from: http://nobelprize.org/nobel_prizes/peace/laureates/1986/wiesel-lecture.html.

civil disobedience may be defended for any reprieve from harm that it brings to victims of a bad policy and for any positive effect it has on expanding society's moral horizons. Vaclav Havel notes, rightly, that 'Even a purely moral act that has no hope of any immediate and visible political effect can gradually and indirectly, over time, gain in political significance'.[42]

Fifth, in cases of mixed motivation where more than one consideration or reason animates our action, things are more complicated. For instance, as I noted in the last chapter, there are cases in which the reason that would otherwise offer a successful justificatory defence is coloured by negative factors. I gave the example of the bored police officer who decides to arrest only bearded speeders.[43] When she next arrests a bearded speeder, she acts not only for the undefeated reason that he is speeding, but also for what she takes mistakenly to be a reason, which is that he is bearded. Another example closer to civil disobedience is that of a fair-weather pacifist. Suppose that a person in a country with mandatory military service decides that he will refuse to fight only in those unjust wars that his society prosecutes against a blue-coated military. When he is next called to war it is an unjust war that his society is pursuing, and they are pursuing it against a blue-coated military. He refuses to fight not only for the undefeated reason that this is an unjust war, but also for what he takes mistakenly to be reason, which is that the opposing side wears blue. Although the police officer's and the pacifist's acts are acceptable in one sense, nevertheless neither act is justified all things considered. Certainly, neither act is the fruit of conscience that is fully responsive to urgent moral concerns.

These two cases of mixed motivation differ from those in which the motivating reasons are good reasons, though they may dilute the defence of necessity. For example, in the Ratcliffe power station case noted at the outset of this chapter, the judge did not question the moral quality of the environmentalists' motives. He said that he had been placed in a unique position in which 'neither judge nor jury need question the veracity and motivation of any defendant'. He said: 'You are all decent men and women with a genuine concern for others, and

---

[42] Havel, Vaclav (1968) 'Letter to President Alexander Dubček' August 1968 following Dubček's removal from office after the Soviet invasion of Czechoslovakia. Cited from Knowles, Elizabeth (ed.), *Oxford Dictionary of Modern Quotations*, (3rd edn). Oxford: Oxford University Press.

[43] Nathanson, Stephen (1985) 'Does it Matter if the Death Penalty is Arbitrarily Administered?' in *Philosophy and Public Affairs* 14: 2, 149–64.

in particular for the survival of planet Earth in something resembling its present form.' However, he also said that he agreed with the jury that, while motivated to stop carbon emissions, an 'equal aim' of the activists was to gain publicity for their campaign.[44]

This motivation is an admirable one, which is why the judge could speak so fulsomely about the campaigners' characters. Their mixture of motivations does not include a defeated reason or base motivation alongside a good reason, like the police officer's and the pacifist's do. Rather their mixture includes a reason that can be understood directly in terms of necessity, namely, stopping carbon emissions, and a reason that is good but can be related only indirectly to necessity, namely, raising general awareness about climate change. Even so, such acts are, in principle, the fruit of conscience. Although there may be other ways to raise awareness about climate change, this act can nonetheless be a reasonable and parsimonious one. Thus, whereas the pacifist could not plead necessity for his refusal to fight, in my view, the environmentalists could plead necessity for their trespass and vandalism.

There is a subtle difference (probably beyond the interest of the law) between these environmentalists and the animal liberationist I mentioned in Chapter 5, who rescues animals from laboratories in which they are being tortured and who does it not only for the reason of protecting the animals from suffering but also for the reason of bringing publicity to her cause. Her act is not fully justified because the animals she saves are not treated with respect, as they are instrumentalized as campaign promotional material. By contrast, the environmentalists discussed earlier in the chapter do not fail to respect any party by having the particular mix of motivations that they have.

Finally, a disobedient may believe *mistakenly* that her disobedience is a reasonable and parsimonious response to a crisis. She may be mistaken about her belief that there is a crisis, in which case her conduct is best examined in relation to the excusatory demands-of-conviction defence. Or, she may be correct in her belief that there is a basic needs crisis, but mistaken in her belief that her chosen mode of disobedience is a reasonable and parsimonious response. In such cases, she would not have access to a justificatory defence of necessity even though she acts in response to legitimate concerns about non-contingent basic needs.

---

[44] Lewis and Prakash (2011).

In more detail, a disobedient must consider the appropriateness of her chosen method, eg vandalism, sit-ins, trespassing, illegal boycotts, or illegal strikes, since the specific action that she performs and the manner in which she performs it will inform its effectiveness as a vehicle to communicate censure. A person may have reasons for engaging in one form of disobedience, but choose to engage in another form that is not supported by these reasons. For example, she may have an undefeated reason to take part in a road-block because this action is well suited to her political concerns and is one that her government and society respond well to or because this action has a public impact that does not greatly harm the interests of others. But, she has no undefeated reason, say, to trespass on government property or to engage in strategic violence. In taking the latter actions, she is guilty of a certain error of judgement about which actions are supported by reasons that admittedly apply. Given her error, the best she could claim is that her conduct is excused, as she had reason to believe that she had reason to undertake that particular act of civil disobedience. When, by contrast, her civilly disobedient action is supported by undefeated reasons that apply to her situation then, provided she acts *for* those reasons, her choice of action is justified.

3.2 *Legal rights*

My reasoning in support of a necessity defence for needs-responsive civil disobedience takes a different path from that pursued by Simon Gardner in his case law based exploration of direct action. But nevertheless we arrive at a similar destination. Gardner argues:

[a person] should have the [necessity] defence if, committing what would otherwise be an offence, [she acts] to vindicate a right that is recognised by the law but not otherwise reflected in the offence's definition, and that is superior to any right or interest that the offence exists to protect and that [she injures] by [her] action; and no less aggressive course of action (i.e. no course of action likewise calculated to vindicate the right, but less injurious of the rights and interests protected by the offence) was open to [her].[45]

---

[45] Gardner, Simon (2005) 'Direct action and the defence of necessity' in *Criminal Law Review*, May, 371–80.

Unlike Gardner, I would not take the rights recognized in law as the reference point for the rights and needs that, in principle, could ground an appeal to a necessity defence in their name. Even in a liberal society, there may well be moral rights that are not entrenched in law but should be entrenched in law, such as many rights of prisoners. Since the competition of values problem has been settled, we may look beyond the law for values that could inform an appeal to necessity. These include values that give rise to duties to respect human rights. We could take international treaties, irrespective of whether our society has ratified them, as one source of rights that our society should respect. But, we could also take the best theoretical account of human rights or moral rights for a society like ours, as I have done earlier, to determine the rights we should respect.

That said, there is at least one reason to favour Gardner's legalistic approach, namely, that it is more readily practicable. In addition to being theoretically more credible than a utilitarian 'lesser evil' analysis, the coming into force of human rights legislation means, as Gardner notes, that an analysis of necessity in terms of rights is increasingly capable of ready practical operation.

There are, of course, limitations to an analysis like Gardner's that focuses on legally recognized *human* rights. The most obvious limit is that it takes a narrow view of the beings who are proper objects of concern. His analysis does not support a necessity defence for civil disobedience in defence of animals or the environment as such, though his analysis could provide a necessity defence for environmental civil disobedience on the grounds that there is a fundamental *human* right to subsistence and basic resources, including breathable air and food, that governments are failing to respect.

4. Avoidance of Punishment and Slippery Slopes

Two final objections to my view may be called the avoidance of punishment objection and the slippery slope objection.

4.1 Avoidance of punishment?

The avoidance of punishment objection says that the civil disobedient who asserts a necessity defence seeks, as a consequence, to avoid conviction and punishment for breach of law. She contrasts with the civil disobedient who offers no such defence and who, thus, does not seek to avoid conviction and punishment but rather submits himself for judgement. The worry is that the former disobedient is disingenuous and hypocritical; she has deliberately broken the law, but then seeks to avoid bearing the legal consequences, and this casts doubt on her sincerity, civility, and communicative aspirations. And, hence, it also casts doubt on her conscience-driven needs-responsiveness.

In reply, first, not too much should be read into a willingness or unwillingness to accept punishment. A person may accept punishment for strategic reasons, ie it can heighten the publicity of her cause, can give her a brief reprieve to regroup and gain further followers, and can lessen tensions with those who are antipathetic to her view and crave retaliation or revenge on this social outcast.

Second, the reasons governing the conduct of the suitably constrained, needs-responsive civil disobedient are not concerned with avoiding punishment. It is a by-product of making the argument that the act was necessary that the disobedient may well not be punished. Not to offer a necessity defence when the disobedient believes her act is necessary *would* be a strategic decision to try to avoid punishment so as to keep protesting. And, *that* would undermine the consistency of her view that there were sufficiently important needs at issue to warrant a deliberate breach of law in their defence.

4.2 *A slippery slope?*

The slippery slope objection is a more general worry that allowing a necessity defence, in principle, for needs-responsive civil disobedience would open up space for abuse through the assertion of spurious defences. This problem is no more pressing in the case of civil disobedience than in any other context in which necessity is available as a defence. Moreover, as I argued in the last chapter, the specious problem of the slippery slope falls afoul of a Kantian requirement to treat people as ends and neither to use them as scapegoats nor to hold them accountable for others' independent decisions to engage in non-conscientious, disruptive behaviour.

Now this Kantian requirement not to treat the disobedient as a means may appear to conflict with my claims earlier that violent civil disobedience can 'encourage' other violence that may or may not be legitimately motivated. There is no tension here. The issue is one of intention. Does the civil disobedient intend to encourage others? If so, then she may be punished in response to such intentions. This is a different story from the one in which, irrespective of her intentions, she is punished merely to deter others from offending. Where the civil disobedient is punished as a scapegoat and a warning to other prospective dissenters, her intentions are ignored and she is treated as a means.

In the next two chapters, I turn to more general questions about how civil disobedience is to be perceived by the law. Specifically, I consider how judges ought to think about the disobedients who come before them. I also highlight a parallel between the communicative aspects of civil disobedience and the communicative aspects of lawful punishment, while noting that, of the two, only civil disobedience can claim to have dialogic ambitions.

Conclusion

In this chapter, I argued for the second of two legal defences for civil disobedience. This defence is a justificatory defence for (some) civil disobedience, grounded in necessity. I explored the complex conceptual terrain of *necessity*, and argued for a thoroughgoing pluralistic account of necessity defences that is framed by the centrality of non-contingent basic needs. These include not only brute survival needs, but also the equally fundamental humanistic needs of basic political recognition, social inclusion, and respect. This account contrasts with a narrower, less humanistic account that frames necessity simply in terms of *emergencies* and conflicts where a danger of death or serious injury is present.

I argued that a defence of necessity applies, in principle, to acts of civil disobedience that are responsive to non-contingent basic needs and rights. I addressed two main objections: the competition of values problem and the proportionality problem. In my replies, I highlighted that the law can grant the legitimacy of competing values (the modesty of law thesis), which, in principle, allows dissenters to appeal to non-legal values in the name of necessity when they satisfy appropriate standards of reasonableness and parsimony.

The next two chapters focus on punishment. In Chapter 7, I consider the justifiability of punishing civil disobedience for which no defence is given or for which only a partial defence could be given. In Chapter 8, I consider whether, irrespective of the justifiability of punishment, we have a moral right not to be punished for civil disobedience. I argue that we do.

7

Dialogue

> We are here, not because we are law-breakers; we are here in our efforts to become law-makers.
>
> —Emmeline Pankhurst[1]

> There is all the difference in the world between the criminal's avoiding the public eye and the civil disobedient's taking the law into his own hands in open defiance. This distinction between an open violation of the law, performed in public, and a clandestine one is so glaringly obvious that it can be neglected only by prejudice or ill will.
>
> —Hannah Arendt[2]

Recently, a Texas trial court judge, Judge Ralph Taite, adopted an anti-civil-disobedience policy, which he applied to the cases he heard irrespective of the disobedients' aims and offences. In his sentencing of a long-time anti-fur trade activist named Megan Lewis, who blocked the entrance to a Neiman Marcus store to protest against its support of the fur industry, Judge Taite ordered her to stay away from animal rights protests. *Texas Observer* reporter Will Potter writes,

[Judge Taite] said Lewis was involved in non-violent civil disobedience in front of Neiman Marcus once before, so he used the sentence to make sure that she wouldn't 'be back doing the same things again.' Sentencing an activist to stay away from protests, Taite said, is no different than sentencing

---

[1] Pankhurst, Emmeline (1908) 'Speech from the Dock (Police Court' in *Votes for Women* (29 October 1908). Reprinted in Bell, Susan G. and Offen, Karen M. (eds.), (1983) *Women, the Family, and Freedom: The Debate in Documents*. Vol II. 1880–1950, 239.

[2] Arendt, Hannah (1972) *Crises of the Republic: Lying in Politics; Civil Disobedience; on Violence; Thoughts on Politics and Revolution*. New York: Harcourt Brace Jovanovich.

a drunk driver to stay away from bars, or sentencing a pedophile [*sic*] to stay 100 feet away from schoolyards.[3]

According to the *Texas Observer*, Judge Taite used similar sentences to keep anti-abortion protesters away from abortion clinics. Taite's comparison of political protest to paedophilia and drunk driving signals a startling dismissal both of legal and moral rights of free speech and of society's interest in the dialogic efforts of civil disobedients. His stance is a potent example of the dialogue-stifling potential of lawful punishment that I explore in this chapter.

There are two dominant theories in the philosophy of punishment, one of which highlights its preventative aims and the other its retributive aims. The preventative theory—often called deterrence theory—is a forward-looking, narrowly consequentialist theory that says that punishment is justified if, and possibly only if, it achieves (or is likely to achieve) the sufficiently weighty good of preventing or discouraging the offender or other people from breaching the law. Deterrence theory is criticized, rightly, on several grounds. First, it draws the parameters of appropriate punishment too broadly in allowing, in principle, that whatever punishment is needed to deter someone from offending is a justifiable punishment. Second, in principle, it allows that persons who are not proper objects of punishment could be justifiably punished if this deters other people from breaching the law. Deterrence theorists may try to refute this charge by conceptual fiat by defining *punishment* so that burdens imposed on innocent parties cannot be punishment: for it to be *punishment*, the burden must be imposed on a convicted *offender* in response to that offence. This conceptual fiat is unconvincing since, in practice, punishment is imposed on a *convicted* person who may or may not be guilty. Also, this fiat does not address the fact that people who *do* offend can also not be proper objects of punishment. Third, deterrence theory seeks to give us not a moral reason but a prudential reason relating to the prospect of punishment to refrain from breaching the law. Hence, it treats us more as brutes than as reasoning moral agents capable of responding to moral reasons. In his subtle and nuanced version of the deterrence theory, Victor Tadros holds that we are *not* treated as brutes when we are punished in the name of deterrence because we have a

---

[3] Potter, Will (2001) 'The New Backlash: From the Streets to the Courthouse, the New Activists Find Themselves Under Attack' in *Texas Observer*, 14 September.

protective duty to our victims. We have a duty to protect our victims from future harms. We honour that duty by accepting punishment for our offence because, by doing so, other people will (hopefully) be deterred from offending.[4] The difficulty with this reply is that it treats those other people as brutes since our being punished is meant to cow them into not offending.

In relation to civil disobedience, deterrence theory would license whatever punishment is necessary and sufficient to deter disobedients and others from offending. Whether that punishment would be milder, harsher, or equal to that imposed on ordinary offenders would depend on empirical considerations rather than on any principled differences between types of offenders. Sometimes harsher punishment might be in order since disobedients who are serious in their moral conviction might not be deterred by standard punishments. Other times, milder punishment or no punishment might be in order since disobedients usually are not 'hardened' criminals and thus may need less or no punishment as a deterrent.[5] These fluctuations in response are unsatisfactory since they do not track the relative or absolute seriousness of civilly disobedient acts, but instead send ambiguous messages about why civil disobedience is condemned if it is condemned.

By contrast, the retributive theory of punishment—often called desert theory—is concerned with the backward-looking objective of punishing only those persons who are proper objects of punishment and only punishing them as much as they deserve. Desert theory aims to respond to an offence in a way that is proportionate to its seriousness. Desert theory is rightly criticized on its own terms for insufficiently defending the view that the guilty should be punished. Although the intuition that the guilty deserve to suffer is widely shared, it is not obvious that this intuition is well-founded. Traditional desert theory says little about *why* the guilty deserve to suffer. Desert theory is also rightly criticized for assuming both that fact-finders can determine

---

[4] See Tadros, Victor (2011) *The Ends of Harm*. Oxford: Oxford University Press.

[5] One might think, mistakenly, that civil disobedients are the paradigm of the 'hardened criminal' since their convictions can make them less responsive to punishment than ordinary offenders are. But, despite this, they are not 'hardened criminals' because, if they are successful in shifting public opinion or changing policy, then they will cease to offend, which is not true of the hardened criminal. The adjective 'hardened' should not be taken to mean 'having a higher punishment threshold', but rather to mean 'less likely to shift toward a law-abiding lifestyle'.

what offenders deserve and that the *deserved* punishment is necessarily the *justified* punishment. We can ask whether, all things considered, people should be punished as they deserve according to retributive justice. It may be that deserved punishments are often too harsh since retributive justice is not the only moral value at issue.[6] We can also ask whether human societies are in a position justifiably to impose punishments even if those punishments are deserved and justified in principle. In relation to civil disobedience, desert theory faces the challenge of explaining how fact-finders can determine what disobedients deserve by way of response, and why that response should take the form of punishment.

In contrast with these two traditional theories of punishment, there is a third, newer theory, known as the communicative theory of punishment. It holds that the purposes of punishment are both to convey the state's condemnation for a certain type of conduct and to lead the offender to repent and reform her conduct. In the standard monistic version of the communicative theory, espoused most famously by Antony Duff, the justification for punishment is backward-looking. It turns on the appropriateness of communicating condemnation for the wrong done. This itself is sufficient to justify punishment. In Duff's view, punishment may be seen as a secular form of penance that vividly confronts the offender with the effects of her crime.[7]

Duff's account contrasts with hybrid communicative theories, such as that defended by Andrew von Hirsch, which are both forward-looking and backward-looking in their justification for punishment. According to hybrid theories, communication of censure alone is insufficient to justify punishment. Added to it must be the aim of deterring offending.[8] If the communication of condemnation will not deter because, say, the censure drowns out the moral appeal, then punishment is not justified.[9]

---

[6] See Tasioulas, John (2006) 'Punishment and Repentance' in *Philosophy* 81: 279–322; and Tasioulas, John (2003) 'Mercy' in *Proceedings of the Aristotelian Society* 103, 101–32.

[7] Duff, Antony (1998) 'Desert and Penance' in *Principled Sentencing: Readings on Theory and Policy*. Andrew Ashworth and Andrew von Hirsch (eds.), Oxford: Hart Publishing, 162.

[8] von Hirsch, Andrew (1998) 'Proportionate Sentences: A Desert Perspective' in *Principled Sentencing: Readings on Theory and Policy*. Andrew Ashworth and Andrew von Hirsch (eds.), Oxford: Hart Publishing, 171.

[9] According to John Tasioulas, the introduction of deterrence into von Hirsch's account of justified punishment threatens to render his account incoherent because what is added to censure (namely the prevention of crime) threatens to undermine the communicative character of punishment. Tasioulas (2006), 279–322.

A third type of communicative theory eschews the hybrid strategy, and instead supplements the backward-looking communicative theory with considerations other than retributive justice. On the pluralistic account defended by John Tasioulas, a distinction is drawn between the punishment that is deserved according to retributive justice and the punishment that is actually morally justifiable. In some cases, the morally justifiable response will be a merciful one based on a charitable concern for the well-being of the offender as a potential recipient of deserved censure, which punishes her less than she deserves according to justice. When, for example, an offender demonstrates repentance for her offence prior to punishment, the law has reasons of charity and concern to be merciful towards her and to impose a less severe punishment on her than that which she deserves.[10] Given this offender's repentance, the justified punishment is less than it would be were there no such grounds for mercy.

One question, of course, is why there would be no reason of charitable concern to be merciful to the wholly unrepentant offender. Why should we be any less concerned about her well-being than we are about the repentant offender's well-being since they are both people about to be subjected to punishment? I believe that there are well-being-based reasons to be merciful to the unrepentant offender. But, they face a difficulty. There is the risk that in being merciful to the unrepentant offender we will obscure our communicative message of censure. This risk of obscurity or mis-communication is less pressing in other cases whose distinguishing features can legitimate our departure from communicating full censure. For instance, the risk of mis-communication is less pressing in the case of the wholly repentant offender since we have achieved part of what we sought through our communication, which is her acknowledgment of her wrong.

Of the three theories of punishment just outlined, I regard the communicative theory as the most promising. In what follows, I shall focus, first, on the monistic communicative theory espoused by Duff, which understands punishment in a liberal regime to be the state's effort to engage an offender in a moral dialogue about her conduct. I identify three problems with this dialogic picture of the monistic

---

[10] Tasioulas (2006), 279–322. Tasioulas (2003), 101–32. This position discounts the suggestion that full punishment must be imposed for the offender to demonstrate the sincerity of her repentance.

communicative theory.[11] These problems are notable both in themselves and in relation to civil disobedience. The first problem is the Scripting Problem, which is that punishment *requires* an offender to engage in the public ritual of apology and penance with its expected expressions of remorse irrespective of her attitudes toward the judgement on her (Section 1). A forced response that is indifferent to her attitudes not only fails to respect her as a person and a citizen, but also fails to satisfy a plausible set of conditions for genuine moral dialogue (Section 2). In relation to civil disobedience, the Scripting Problem takes a second, more focused form, which I call the Generic-Script Problem. Certain offenders such as civil disobedients should not want to follow the formal script assigned to offenders by the state, the content of which signals growing awareness of, and remorsefulness for, wrongdoing as well as apology and commitment to reparation and reform. They should not want to follow this script because they differ relevantly from ordinary unrepentant offenders in their attitudes and their reasoning about their acts (as discussed in Chapters 5 and 6). Generic punishments that do not distinguish civil disobedients from other offenders misrepresent civil disobedients as being unrepentant or perversely defiant when in fact they seek to engage society in a dialogue different from that ostensibly pursued through censuring them (Section 3). A third problem for the monistic communicative theory is what I call the Status Change Problem. The state's communication of condemnation to an offender is a performative act. And, unless it is responsive to the offender's communicative efforts, this performative act alters the offender's legal status in a way that undermines the conditions for genuine moral dialogue. In relation to civil disobedience, punishment that ignores the communication of the disobedient temporarily undermines her standing to try to engage society in a dialogue about the cause that prompted her to breach the law (Section 4).

After responding to the replies that Duff has made to some of my charges, I then turn to the pluralistic communicative theory, and ultimately embrace it (Section 5). I embrace it because although not ideal,

---

[11] In this chapter, I elaborate arguments in Brownlee, Kimberley (2011) 'The Offender's Part in the Dialogue' in *Crime, Punishment, & Responsibility: The Jurisprudence of Antony Duff*. Rowan Cruft, Matthew Kramer, and Mark Reiff (eds.), Oxford: Oxford University Press, 2011, 54–67. I also offer here some responses to the replies that Antony Duff made to my arguments in his (2011) 'Reply' in that Festschrift.

it does not face either the Generic-Script Problem or the Status Change Problem.

1. The Scripting Problem

As noted in Chapter 1, there is a parallel between the communicative aspects of civil disobedience and the communicative aspects of lawful punishment. In civilly disobeying the law, we seek to convey both our condemnation of a certain policy and our desire for recognition that a lasting change in policy is required. Similarly, through lawful punishment, a liberal state endeavours to communicate both its condemnation of an offence and its desire for repentance and reformation by the offender. Both involve a performative act of condemnation, dissociation, and disavowal.

However, communicative theorists such as Duff claim something stronger on behalf of lawful punishment, that it is not simply a communicative practice, but a dialogic practice. As Duff puts it, 'the [criminal] trial seeks to engage the defendant in a rational dialogue about the justice of the charge which she faces, and to persuade her—if that charge is proved against her—to accept and make her own the condemnation which her conviction expresses'.[12] Punishment, he says, not only communicates both condemnation and a desire for repentance and reformation by the offender, but also gives the offender an opportunity to communicate her repentance by accepting the punishment, apologizing, and making reparation where possible.[13]

My first objection to Duff's view is one to which he is sensitive. It is the Scripting Problem. The problem is that punishment is *imposed* on an offender irrespective of her will. It *requires* her to engage in the public apology ritual with its expected expressions of grief regardless of whether she feels those emotions or accepts the judgment on her, and therefore, it fails to respect her as a person and as a full and equal citizen.

---

[12] Duff, Antony (1986) *Trials and Punishments*. Cambridge: Cambridge University Press, 233.
[13] Duff, Antony (2001) *Punishment, Communication, and Community*. Oxford: Oxford University Press. It is worth noting that Duff defines *communication* in rich, dialogic terms as a *rational* and *reciprocal* act that aims to engage another person 'as an active participant in the process who will receive and respond to the communication...[I]t appeals to the other's reason and understanding—the response it seeks is one that is mediated by the other's rational grasp of its content'. Duff (2001), 79–80.

It fails to respect her because it is indifferent to whether she is misrepresented in the exchange, forced to be duplicitous in her interactions with society and victims, or forced to be untrue to herself. As Duff himself puts the objection: 'To require [offenders] to apologize is to write their side of the communicative dialogue for them—whereas if we respect them as fellow citizens of a liberal polity, we must leave them free to write their own side of the dialogue.'[14]

Duff offers two responses to the Scripting Problem. First, he says that the objection would be forceful if the apology required the offender to demean, degrade, or humiliate herself as no doubt many existing penal practices do. But, since punishment is not, by nature, necessarily demeaning, a required public apology need not be self-degrading. Second, he argues that the *required* nature of the public apology ritual pertains to the offender's participation in that process, not to her attitudes towards it. She is not required to be genuinely apologetic and remorseful. The formality of the ritual leaves open, and is intended to leave open, the question of sincerity, because it would be overly intrusive to inquire into the offender's actual attitudes and because, like any other process of rational persuasion, it is fallible. The offender must be free to remain unpersuaded and unrepentant.[15]

Duff has doubts about these two responses, some of which track my own doubt that we respect an offender as a person and equal citizen when we, first, *tell* her what she ought to say in words or do in deeds by way of apology and reparation, and then, second, *compel* her to say and do those things. To suggest that such treatment is consistent with respecting the offender's liberty to write her side of the dialogue is akin, I think, to suggesting that a person who has food stuffed in her mouth is nonetheless respected in being at liberty not to swallow.

Duff addresses this lingering worry by recommending a practical modification to the apology ritual. In brief, at the time that sentence is passed on an offender, she should have the opportunity to state that she does not undertake the various requirements of the punishment as an act of apology.[16] Nevertheless, once she has undertaken those requirements, she should be treated by society as having 'paid her debt' since she has done the acts required of her that are consistent with a genuine apology. Thus, although the state compels her attention, it does not, and ought not, to require her either to feel apologetic or to represent her acts as acts of apology.

---

[14] Duff (2001), 110.   [15] Duff (1998), 165.   [16] Duff (2001), 111.

This practical suggestion allays the worry that the unrepentant offender is both misrepresented in the process and forced to be untrue to herself, at least at the time of sentencing. But it does not allay either the worry that a fully repentant offender is misrepresented as needing to undergo this process of punishment to be brought to repent[17] or the worry that the civil disobedient is misrepresented as being merely defiant when she actually seeks to engage society in a dialogue of a different kind from that purportedly pursued by the state. I return to such cases later. Duff's practical suggestion also does not allay the more modest worry that, in time, the ordinary, unrepentant offender may come to disavow her declaration of defiance, but will not again have a public forum like her sentencing in which to communicate her stance on her punishment. As a vehicle for offenders to communicate to society and victims, this platform at the time of sentencing is an imperfect one.

Moreover, despite providing this communicative opportunity at the time of sentencing, the standard, monistic communicative theory of punishment remains dismissive of the offender's actual attitudes and communicative efforts. The state still *tells* her how she should communicate to society and victims in terms of penances and reparation, and then *makes* her go through the motions of taking those communicative steps.[18] This contrasts sharply with a commonsense notion of *rational dialogue*, the central features of which I sketch out in Section 2. I shall use this notion of *dialogue* to explore the two further objections of the Generic-Script Problem and the Status Change Problem.

2. Conditions for Moral Dialogue

A *dialogue* is a sustained, purposive conversation or verbal exchange of thought carried out by two or more persons. From this spare description, I distil at least five broad conditions for genuine dialogue.

---

[17] Presumably, though, she is not forced to be untrue to herself since her repentance should prompt her to embrace society's censure of her conduct. For a discussion of repentance and mercy, see Tasioulas (2003), 101–32; Tasioulas (2006), 279–322.

[18] In 'In Defence of One Type of Retributivism: A Reply to Bagaric and Amarasekara', Duff does respond briefly to the objection that the *imposed* nature of punishment precludes it from being plausibly characterized in dialogic terms. I address Duff's response in Section 4. See Duff, Antony (2000) 'In Defence of One Type of Retributivism: A Reply to Bagaric and Amarasekara' in *Melbourne University Law Review* 24: 2, 411–26.

The first is reciprocity between the parties. Reciprocity in this context has two dimensions. One dimension relates to the roles that each party plays. For a dialogue to occur, each party must be an active participant in the interaction by intentionally playing the dual roles of communicator and receiver. The other dimension relates to each party's recognition of the other's dual roles. A reciprocal exchange is marked by mutual recognition of the conventional communicative claim-rights, duties, and privileges that each has as an active participant in this interaction.

Second, a dialogue is a more sustained and extensive interaction than other kinds of broadly reciprocal exchanges such as a simple call and response or an exchange of threats, or a wordless meeting of minds.

Third, as a purposive interaction marked by mutual recognition of each party's rights and duties, a dialogue is an argument-based, progress-oriented conversation. The parties attend to each other's contributions and modify their responses in light of those contributions. Their exchange is neither a quarrel nor a one-sided monologue. Its aims are constructive, didactic, and rationally persuasive. This does not mean that a dialogue necessarily leads to a reasoned resolution, an agreement, or even an improved understanding amongst the parties. It might not succeed in its aims. Rather, parties' engagement in this kind of interaction implies a certain mutual orientation toward progress in common understanding.

Fourth, there are connotations of fairness and equality in a dialogue. Implicitly, the parties are represented as equals in the relevant sense of being equally active and equally empowered participants to the exchange. This implied equality arises not only from the first condition of reciprocity in the parties' reciprocal recognition of each other's communicative rights and duties, but also from the third condition of the reason-giving, argument-based nature of the exchange where each party is addressed as a reasoning agent. Being equally active does not mean that each party must have and make use of equal space in the communications. Rather, it means that each has an equal right not only to speak when she wishes, provided that she respects the equal rights of the other, but also to be heard and understood as well as can be expected. Communication is not only an other-directed activity, unlike expression, it is also a *successful* other-directed activity (see Chapter 4). Communication is the successful transmission of data from a communicator to a receiver, which, in a dialogue, is done with the intention of eliciting certain responses from the receiver and of attending appropriately to those responses.

Finally, so that what each party actually communicates may credibly be taken to be what each party intends to communicate, the parties to a dialogue are necessarily not subjugated to the will of either each other or a third-party. That is, they cannot be unduly manipulated or under extreme duress.[19] They can be unenthusiastic or even forced participants in the exchange, but their will *as communicators* must be their own.[20] Such non-subjugation is necessary for their exchange to be genuine and genuinely reciprocal. It is necessary for them to be and to be seen to be equal in the relevant sense. In light of these five conditions, dialogue is paradigmatically a verbal exchange marked by mutual respect.

In simple terms, a *moral* dialogue is a dialogue that has as its subject either a moral issue or an issue that has moral implications. Often a moral dialogue will involve some moral disagreement. The moral disagreement may be about the nature of morality, the status of a moral principle, the application of a moral principle, the moral evaluation of an act in light of a particular moral principle, and so on. In broader terms, every dialogue is a moral dialogue in the sense that both parties are engaged in respectfully attending to the communicative efforts of the other. Jacob Needleman suggests, correctly I believe, that listening to a person well enough that we could summarize to her satisfaction what she has said is a deeply moral act. It is a necessary and attainable form of care between human beings.[21]

One possible challenge to my account of *dialogue*, suggested by José Luis Martí, is that it outlines an *ideal* standard for dialogue and not a set of necessary conditions for dialogues as such.[22] This is because,

---

[19] I thank Michelle Madden Dempsey for helping me to clarify this point.

[20] I thank an anonymous reader for OUP for pressing me to clarify this condition. The reader offered the following case. Suppose that I know you never pay attention to what I say. So one day I decide to lock us both in a room, or I simply grab your arm, and bring up the problem that I intend to discuss. My act is morally problematic in many ways, but it does not necessarily prevent a dialogue from taking place between us. You could choose to remain silent, in which case we will not have a dialogue. But, if you respond adequately to the issue I raise by offering valid reasons in reply, then we do have a dialogue. Now, if you remain silent and I threaten you credibly that I will never let you leave until you discuss the issue with me, then your will has been subjugated to mine and any ensuing exchange is not a dialogue.

[21] See Needleman, Jacob (2007) 'Why Can't We be Good?' Authors@Google Lecture Series, 30 April.

[22] Martí, José Luis (2011) 'Comment on Brownlee, "The Offender's Part in the Dialogue"' Workshop on Philosophy of Criminal Law, Pompeu Fabra University, Barcelona, 10 June.

ordinarily, dialogues are messier than these conditions allow. They can occur even when the exchange is not marked by mutual respect, a desire for progress, or argumentation.

In reply, first, it is important not to conflate *dialogue* with other kinds of interpersonal communication such as quarrels, fights, and exchanges of threats. Dialogues are characterized not only by their communicative success, but also by the participants' intentions to respect the other party. Second, the five conditions do not identify an ideal because they allow for significant defects in the exchange, which a genuine ideal of dialogue would transcend. For instance, the third condition allows that genuine progress in understanding might not actually occur. The fourth condition grants that parties might not communicate equally. And, the fifth condition grants that, to an extent, parties in a dialogue can be forced participants even though they must have control over what they communicate.

Now, some of these conditions for dialogue are clearly problematic for the claim that lawful punishment is dialogic. For instance, the fifth condition of non-subjugation cannot be presumed to apply to the typical offender confronting the prospect of punishment. Nor can the fourth condition of equal empowerment be presumed to apply to citizens in general in their relations with their state let alone between offenders and their state. However, the imbalance in power between a state and its citizens is not the kind of inequality that concerns us here because it is not an inequality that precludes the possibility of genuine dialogue, though, it does have a bearing on the conditions for dialogue. There is a similar, albeit less extreme, imbalance of power between a parent and a child, yet this does not prevent a parent and child from engaging in a dialogue as equals in the relevant sense of being equally active participants. But, there is a limitation to their equality in that the child's communicative claim-rights depend for their enforcement on continued recognition of them by the parent. The parent's communicative claim-rights against the child depend far less on continued recognition of them by the child since the parent has considerable power to ensure that she is heard regardless of whether the child acknowledges her communicative rights. (See Chapter 4 on valuable hierarchical relationships.) This imbalance in power, like that between the state and its citizens, suggests that, between such parties, the conditions for dialogue may be only shakily met.

The five conditions for genuine dialogue are not nearly as problematic for the idea that civil disobedience is dialogic as they are for the idea that punishment is dialogic. The first condition of reciprocity is met because civil disobedients 1) desire to engage in a dialogue, 2) are constrained in their communicative efforts, and 3) are not in a position of power relative to their audience. The second and third conditions of sustained purposiveness and reason-giving engagement are met because civil disobedients, by nature, have forward-looking and backward-looking communicative aims that they seek to advance, and because the conscientious convictions that animate their disobedience place process-related restrictions on the modes of communication they may use to promote those aims. It is an implication of their communicative conscientiousness that civil disobedients aim rationally to persuade their hearers of the merits of their cause. To aim to coerce authorities and society rather than to persuade them would be to treat them as less than fully autonomous beings to whom disobedients could make a reasoned defence of their view. If disobedients are to claim legitimately that they endeavour to engage in moral dialogue, their modes of communication must aim to respect the autonomy of their hearers as rational beings capable of responding to the reasons they believe they have to challenge current policy.[23] The fourth condition of fairness is met because civil disobedients are neither necessarily antidemocratic nor improperly putting themselves above the law (see Chapter 5). Finally, the fifth condition of non-subjugation is met because, although civil disobedience can force an issue onto the table, the parties to whom it is directed are not communicatively subjugated to the will of civil disobedients. Briefly, it is true that civil disobedience can be divisive and exert pressure on governments that is sometimes effective because it is pressure and not because it is reason-giving. As noted in Chapter 1, disobedients sometimes can find it unavoidable to employ limited pressure tactics to get their issue onto the table. Only when they have the ear of society may they undertake

---

[23] As noted in Chapter 1, the constraints imposed by civil disobedients' persuasive aims also have a consequential aspect. Since, as a strategy, coercion and intimidation can turn society against a position, disobedients who sincerely aim to have a long-term impact on policy have reason not to try to force people to adopt their position, but rather rationally to persuade them of the merits of their view. In short, to be serious in their aim to bring about a lasting change in policy, they must recognize the importance of engaging policy-makers and society in a moral dialogue. Too radical a protest could obscure the moral appeal of their objection. Both the non-consequential reason of respect and the consequential reason of succeeding in their persuasive project are reasons to prefer civil disobedience as a communicative strategy to more radical disobedience.

meaningfully to persuade people of their view. And, their actions may have this coercing effect irrespective of their intentions since many kinds of civil disobedience, such as illegal boycotts, illegal strikes, refusals to pay taxes, draft dodging, road-blocks, and sit-ins, make it difficult for a system to function and hence can have a potent effect on leaders' decisions. However, such modest, incidental pressure does not muffle disobedients' moral plea in the way that radical protest can do, and so its limited use can be consistent with both the persuasive aims of civilly disobedient communication and a respect for the hearers.

3. The Generic-Script Problem

The five conditions for dialogue impose some success-related constraints on the intentions and actions of any party who can claim with legitimacy to be *trying* to engage in a dialogue. Thus, these conditions check the power of any so-intentioned party to mistreat their putative dialogue partners. First, the conditions bar a sincere party from wilfully ignoring or immunizing herself from the would-be communications of the dialogue partner. As Onora O'Neill observes in more general terms:

Doing nothing isn't standardly a way of having no effect on others' possibilities for self-expression, given that the standard point of expression is communication. Doing nothing may convey disapproval and hostility. In extreme cases lack of response may reasonably be read as ostracism or rejection, as conveying the message that the other is not (or not fully) human. More commonly, doing nothing signals that what the other seeks to convey will be viewed as mere expression and not as a communication.[24]

Readiness to heed and interpret correctly the other party's would-be communications is necessary for communication between two parties to succeed. Without such readiness, communication fails and no dialogue occurs.

---

[24] O'Neill, Onora (1986) 'The Public Use of Reason' in *Political Theory* 14, 523–51.

Second, the conditions for dialogue constrain a sincere party in both her chosen *means* of communication and her chosen *mode* of communication. To claim legitimately to be endeavouring to engage in a dialogue, she must consider whether the means that she uses to communicate—words, actions, images, body movements, facial expressions—are likely to foster understanding of her message. And she must consider whether her mode or manner of communication—be it aggressive, assertive, conciliatory, or cowardly—will serve her communicative aims in a way that is compatible with the reason-governed, reciprocal, purposive nature of dialogue. For example, aggressively communicating a view is incompatible with genuine dialogue when the communication constitutes a failure to recognize the communicative claim-rights and equal status of the other party.

Third, the conditions for dialogue impose some success-related constraints on the *content* of a sincere party's communications. She must consider whether the content of her message is something that the other party has the capacity not only to understand, but also to reply to if he wishes. Each party must modify the content of his or her would-be communications when comprehension and response-ability from the other party are unlikely to follow.

These three success-related constraints on sincere dialogue partners create further difficulties for a dialogic conception of state punishment. Although the second and third constraints on means, mode, and content can, in all likelihood, be accommodated by state punishment since they require only modification in the processes of communication, the first constraint—readiness to heed the other—is more problematic for an account such as Duff's that subsumes such readiness under a formal process that largely disregards offenders' attitudes as irrelevant to their relations with the state. This is the Generic-Script Problem. In particular cases—such as full repentance prior to punishment or suitably constrained conscientious disobedience—the convicted person should not wish to recite the formal script assigned to her. And to require her to do so through the ritual of punishment not only disrespects her, but also makes a mockery of genuine moral dialogue undertaken reciprocally on a plane of roughly equal footing by parties who are responsive to the communicative efforts of the other.

In the case of the wholly repentant offender, the apology ritual misrepresents her by presenting her as being of a similar mind and attitude to unrepentant offenders who need to be brought to appreciate the wrongness of their acts and the reasons for reparation and repentance. As such, her punishment, when comparable in harshness to that of unrepentant offenders, is indefensibly dismissive of her sincere repentance and fervent desire to remedy relations.[25] If the state, through its criminal justice system, does nothing to alter its communications to such an offender in light of her attempted responses, then her communicative efforts seem to be, in the eyes of the state, mere acts of expression and not communication.

In response to this part of my argument, Duff says that we must first ask whether the problem is best expressed by complaining that a repentant offender is required to follow the same script as the unrepentant offender:

this [complaint] implies that the unrepentant offender's sentence is the default—in which case a repentant offender might reasonably object that she is required to speak as if she were unrepentant. But we could put the matter the other way round. The normal prescribed sentence, we could say, is one appropriate for a repentant offender: it constitutes what the repentant offender should undertake in order to communicate, in an appropriate formal public language, her apologetic recognition of her crime. We now face a quite different question: why should an unrepentant offender's punishment be no more severe than that of a repentant offender? But the answer to this question is relatively easy: a liberal polity that respects its citizens' privacy and freedom should not inquire into the sincerity of their public performances, it should address them and require conduct of them as if they were sincere.[26]

---

[25] Christopher Bennett is sensitive to this kind of objection in his defence of the 'apology ritual'. Bennett argues that concerns about sincerity and misrepresentation do not make the apology element (the imposition of duties to make amends) an empty ritual that could be left out. Rather, it highlights the limits of what the state may take its responsibilities to be in bringing about a resolution. The state does not have the responsibility to condemn all wrongs; its responsibilities extend only to addressing those wrongs that are of concern to the community—public wrongs. The state tasks the wrongdoer to remedy the public wrong. Given the intrusiveness of demanding a sincere apology, only apologetic action may be legitimately required of the offender. Whether the offender is genuinely repentant and remorseful is irrelevant to his relations with the state. See Bennett, Christopher (2008) *The Apology Ritual*. Cambridge: Cambridge University Press, 172–3. This position is examined critically in Brownlee, Kimberley (2010c) 'Retributive, Restorative, and Ritualistic Justice' in *Oxford Journal of Legal Studies* 30, 385–97.

[26] Duff (2011), 373. Duff continues: 'The script is generic: the sentence leaves no room for offenders to communicate more nuanced messages. But that is because it is a formal public procedure, appropriate between citizens who are (relative) strangers: the language of punishment is a ritual, conventional language in which appropriate formal messages about the crime are communicated. An offender might want to find other ways of communicating some

This reply is unconvincing because a communicative theory such as Duff's could not take the repentant offender as the default case since a key aim of punishment on that theory, though it does not form part of the core justification, is the forward-looking aim of bringing the offender to repent her offence. Such an aim would be redundant in the default case if the default case were that of the fully repentant offender.

The same Generic-Script Problem holds, to a different degree and for different reasons, in the case of a conscientious offender. Duff's monistic communicative theory is more accommodating of conscientiousness than it is of repentance. For instance, he observes that,

what the law says (and thus what punishment says) to a principled dissident whose values the community should respect will be different from what it says to other kinds of dissident. Suppose . . . that someone kills a terminally ill friend, in the honest belief that this is morally justified (or even required), although the law counts it as murder. The law still says to her, as it says to all citizens, that such killing is wrong, and her punishment still aims to bring her to see and accept that it was wrong. But it now portrays that wrongfulness to her as more like a *malum prohibitum* than a straightforward *malum in se*. Even if, for respectworthy reasons, she dissents from the content of the law, she ought to obey it out of respect for the law and as a matter of her duty as a citizen. Her punishment must therefore embody this more complex message, and will properly be lighter than that imposed on someone whose crime did not flow from respectworthy values.[27]

This departure from the Generic Script provides partial accommodation for conscientious offenders. However, the accommodation is inadequate in two respects. First, this script of lesser censure is still a blanket script of censure, which disregards the fact that some conscientious offenders, notably civil disobedients, can embody a more nuanced conception of citizens' duties than the duty to obey the law out of respect for the law.[28] The more nuanced conception recognizes that citizens may well have duties to know the law, to contribute to the

---

more personal message to the victim or to others (and the sentencing process could include a meeting with the victim at which each could speak more personally); but this is the way in which she must formally communicate, as an offender-citizen, with her fellow citizens.'

[27] Duff (2001), 122.

[28] For a discussion of political obligations other than a duty to obey the law, see Green, Leslie (2002) 'Law and Obligations' in *The Oxford Handbook of Jurisprudence and Philosophy of Law*. Jules Coleman and Scott Shapiro (eds.), Oxford: Oxford University Press.

development of the law, and to try to improve the alignment between the law and the central values of a liberal polity, but not a general, unqualified duty to obey the law out of respect for the law. Second, this script of lesser censure does not distinguish conscientious, communicative disobedients who wish to engage society in a moral dialogue from non-communicative offenders and evasive personal disobedients. Punishment of a civil disobedient is more problematic in this respect than punishment of a personal disobedient because it misrepresents the civil disobedient as being either remorseful or perversely defiant for modest breaches of law that she undertook to draw attention to a perceived injustice. Such misrepresentation might not only stifle reflection and debate on the merits of her cause, but also perpetuate injustice. As the history of liberal and illiberal societies shows, it is sometimes the law and not the offender's conduct that should undergo revision. Recognition of this fact is lost if the offender's attitudes are viewed as irrelevant to her relations with the state.[29]

Duff seems broadly receptive to my application of the Generic-Script Problem to civil disobedience. He states:

We must first decide whether and when someone's conscientious motive for offending should affect her legal fate, whether by grounding a defence, or as warranting a mitigation of sentence. If the law should formally recognize such conscientious offending, the criminal process must of course allow the principled defendant to explain herself; if it should not, the principled offender suffers no communicative injustice in not being allowed to argue her case. That answer is too quick, for two reasons. First, the principled dissident must have a forum in which she can make her case to her fellow citizens; if she is not allowed to make it at her trial the court must be able to say to her, truthfully, that there is another forum in which she can make it. Second, if we should still convict some principled offenders, we must take a view on whether what the law should say to them is that they committed substantive public wrongs (even if they deny this), for which this is an appropriate apologetic ritual; or that even if their rejection of the law reflects

---

[29] Additionally, when deciding how to respond, authorities should be sensitive to the fact that an offender may be defiant toward certain kinds of responses, but not towards others. The defiant offender's apparent unreceptiveness may be due to the modes of communication that authorities have adopted to address her. If her reasons for being unreceptive are well-founded, and if she would be receptive to other responses that are more respectful of her conscientiousness, then authorities must consider whether those other responses would be more appropriate.

a not-unreasonable normative stance, they should respect the polity's democratic decision on the matter until they can secure a democratic change—in which case their principled motivation should make a difference to their sentence. (There is also a further question: whether courts in imperfectly democratic polities should sometimes, morally, violate their legal duty and allow a principled disobedient a hearing, or nullify the law by acquitting her.)[30]

However, he continues:

There are important problems here about the criminal law's role in polities that are far from just (procedurally or substantively), or are riven by deep normative disagreements... [A]ny normative theory of punishment must confront those problems, but I don't think that they undermine the ideal of criminal punishment as an attempt at moral dialogue.[31]

Duff is more sanguine than I am about the prospects in liberal democracies for having dialogic ambitions through punishment, as my discussion of the Status Change Problem will make clear. In general, I see all liberal democracies as necessarily imperfect, given the near-inescapable imbalance of power between majorities and vulnerable minorities, and given the near-inevitability that liberal democracies will engage in some injustices, rights-abuses, and neglect of non-contingent needs (see Chapter 3 on the *gap thesis* and see Chapter 6). Therefore, the further question of whether courts should sometimes violate their legal duty and allow a principled disobedient a hearing or nullify the law by acquitting her is always present. Let me now take up the Status Change Problem, which is a more general problem for Duff's monistic communicative theory.

4. The Status Change Problem

The conditions for ordinary interpersonal dialogue do not rule out the communication of condemnation by one person to another. Although *condemnation* has a stronger negative connotation than does *adverse*

---

[30] Duff (2011), 374. [31] Duff (2011), 374.

opinion or *negative judgement*, one ordinary person's condemnation of another ordinary person does not alter the latter's status as a party to any dialogue between them provided that the condemnation signals an invitation to discuss the charge and not a termination of relations. When the condemnation does signal a termination of relations it is a performative act of silencing because all subsequent communicative efforts by the condemned party become, in the first instance, mere acts of expression. When, by contrast, condemnation signals an invitation to discuss the charge, the condemned party retains her ability to respond to the charges on a footing of rough communicative equality and reciprocity because her dialogue partner has not exercised his limited power to alter her moral standing in relation to him.

This contrasts sharply with the nature and force of condemnation in either a religious context or a legal context when the latter is conceived of in quasi-religious terms of *secular penance, absolution,* and *atonement* as Duff conceives of it. In a religious context, to be condemned by a properly empowered party is not simply to be judged harshly and invited to discuss the charge. Rather, it is to experience a radical, uncontestable demotion in our moral status (and sometimes our legal status) and with it a reduction in our rights and duties. This unequivocal demotion tracks the etymology of the word 'condemnation', which shares its etymological lineage with the word 'damnation'. To condemn someone in this sense is to doom her to punishment, to damn her to hell, or to inflict damage or loss on her. When a spiritual authority condemns a member of the congregation, that performative act not only negates her standing in the religious community, but also ostensibly interrupts her relationship with the Deity. The spiritual authority's act undermines the possibility for dialogue about the conduct that prompted the condemnation since the condemned party no longer has the standing to engage in an equally empowered, rational, and reciprocal exchange about it.

The same is true, I argue, of state condemnation and punishment in Duff's monistic communicative theory.[32] The notion of *condemnation* is

---

[32] Duff's use of other quasi-religious notions such as *secular penance* indicates that this quasi-religious reading of *condemnation* is not inappropriate in an analysis of his theory of punishment. In his paper 'Penance, Punishment, and the Limits of Community', Duff defends the view that religious ideas such as *penance, atonement,* and *absolution* can have a place in a liberal normative theory of criminal punishment, but regrettably he does not discuss the religious connotations of the notion of *condemnation*. Cf Duff, Antony (2003) 'Penance, Punishment, and the Limits of Community' in *Punishment and Society* 5, 295–312.

most apt in capital punishment cases where the sentence really does doom the convicted person. But, even in much milder contexts, when there is no opportunity for the offender to respond, condemnation and hard treatment radically demote the offender's standing, rights, and duties in ways that undermine the present possibility for dialogue about the offence. Some of this demotion is conventional. The status of 'criminal' carries life-long, stigmatizing features in our society. But it is not only the offender's conventional social status that changes. It is also the offender's standing to engage in a dialogue about her conduct. Since Duff's view is broadly insensitive to the communicative efforts of offenders (as noted in the Scripting Problem and Generic-Script Problem), state condemnation represents in his view a suspension of relations, not an invitation to discuss the charge.

In cases of civil disobedience, the status changing effects of such condemnation are particularly troubling because these offenders, more than any other, seek to engage their society in a dialogue. To deny them the standing to do so, is to deny them what they have a moral right and sometimes a duty to do.

Let me be clear about what the Status Change Problem is not. First, I am not saying that the state, as a morally complex and often morally tainted entity, lacks the moral credibility to engage in a moral dialogue. Second, I am not invoking a *tu quoque* argument to the effect that, although condemnation of an offence may be appropriate, the state lacks the moral standing to issue it because it is engaged in offences far worse than those for which it would condemn an offender.[33] For present purposes, it is not necessary to take a stand on the *tu quoque* argument. What I am saying is that, when punishment is imposed in a way that is insensitive to the communicative efforts of the offender, the state's act of condemnation disrupts the conditions of rough communicative equality and reciprocity necessary for genuine moral dialogue.

There are at least four possible replies that Duff might make to the Status Change Problem, which differ in their degree of plausibility. The first reply is that this objection is a matter of semantics. If the inner logic of *condemnation* by the state is ineliminably performative, and cannot but disrupt an offender's claim-rights and privileges as a dialogue partner, then we should put aside the language of *condemnation* and use the more modest language of *censure* and *disapprobation*. Thus,

---

[33] See Cohen, G. A. (2006), 'Casting the First Stone: Who Can, and Who Can't, Condemn the Terrorists' in *Royal Institute of Philosophy Supplement* 81, 113–36.

what the state does when it punishes an offender is communicate its censure and disapprobation of her conduct. Duff endorses this reply, saying: 'I am not sure that condemnation still carries the connotations of demotion and expulsion that [Brownlee] finds, but agree that legitimate punishment cannot have that character; if "condemnation" suggests it, I should drop that term and talk of "authoritative censure".'[34]

Although it is true that 'condemnation' can take the gentler form of inviting the condemned person to discuss the charge, Duff's reply is unconvincing because, in Duff's theory, the communication of censure and disapprobation is not all that is going on when the state convicts, sentences, and punishes an offender. As Duff himself notes, in his view, society doesn't simply communicate to an offender the censure that her offence deserves and then hope that she will make the censure her own in remorse; and society doesn't simply offer her a forum in which to communicate back her remorse should she come to repent her crimes. Rather, society *requires* her to go through the process of punishment as a form of secular penance. That quasi-religious process is said by Duff to be *necessary* for her absolution and reinstatement in the community. Therefore, she is not simply judged negatively or invited to respond. She is required to act in order to be absolved.

A second reply that Duff might make to the Status Change Problem grants that, in his view, lawful punishment does constitute a communication of condemnation in a rich, performative sense, but denies that an accurate fleshing out of the structure of condemnation—x condemns y for conduct z—gives rise to the Status Change Problem because what is condemned is not the offender, but the offensive conduct.

One difficulty with this reply is that, although Duff does speak of condemning an offender's conduct, he also speaks often of condemning the offender herself. He states, 'A conviction does not merely record a finding that this person committed the crime charged: it condemns him for that crime; it is a communicative act, communicating censure to the convicted defendant.'[35] There is also the deeper issue of whether it makes sense to speak of condemning an offence independently of condemning an offender since it is the offender, and not the offence, that is doomed to punishment. A second, more important difficulty is that, irrespective of whether it is plausible to

---

[34] Duff, (2011), 373.   [35] Duff (1998), 162.

speak of condemning an offence independently of condemning an offender, the effect of relation-suspending condemnation is that the offender suffers a demotion that affects her present capacity to enter into a dialogue with society about her conduct.

A third reply Duff might give to the Status Change Problem is that, although my concerns about condemnation identify a legitimate practical problem of how the state's communication will be taken by both the offender and others since both may regard the state's condemnation in the rich, performative terms I have outlined, nevertheless my concerns do not identify a deeper logical problem about the state's use of relation-suspending condemnation in its effort to engage the offender in moral dialogue. Duff states:

... while there is clearly room, and need, for empirical investigation into the actual impact of criminal censure on offenders and on the wider public (what message is actually heard, and to what further effect), and while there is also room, and need, for empirical investigation into the effect of different kinds of styles of censuring, the justification of censure I have offered does not depend on such empirical facts.[36]

Rather, what justifies censure or condemnation within Duff's communicative theory is the *wrong* that the offender has done. Specifically in reply to my account of the Status Change Problem, Duff states:

The 'Status Change Problem' is...a problem for our practices rather than for my normative account: the punishments that we now impose, given their social and political contexts, do all too often demote offenders to a lower moral and social status; but punishment need not, and should not, have this character.[37]

This reply, while it is consistent with the claim that punishment seeks to be transparently persuasive, does not allay the worry that such persuasion, given its condemnatory force and imposed nature, cannot be reciprocal when it ignores the communicative efforts of the offender.

---

[36] Duff (1998), 163.   [37] Duff (2011), 373.

A fourth reply, which Duff makes to a related objection,[38] is that 'there is certainly room in the criminal process for the offender's voice to be heard: at her trial, in deciding her sentence, and through her response to her punishment'. Duff continues:

There are of course strict limits on what she will be heard to say and, in the end, neither verdict nor sentence are up to her: the court, speaking for the law and for the community whose law it is, claims the authority to determine these matters. However, enforced claims to effective authority do not make dialogue of a morally significant kind impossible. I can, for instance, engage in philosophical dialogue with my students, addressing and respecting them as rational beings, whilst still claiming the authority to require work from them, and to assess and grade that work.[39]

The difficulty with this response can best be stated by expanding on Duff's academic analogy. It is true, as I noted on page 220 with the example of the parent and child, that, in principle, an authority such as a professor or a government can engage in a dialogue with those under her authority because, although the communicative rights of dependants are conditional on the authority's recognition of them, there are success-based constraints for dialogue that require any authority who sincerely seeks to engage in dialogue to recognize the dependants' communicative claim-rights. But this is where the difficulty for relations-suspending condemnation arises. If Duff were to bar a disruptive student from coming to the next class or were to ask an unprepared student to leave the class or were to fail a poorly performing student, he would engage in communicative acts that temporarily undermine the possibility for dialogue. Certainly, the conditions for dialogue might subsequently be restored, say, when the recalcitrant student comes to see Duff in his office to show that she understands the reason for the condemnation and to discuss reinstatement. But, those conditions are not achieved at the time that the student's status in the class is radically demoted by Duff's exercise of censuring authority.

It may be possible to re-present this fourth reply by distinguishing the two central parts of the criminal justice process—the first being the

---

[38] Bagaric and Amarasekara argue that, since punishment is imposed, it cannot be represented as a communicative dialogue. Bagaric, Mirko and Amarasekara, Kumar (2000) 'The Errors of Retributivism' in *University of Melbourne Law Review* 24, 173.

[39] Duff (2000), 414–15.

criminal trial and the second the conviction, sentence, and imposition of punishment—and by arguing that the *first* is the proper institutional analogue to interpersonal dialogue since, at trial, a person is called to account as a suspect and is provided a public forum in which to answer charges and, if necessary, to make a defence. In Duff's view, the criminal trial is a two-stage process of 'answerings':

We should ... see the criminal trial as a formal process through which an alleged wrongdoer is called to answer to his fellow citizens, by the court that speaks in their name. He is called, initially, to answer to the charge of wrongdoing—either by pleading 'Guilty', thus admitting his culpable commission of the wrong; or by pleading 'Not Guilty', thus challenging the prosecution to prove his guilt. If the prosecution does prove that he committed the offence, he must then answer for that commission: either by offering a defence—a justification or excuse which shows that he should not be condemned for committing the offence—or by submitting himself to the court's formal condemnation and to the sentence it imposes. The criminal trial is thus a formal analogue of the informal moral processes through which we call each other to account for wrongs that we have committed: it addresses the defendant not simply as someone who is the subject of a formal inquiry, but as a citizen who is to participate in the process, and who is expected to answer to his fellows for his alleged violation of the values that define their polity.[40]

During the trial process, there is no communication of condemnation yet, and therefore, the Status Change Problem does not arise. (However, it cannot be denied that a suspect's standing is altered by her having charges to answer.) Such a forum, which precedes condemnation, does seem broadly acceptable as an analogue of interpersonal dialogue, if we put aside cases of unwillingness to plead.[41] The next

---

[40] Duff, Antony (2010) 'Inaugural Address: Towards a Theory of Criminal Law?' in *Proceedings of the Aristotelian Society Supplementary Volume l*, xxxiv, 11.

[41] William Smith argues credibly that there should be dialogic possibilities between police and civil disobedients prior to the arrest, detention, or charging of disobedients. He says that, where possible, the police should adopt a strategy of 'negotiated accommodation', which requires the police to try to engage protest groups in a dialogue either before or during their civil disobedience. Such a dialogic effort by the police must be underpinned by a sincere commitment to balancing public order policing against the good of accommodating civil disobedience. See Smith, William (2012) 'Policing Civil Disobedience' in *Political Studies*, doi: 10.1111/j.1467-9248.2011.00937.x.

stage in the process is that of punishment, which, in this reply, is not to be conceived of in dialogic terms, but in simpler, one-sided, communicative, reason-based terms. This kind of reply, while potentially compelling, is not entirely open to Duff because, first, he does speak of punishment itself as being dialogic, and second, in his view, the aims and purposes of the trial are continuous with those of punishment, and hence the whole process is intended to be viewed in the reciprocal terms of moral dialogue.

The Scripting Problem, Generic-Script Problem, and Status Change Problem do not undermine the claim that the aims of lawful punishment can be communicative and rationally persuasive. This is because, just as the laws and the trial process (ideally) respect persons as autonomous agents, so too punishment can reflect transparent efforts at moral persuasion that seek the offender's assent, acknowledgment of wrongdoing, and acceptance of the moral reasons to follow the law. This is a powerful way to think about the most defensible form that punishment might take. My point is that, unless tempered by other values, it is not dialogic. A monistic communicative account of punishment that is untempered by non-retributive values and gives little attention to the offender's communicative efforts cannot be characterized in terms of a moral dialogue.

5. A Pluralistic Theory of Punishment

It is possible to move towards a communicative theory of punishment whose aims more closely approximate those of a genuine moral dialogue. A pluralistic communicative theory does this by supplementing retributive desert with other, independent moral values to determine what punishment, if any, is morally justified all things considered. In principle, such an approach to punishment can be more sensitive to the offender's communicative contributions, and hence can more closely approximate a genuine dialogue.

As noted at the outset of this chapter, one independent moral virtue that tempers justice is mercy. Tasioulas argues, rightly, that there are reasons sometimes for the state to be merciful to an offender and to show a charitable concern for her well-being as a potential recipient of deserved punishment.[42] When the law has reason to be merciful this can reduce the justified punishment in relation to the deserved punishment. The case that Tasioulas focuses on is the repentant offender. Since a key aim of punishment, in a communicative theory, is to lead the offender to repent her action and to reform her conduct, when the offender demonstrates prior to punishment that she does repent and has reformed, this gives the law reason to show mercy and to impose a lesser punishment on her than that which she deserves according to justice. Other possible cases for mercy that Tasioulas looks at are: 1) the offender who is a recipient of natural punishment, such as the father who has accidentally killed the son he loves; 2) the offender whose circumstances make her an inappropriate object of punishment, such as the abused wife or the kid whose upbringing contained formidable obstacles to forming a decent and law-abiding character; and 3) the offender who is already suffering from some grave misfortune that would be cruelly exacerbated with the imposition of punishment.[43] A further case for mercy, I argue, is civil disobedience.

Undeniably, punishment for civil disobedience can be *deserved*. If civil disobedients engage in vandalism, property damage, trespass, or violence, punishment may well be deserved especially if the disobedience has significant negative effects for others (some of which might not be foreseeable) for which the disobedients cannot be fully exculpated. However, given that, to be civilly disobedient at all, these agents must satisfy conditions of sincerity, consistency, and self-restrained communicativeness, they are distinct from ordinary offenders, evasive disobedients, and radical protesters. Judges have reasons to appreciate the onerousness for civil disobedients of abiding by the law. This is because, even when their acts are not fully exculpable, civil disobedience is disobedience grounded in deeply and conscientiously held commitments that understandably make it difficult for disobedients both to follow laws that contravene those commitments and to refrain from communicating in effective ways their objections to those laws. Concern for disobedients' well-being as conscientiously motivated persons gives the state reason to be merciful towards them irrespective

---

[42] Tasioulas contrasts mercy with justifiable leniency. Only mercy takes as central a concern for the well-being of the offender as one about to be subjected to deserved punishment.

[43] Cf Tasioulas (2003).

of whether their cause is well-founded and their acts fully parsimonious and reasonable.

This ground for mercy is not a mirror of the demands-of-conviction defence because that defence is premised on an egalitarian respect for autonomy, psychological integrity, and the value of practical judgement. The limits of the defence lie where one person's expression of conscientious conviction intrudes on the equal rights of others to be respected as autonomous. The case for mercy applies to those disobedients who cannot make full use of the demands-of-conviction defence because they do intrude on others' equal rights to respect and autonomy.

The inappropriateness of demanding repentance from civil disobedients through punishment is particularly clear when disobedients' cause is well-founded. Demanding repentance from such disobedients would attack values that the state and society should advocate. But, the inappropriateness of imposing customary sanctions does not leave the state speechless because there are other responses that the state can make to civil disobedience. As John Gardner notes, there are many types of normative consequences for breach of law apart from liability to punishment, such as a duty to show regret, to apologize for the harm or damage done, to make restitution, and to provide reparation.[44] These actions may be required of civil disobedients even when whatever wrong they do is also justified. I expand on these thoughts in Chapter 8 in relation to non-punitive restorative responses to civil disobedience.

Conclusion

In this chapter, I have identified three problems with a monistic communicative theory of punishment. These are the Scripting Problem, the Generic-Script Problem, and the Status Change Problem. These problems are noteworthy both in themselves and in relation to the punishing of civil disobedience. These three problems show that a monistic communicative theory, which justifies punishment in purely backward-looking retributive terms, cannot claim to have dialogic

---

[44] Gardner, John (2007) 'In Defence of Defences' in *Offences and Defences*. Oxford: Oxford University Press.

ambitions because it disregards the communicative efforts of the offender. By contrast, a pluralistic communicative theory, which grants that moral values other than retributive justice must figure in the assessment of the overall morally justifiable response to offending, can have dialogic ambitions because it is more sensitive, in principle, to offenders' communicative efforts. The pluralistic theory tempers retributive aims with charitable aims that are responsive to the offender's communication of repentance, natural suffering, and so on. Such an approach to punishment can recognize that civil disobedients' conscientious moral commitments make it very difficult for them not to dissociate themselves communicatively from laws that violate those commitments. These facts about their circumstances give the law reason to show mercy towards them and lessen the severity of any deserved response from the law. This possibility for a nuanced approach shows that a pluralistic communicative theory of punishment better approximates a genuine dialogue between civil disobedients and their society.

8

Punishment

This chapter continues the discussion of punishment. Here, I defend a moral right against punishment. I show that civil disobedients such as anti-fur trade activist Megan Lewis, who blocked a Neiman Marcus store and was ordered by the judge to stay away from animal rights protests, have a moral right not to be punished.

In brief, the moral right to civil disobedience advanced in Chapter 4 grounds defeasible normative protection against interference by others including legal interference such as prevention or punishment.[1] This blanket defeasible protection flows from the very concept of a *right of conduct* on the standard liberal conception of *rights*, which I endorse. Rights of conduct provide defeasible normative protection of a sphere of liberty or autonomy against *all* forms of coercive interference by others (Section 1).[2] A question that arises from this is whether the protection of the right to civil disobedience holds against formal

---

[1] We saw in Chapter 4 that there exists a moral right to engage in civil disobedience. First, this right acknowledges the communicative dimension of conscientious conviction. To require us always either to respect a law that we oppose or to engage only in private, surreptitious disobedience of that law (where possible) is to deny us appropriate space to act in keeping with our conscientiously held beliefs. And although legal protest, like civil disobedience, offers a vehicle through which to communicate conviction, legal protest lacks the conscientious and performative dissociation that civil disobedience has as a constrained breach of law. In essence, to make rights of conscientious action real and meaningful, some space must be made for civil disobedience. Second, to some extent, this right can redress the participatory-power imbalance between majorities and minorities by reducing the impact that luck, time, and limited resources can have on the effectiveness of our participation. Third, the right serves the double harmony between dissenters' interests and society's interests in the stabilizing, democracy-promoting collision of opinions to which civil disobedience contributes.

[2] Cf Raz, Joseph (1979) *The Authority of Law*. Oxford: Oxford University Press, ch. 14.

censure or symbolic censure since such censure is ostensibly non-interfering and since our rights do not protect us from criticism about how we exercise them. I argue that the right to civil disobedience does protect against formal or symbolic censure,[3] but the right is not absolute (Section 2). In principle, the grounds for communicating censure could override the right.[4] But, in practice, the reasons to respect the right, including its humanistic foundation and its double-harmony with society's interests, recommend a non-punitive restorative approach that clearly distinguishes civil disobedients from ordinary offenders (Section 3).

1. The Right to Civil Disobedience

Let me begin by exploring an account of the right to civil disobedience that contrasts with my own. This account is advanced by David Lefkowitz, who says that the moral right to civil disobedience consists of two parts.[5] The first is a claim-right specifically against punishment, which is grounded in the non-instrumental value of individual autonomy. This claim-right, he argues, does not extend to a right against *non-punitive* forms of state interference such as forcible prevention or penalization. Penalization is one thing, he says, and punishment is another. This distinction between punishment and penalization is drawn by Joel Feinberg on the grounds that, although both penalization and punishment are authoritative deprivations for failures, punishment alone involves the communication of condemnation through hard treatment.[6] Drawing on this distinction, Lefkowitz holds that, although the state may not *punish* civil disobedients, it is at liberty to *penalize* them for their conduct through heavy fines and even temporary incarceration. Penalization is permissible, he says, on both

---

[3] In taking this view, I depart from a position I have advanced in previous writings where I suggested that the right to civil disobedience did not extend to protection against formal condemnation.

[4] Some of the material in the current chapter elaborates themes in Brownlee, Kimberley (2008) 'Penalizing Public Disobedience' in *Ethics* 118: 4, 711–16.

[5] Lefkowitz speaks about a right to public disobedience, not a right to civil disobedience. Since his conception of *public disobedience* broadly aligns with my conception of *civil disobedience*, I shall speak of a right to civil disobedience.

[6] Feinberg, Joel (1994b) 'The Expressive Function of Punishment' in *A Reader on Punishment*. Antony Duff and David Garland (eds.), Oxford: Oxford University Press, 73–4.

instrumental grounds and symbolic grounds (which I elaborate later) because, unlike punishment, it does not aim to communicate condemnation to civil disobedients for their breach of law. The second part of the right to civil disobedience, Lefkowitz says, is a (special) Hohfeldian liberty-right to do wrong.[7] This is a permission to act sincerely and reasonably on a mistaken conception of what justice requires. In this section, I show that both parts of Lefkowitz's account of the right to civil disobedience are mistaken. Let's begin with the liberty-right.

1.1 Liberty-rights

Lefkowitz says that we enjoy a liberty or permission to engage in civil disobedience because other people have no claim on us not to do so. To make this argument, Lefkowitz revises the traditional conception of what it means to 'have a claim on someone's action'. He argues that there are limits to what we plausibly may demand of each other as persons making decisions in light of the 'burdens of judgment'.[8]

If we accept that 'ought' implies 'can' and that the most that creatures like us can do, in circumstances characterized by the burdens of judgment, is to make reasonable judgments as to what justice, or morality, requires, then this fact ought to be reflected in the content of our claims against one another.[9]

Therefore, although we ought to act as morality truly requires, the most that we may demand of each other is that we all act reasonably, Lefkowitz argues. To say that someone has a liberty-right to act is not to say that she acts rightly. It is to say that she acts reasonably.[10] The right to civil disobedience may be construed as a liberty-right in this sense, Lefkowitz says, because when a person champions through civil

---

[7] Lefkowitz, David (2007) 'On a Moral Right to Civil Disobedience' in *Ethics* 117, 202–33. For a brief defence of the coherence of the notion of a liberty-right to do wrong, see Jones, Peter (1994) *Rights*. New York: Palgrave, 204–7.

[8] Lefkowitz specifies two senses of 'reasonable'. A person is *morally reasonable* if, and only if, she is committed to limiting her pursuit of the good life appropriately to accommodate others who are also rational and reasonable. A person's belief or action is *cognitively reasonable* when it is 'a judgment made under conditions of less than full information, and/or awareness of the full range of reasons that apply to someone in that situation, and/or with less than perfect reasoning'. Cognitively reasonable judgements are ones made in circumstances characterized by the burdens of judgement. Cf Lefkowitz, David (2005) 'A Contractualist Defense of Democratic Authority' in *Ratio Juris* 18: 3, 346–64.

[9] Lefkowitz (2007), 229.

[10] Lefkowitz (2007), 232.

disobedience a reasonable but erroneous conception of justice, she satisfies all claims that others plausibly can make of her, but nonetheless, in some sense, acts 'wrongly' since the policy she defends is less just or moral than existing policy.

I have three criticisms of this view. First, the difficulties, which Lefkowitz notes, in applying traditional deontological terminology to this account might be alleviated if he relinquishes the idea that the realm of duty is exhausted by the realm of rights-claims.[11] His suggestion that these two realms are co-extensive is problematic for him because he also says that, for the purposes of his discussion, he limits the terms 'wrong' and 'immoral' to violations of moral duty.[12] If wrong actions are actions that breach moral duty, and if moral duties are exhausted by rights-claims, then it cannot follow that we act wrongly when we act sincerely and reasonably in defence of an unjust cause where no one has a rights-claim on us to do otherwise.

By contrast, if we *can* have moral duties to act in certain ways even when others have no rights-claim on us that we do so, and thus we act wrongly when we breach those duties, then a person who reasonably endorses an unjust policy can be said to act wrongly (even though no one may demand that she act otherwise) since she breaches a duty, and thus fails to act as morality truly requires. Adopting this view of duty would prevent Lefkowitz from having to assert that the conduct of the reasonable person involves some special and rather obscure sort of wrongness.

Second, related to this, it is unclear that 'ought implies can' actually supports Lefkowitz's position. Suppose I have to give a lecture this morning, but my train to the university is delayed so that I am unable to give the lecture this morning. In some sense, I still ought to give the lecture, but the fact that I am unable to do so is a constraint on this. I have reason to give my lecture even though I cannot do so; and it is because I have reason to give the lecture that it would be appropriate for me to feel distressed at being unable to do so. But, since I cannot give the lecture, I have no reason *to try* to give the lecture since this would be fruitless.[13] This characterization of the relation between ought and can (ie that ought to *try* implies can succeed (broadly

---

[11] Lefkowitz (2007), 224.
[12] Lefkowitz (2007), 225.
[13] Gardner, John (2004) 'The Wrongdoing that Gets Results' in *Philosophical Perspectives* 18, 53–88.

construed), but ought does not necessarily imply can) is more compatible with Lefkowitz's position than 'ought implies can' since Lefkowitz seeks to highlight that what we ought to do according to morality lies beyond what we may demand of each other given the burdens of judgement; therefore, what we ought to *try* to do is to act reasonably.

Third, I assume that Lefkowitz intends the liberty-right to civil disobedience to apply to the same set of actions as the claim-right to civil disobedience. But, if the correct way to conceive of the claim-right to civil disobedience is, as I noted at the outset of this chapter, as a right of conduct that protects a certain sphere of action from all coercive interference irrespective of the legitimacy of the disobedient's cause, then necessarily there will be acts of civil disobedience, namely those advocating highly objectionable or unreasonable causes such as neo-Nazism, that are protected by the claim-right but not by Lefkowitz's liberty-right. The implication is that there can be no liberty-right to civil disobedience as such because only the civil disobedience that is just or reasonable could fall within the parameters of such a liberty-right. Therefore, we may reject the idea of a liberty-right to civil disobedience and turn to the claim-right to civil disobedience.

1.2 *Penalization*

According to Lefkowitz, the claim constitutive of the moral right to civil disobedience is a claim against punishment, but not a claim against either state penalization or *ex ante* interference. This distinction between *punishment* and *penalization* turns on the observation that ordinary penalties such as parking tickets, offside penalties, and disqualifications have a miscellaneous character, but largely lack the symbolic, condemnatory significance of punishment.[14] Trading on this distinction, Lefkowitz argues that the non-instrumental value of individual autonomy gives the state a rights-based duty not to condemn/punish civil disobedience, but no rights-based duty not to penalize it. He argues that, granting the state the liberty to penalize

---

[14] The distinction between punishment and penalization is less clear-cut than Feinberg and Lefkowitz suppose, but I shall accept the distinction for the purposes of this discussion because my challenge to Lefkowitz focuses on the reasons for which he says penalization may be imposed. As an aside, assuming that the distinction is sustainable, it is a mistake to suppose, as Lefkowitz does, that *ceteris paribus* punishment is inevitably worse, and thereby harder to justify, than penalization. The *reasons* for which some act of penalization or punishment is imposed and the particular type of penalization or punishment imposed cannot be neglected in the determination of whether it is justifiable.

civil disobedience contributes to the stability of the state by both better enabling the state to facilitate morally necessary collective action and reducing the likelihood that people will undertake civil disobedience unless they believe a law and policy is significantly unjust:[15]

> the justification for a fine or limitation on liberty rests primarily on considerations of deterrence, i.e., on an instrumental calculation of the effect that penalizing, or not penalizing, a [civil] disobedient will have on the stability and effectiveness of the legal order.[16]

Additionally, accepting harsh penalties allows disobedients symbolically to affirm citizens' collective authority to settle reasonable disagreements about morally necessary collective action schemes.[17] In particular, paying fines allows disobedients symbolically to recognize the costs that they impose on others when they civilly disobey. And, accepting temporary incarceration allows them to show that they do not intend to usurp the authority of the state, but rather act (just) within the boundaries of political debate.[18]

I have five objections to this account of the scope of the moral claim-right to civil disobedience. The first is a conceptual objection about the nature of rights of conduct. The second and third are Kantian objections based on respect for persons as persons. The fourth concerns effective participation. The fifth concerns legitimate participation.

First, as noted above, in the liberal view of rights, which I think Lefkowitz endorses as I do, rights of conduct provide defeasible normative protection of a sphere of autonomy against *all* forms of coercive interference by others, and not just against particular forms of interference such as punishment. Therefore, Lefkowitz cannot argue that the claim-right to civil disobedience protects a person against condemnation or punishment, but not against *ex ante* interference or penalization.

---

[15] Lefkowitz (2007), 219.
[16] Lefkowitz (2007), 223n. Deterring all but the most serious dissenters might not contribute to the stability of the state. First, the most serious dissenters are not necessarily the most justified in their commitments. Second, Rawls would argue that (justified) civil disobedience can serve to inhibit departures from justice and to correct departures when they occur; and thus can act as a stabilizing force in society. Rawls, John (1971) *A Theory of Justice*. Cambridge: Harvard University Press, 383.
[17] Lefkowitz (2007), 220.
[18] Lefkowitz (2007), 222.

A partial reply for Lefkowitz might be that the state is *not* interfering when it penalizes civil disobedients because the boundaries of the right are drawn at the point where disobedients' action would encourage, incite, or inspire others to engage in non-conscientious disobedience.

In response, first, this reply speaks only to penalization and not to *ex ante* interference, against which Lefkowitz also says the right does not protect. Second, to let the parameters of our rights of conscientious action be set by others' decision to act rashly is to hold those rights hostage to the heckler and the zealot, especially since, by definition, civil disobedients do not intend to incite radical protest. Third, the reply misses its mark. The point is not about the permissibility of penalizing *some* civil disobedience, but about the permissibility of penalizing *any* civil disobedience. Lefkowitz thinks that penalizing civil disobedience that is *not* itself likely to incite others does not intrude on the right to civil disobedience.

Second, the claim that disobedients have no moral right against penalization conflicts with what is required to respect them as autonomous, reasoning agents. This objection takes two forms. The first form challenges the legitimacy of *individual* deterrence as a ground for penalization. If the non-instrumental value of individual autonomy makes it impermissible for the state to *punish* civil disobedients, then it equally makes it impermissible for the state to *penalize* civil disobedients. Indeed, penalization taken on instrumental grounds is more problematic than punishment is since it disregards both the conscientious nature of civil disobedients' conduct and their status as equal members of the community. When a judge penalizes a disobedient primarily to deter her from engaging in undesired behaviour he disregards her status as a reasoning, autonomous agent and treats her as a mere brute responsive to a threatened stick. Judge Taite did exactly this when he ordered Megan Lewis to stay away from animal rights protests so that she won't 'be back doing the same things again'.[19] He gave no weight to the conscientiousness of her convictions or the merits of her position or the constrained, non-coercive nature of her chosen conduct. He simply issued an order to deter undesired behaviour.

---

[19] Judge Ralph Taite maintained that sentencing an activist to stay away from protests is no different than sentencing a drunk driver to stay away from bars, or sentencing a paedophile to stay 100 feet away from schoolyards, ignoring the fact that neither of the latter are protected under the US Constitution. Potter, Will (2001) 'The New Backlash: From the Streets to the Courthouse, the New Activists Find Themselves under Attack' in *Texas Observer*, 14 September 2001.

Third, *general* deterrence is a questionable ground for penalizing civil disobedience. The deterrence argument is that, since civil disobedience can encourage frivolous, opportunistic, or radical disobedience, civil disobedients should accept significant penalties as a means of restoring the general levels of deterrence that their actions have undermined. This argument not only misattributes blame for the decline in general deterrence, because copycats are responsible for their own decisions to breach the law, but also uses civil disobedients as a means to deterring undesired, frivolous disobedience. When a judge penalizes a civil disobedient primarily to deter other people from engaging in undesired behaviour he uses her as a means to achieve some future good. Unless further arguments are offered, such use ignores that she has certain rights as an autonomous agent that proscribe her being treated that way.[20] Penalizing civil disobedients in order to restore deterrence levels may be, at best, a necessary evil that the state must impose in order to avoid having to prohibit and punish all civil disobedience, but we should not suppose, as Lefkowitz does, that it is anything other than a necessary evil that fails to respect disobedients as autonomous persons who contribute to collective decision-making in constrained and legitimate ways.

This Kantian objection applies most vividly to incarceration. Lefkowitz compares penalizing civil disobedients through incarceration to quarantining potential disease carriers. This parallel shows, he says, that there is no necessary connection between the state's confining a person and its communicating censure (punishment). However, what Lefkowitz overlooks are, first, whether the unpleasantness of the incarceration in each context is an essential and intended feature of what is done to the person, even if done ostensibly without condemnatory significance, and second, whether the reasons for imposing that unpleasantness are at odds with respect for individual rights. Incarceration imposed as a penalty cannot be compared to quarantine because the deprivations of quarantine are an unintended and highly regrettable side-effect of isolating persons who are potential disease carriers. By contrast, the deprivations imposed by incarcerating civil disobedients are an essential and intended part of what is done to them. The incarceration is *meant* to be burdensome on disobedients so that it deters them or other people from engaging in excessive or frivolous

---

[20] Cf Murphy, J. G. (1994) 'Marxism and Retribution' in *A Reader on Punishment*. Antony Duff and David Garland (eds.), Oxford: Oxford University Press, 44.

disobedience. And this disregards their rights to be respected both as ends and as full members of the community who may contribute to the resolution of collective disputes. It also shows how shaky is the supposed distinction between *penalization* and *punishment*.

These Kantian objections do not imply that the moral right to civil disobedience is absolute. The right may be overridden if the benefits of penalization are sufficiently great (as I discuss in Section 3). The point is that the right provides defeasible normative protection against *all* forms of coercive interference including instrumentally useful penalization.

Fourth, related to the Kantian objections is what I call the effective participation objection. Lefkowitz's willingness to let the state penalize civil disobedients through means sufficient to impose a *genuine sacrifice* on them conflicts with his claim that it is important to reduce as much as possible the barriers to effective political participation. Since penalization, and in particular penalization sufficient to impose a genuine sacrifice, is likely to dissuade many people from engaging in civil disobedience (including many who are serious about their convictions), the use of penalization is a barrier to citizens' effective exercise of their right to political participation including the right to civil disobedience.

Fifth, there is the legitimacy objection. Lefkowitz's defence of penalization and *ex ante* interference would be more credible if civil disobedience were, in his view, a deviant form of political engagement beyond what can be tolerated in a liberal democracy. But, in his view, it is not beyond what can be tolerated. Rather, it offers one of two ways to satisfy the demands of our obligations to the law because it respects other citizens as persons who have equal authority to determine what the law ought to be.[21] This undermines the putative symbolic grounds for penalization. If suitably constrained civil disobedience respects the equal authority of all to determine what the

---

[21] A state, Lefkowitz says, has a justified claim to political authority when it is both minimally democratic and liberal in the sense of manifesting a principled commitment to individual rights. When a state has such legitimacy, citizens have a duty to follow the law. But, in contrast with traditional accounts of legal obligation, Lefkowitz maintains that this duty to the law is disjunctive. Citizens either must follow the law or they must engage in suitably constrained civil disobedience. If they oppose a policy, they may not choose, for example, simply to disregard it; they either must follow it (using legal means of protest if they wish) or use suitably constrained civil disobedience against it. Lefkowitz's explanation for why legal obligation is disjunctive is that both adherence to the law and suitably constrained civil disobedience, and only these two options, demonstrate respect for other citizens as persons who have equal authority to determine what the law ought to be.

law ought to be, as Lefkowitz claims it does, then there could be no real costs of the relevant kind for disobedients symbolically to acknowledge.

2. Symbolic Punishment

The take-away message of the last section is that the moral right to civil disobedience protects against all forms of interference including prevention, penalization, and punitive hard treatment. However, as I noted in the introduction, this conclusion gives rise to a further question which is: Does the protection of this right hold against purely *formal* or *symbolic* censure, such as verbal reprimands or formal convictions? There are at least two reasons to think at first glance that it does not.

First, formal moral censure and symbolic censure are usually distinguished from punitive hard treatment on the grounds that only the latter inflicts something normally regarded as detrimental to our genuine interests 'quite independently of its use as a vehicle of censure'.[22] Formal or symbolic censure is non-interfering, so the argument goes, and hence does not overstep the bounds of the moral right to civil disobedience.

Second, our rights do not protect us from criticism of how we exercise them. In guaranteeing us a protected sphere in which to act, our right does not bind other people to approve of how we make use of that protected sphere. My right to free speech does not bind you to approve of everything I say. This is because there is an important distinction between protecting autonomous choices and assessing or guiding those choices.[23] Therefore, although a moral right to civil disobedience defeasibly protects us from coercive interference and may indeed give us certain claims to positive assistance,[24] it does not

---

[22] Tasioulas, John (2006) 'Punishment and Repentance' in *Philosophy* 81, 288.
[23] Cf Jones (1994), ch 9.
[24] For our rights to be meaningful, we require an effective system of provision and protection within society's accepted morality and (in certain senses) its legal system. Effective recognition of the moral right to civil disobedience requires, for example, that the state, where possible, allow the disobedience to occur, and neither sabotage the disobedience nor respond with excessive force. Additionally, it requires that the state take civil disobedients seriously as a distinct category of offender, and thus, exercise discretion when deciding whether to arrest, charge, go to trial, convict, or sentence. Although the strength of these

immunize us from other people's judgements about how we exercise this right.

Although seemingly forceful, these two points are ultimately not compelling. First, with regard to this last point about others' judgements, when we look at the details it is difficult to sustain a distinction between others' judgements about how we use our rights and others' interference with our rights since others' judgements can affect our opportunities to exercise our rights. Although the formal safeguards of a 'right' should be in place, others' judgements can have cumulative effects in practice on the parameters of our protected conduct. This is especially true when the people expressing critical judgements have power over us. Does the boss who says in a formal meeting 'I don't approve of what you're saying' differ so much from the boss who covers your mouth or shuts off your email? Ostensibly, you have a choice in the first case to continue to speak as you wish, and should be protected in doing so, but the boss's coercive power is such that the censure makes that option highly unattractive. It poses risks for your relations with your co-workers, for your prospects at work, and for your personal security and psychological comfort. Thus, instead of a division between judgements and interference, there is more likely a continuum of degrees of interference in others' communication of censure.

This conclusion bears on the first point that formal or symbolic censure is non-interfering. There are two related reasons to conclude that formal or symbolic censure *does* interfere with our conduct. The first is a conceptual point that the distinction between *formal* or *symbolic censure*, on the one hand, and *hard treatment*, on the other, cannot be sustained because the former, like the latter, involves the imposition of a genuine burden, namely, the burden of public censure. As John Tasioulas rightly notes, 'some predominantly symbolic forms of condemnation shade over into hard treatment insofar as they subject the offender to certain painful forms of public humiliation or ridicule'.[25] Indeed, he continues, the stark distinction between censure and hard treatment can be rejected because 'Even purely formal censure constitutes hard treatment, since condemnation is meant to be experienced as unwelcome, a bringing up short of the

---

duties depends partly on the strategies that civil disobedients employ and their immediate effects, these duties will be in play for any suitably constrained, rights-protected disobedience. At all stages in the legal process, authorities have opportunities to show their tolerance of a little disobedience.

[25] Tasioulas (2006), 289.

wrongdoer, a drawing attention to, and denunciation of, his moral wrong-doing.'

Indeed, it may even turn out on occasion that certain relatively anonymous and formal modes of material deprivation, such as monetary fines, constitute appreciably lighter treatment than some purely symbolic forms of condemnation, such as the naval institution of the 'captain's mast'.[26]

Therefore, there is a spectrum of harshness in punitive hard treatments, and formal or symbolic censure falls somewhere along that spectrum, and not necessarily at the lightest end of it in all cases.

Second, even if a rough distinction between formal or symbolic censure and hard treatment could be sustained, both are expressions of condemnation by the state whose authoritative censure can be status changing (see Chapter 7). In one sense, such demotion of status would be less radical in cases of formal or symbolic censure because offenders subject to it would not be forced to undergo rituals of apology and repentance, which offenders are required to go through when sentenced to more concrete forms of hard treatment. However, in another sense, the demotion of status flowing from symbolic censure could be equal to or greater than material hard treatment because symbolic censure can be shaming and shameful. The burdens of embarrassment, public exposure, and loss of social standing can be not just more burdensome, but more status-affecting than a monetary fine or other anonymous punishment. They can render us even less able to respond to the censure.[27]

All that said, even if symbolic censure as well as concrete punishment proves to be inescapably intrusive, it does not end the debate about the moral right to civil disobedience. There are at least two possible ways forward.

3. Some Ways Forward

One way forward is to note that the moral right to civil disobedience is not absolute. It is defeasible. In principle, the grounds for punishment

---

[26] Tasioulas (2006), 296.
[27] Given the dialogic ambitions of civil disobedience, symbolic punishments can sometimes make martyrs of campaigners and bring others to their cause. But, they can also delegitimize that cause in others' eyes through association with public shame.

could justifiably override the moral right to civil disobedience. If they did, it would be appropriate for judges to acknowledge that punishment is a necessary evil and that an apology is due to the civil disobedients whom they censure. It would be appropriate to signal that 'we appreciate the value of what you do, and regret that we have to censure you for your breach of law, but this is the necessary price of allowing any illegal protest to occur'. The apology signals an awareness that, however mild it is, the punishment is disrespectful of the civil disobedient's agency.

It is true that, in practice, a direct apology could well threaten the values that overrode the right, such as the value of signalling our unwillingness to tolerate too much dissent, or the value of condemning risks posed to other people, or the (putative) value of seeking to deter non-conscientious dissent. The state's censure probably won't be very effective when the state follows it with an apology for imposing that censure.

That said, there are other ways for judges to signal that they regret having to make a public show of censure. They can opt for non-custodial sentences, which Judge Teare did in the Ratcliffe power station case (Chapter 6) after the jury found the campaigners guilty. He imposed lenient sentences ranging from 18 months of conditional discharge to 90 hours of unpaid work. Judges can also praise disobedients' characters, which Judge Teare also did. In his comments, he observed that, although the public might consider his sentencing 'impossibly lenient', he had been put in a highly unique position given the moral standing of the campaigners, whom he praised as decent men and women with a genuine concern for others and for the survival of the planet. Finally, judges can make comments about the value of the practice of civil disobedience itself, which Judge Hunter did in the sentencing of Galland and Stander (Chapter 5). Like Judge Teare, he avoided custodial sentences. And, in his comments, he said: 'I remember that in the 1960s there were actions of civil disobedience that, eventually, made our life better... We all have derived benefits from acts of civil disobedience like the Boston Tea Party. That act of civil disobedience has played an extremely important and vital political role in our history.'

A second way forward is to look to non-punitive, restorative ways for society to engage with civil disobedients.[28] In essence, the aim

---

[28] For discussions of abolitionism, see Bianchi, H. (1994) 'Abolition: Assensus and Sanctuary' in *A Reader on Punishment*. Antony Duff and David Garland (eds.), Oxford: Oxford

would be to 'civilize' state responses to civil disobedience by taking civil law dispute resolutions as the model, and seeing civil disobedience not as a crime to be censured, but as a conflict to be resolved. This way forward does not commit us to rejecting the legitimacy of state punishment for *any* offence. Nor does it commit us to rejecting the very notion of *crime*. Rather, it puts the communicative emphasis on reconciliation, compensation, and constructive collective deliberation even though the communication of censure might be appropriate for any harm done. This approach chooses to see any such harm in terms of *tort* rather than *crime*, that is, as a wrong, but not a wrong to be dealt with through punishment. There are several reasons to favour this non-punitive restorative approach.

First, paradigmatically, civil disobedients breach the law in constrained, conscientiously communicative ways (even when their acts lack full legal defensibility). In doing so, they enter into a conflict with authorities at the level of deeply held conviction. As such, it seems a more fitting objective for the state to promote a reconciliation of antagonistic perspectives than to seek to condemn such constrained disobedience. Of course, not all conflicts between civil disobedients and authorities merit a 'reconciliation of perspectives' as opposed to a revision in perspective on the part of disobedients. But, such a revision need not be achieved through *punitive* restoration.

Second, a non-punitive restorative approach does not represent civil disobedients as *criminals*. In our current practice and theorizing, for better or worse, *criminals* make up a special, stigmatized category of persons. Inclusion in that category is something that personal objectors are increasingly able to avoid given the growing number of legal exemptions for personal refusals of performance. No comparable legal exemption can be given for civil disobedience, despite its conscientiousness, since it is a deliberate breach of law. This gives us a reason to consider other ways of responding to civil disobedience that do not require us to represent disobedients as criminals.

Third, by privileging reconciliation and deliberation, a non-punitive restorative approach affirms society's commitment to its own

University Press; van Ness, Daniel (1993a) 'New Wine and Old Wineskins: Four Challenges to Restorative Justice' in *Criminal Law Forum* 4: 2, 251–76; Ashworth, Andrew (1993) 'Some Doubts about Restorative Justice' in *Criminal Law Forum* 4: 2, 277–99; van Ness, Daniel (1993b) 'A Reply to Andrew Ashworth' in *Criminal Law Forum* 4: 2, 301–6; Christie, N. (1981) *Limits to Pain*. London: Martin Robertson; Hulsman, L. (1991) 'The Abolitionist Case: Alternative Crime Policies' in *Israel Law Review* 25, 681–709.

betterment through constructive, democratic, egalitarian means, which is an appropriate commitment to reaffirm in response to *civil* disobedients. A non-punitive response honours the double-harmony between our individual interests in having a moral right to civil disobedience and society's interests in the deliberative and communicative contributions of disobedients (see Chapter 4).

Fourth, civil disobedients are, almost by definition, members of minorities, and, they are typically members of persistent, vulnerable minorities. By opting for a civil response over a criminal response, there is the prospect that disobedients' rights and others' rights will be better respected as the rights of full and equal members of society.

Fifth, all else being equal, in general, non-punitive responses are to be preferred to punitive ones. The onus lies with those who would oppose non-punitive restoration to explain why a punitive response should be preferred in the case of civil disobedience.

Conclusion

In this final chapter, I have argued that the moral right to civil disobedience includes a right against state punishment. This right protects against not only concretely burdensome hard treatment but also formal or symbolic censure. As a *moral* right, this right puts a negative moral gloss on any lawful imposition of state punishment for civil disobedience. Such punishment wrongs the person as one who has a moral right to conscientious action that includes civil disobedience. However, this moral right is not absolute. In some cases, there could be moral grounds for overriding the right to civil disobedience and communicating censure for this breach of law. But, given the constrained, conscientious, and communicative nature of civil disobedience, there are good reasons to favour a non-punitive restorative response to it.

Bibliography

Applbaum, Arthur (1999) *Ethics for Adversaries*. Princeton: Princeton University Press.
Arendt, Hannah (1972) *Crises of the Republic: Lying in Politics; Civil Disobedience; on Violence; Thoughts on Politics and Revolution*. New York: Harcourt Brace Jovanovich.
Ariely, Daniel (2008) *Predictably Irrational: The Hidden Forces that Shape our Decisions*. London: HarperCollins.
Aristotle *Nicomachean Ethics* (various edns).
——*Eudemian Ethics* (various edns).
Ashworth, Andrew (1993) 'Some Doubts about Restorative Justice' in *Criminal Law Forum* 4: 2, 277–99.
——(1998) 'Desert' in *Principled Sentencing: Readings on Theory and Policy* (2nd edn). Andrew Ashworth and Andrew von Hirsch (eds.), Oxford: Hart Publishing.
Bagaric, Mirko and Amarasekara, Kumar (2000) 'The Errors of Retributivism' in *University of Melbourne Law Review* 24, 124–89.
Baraz, James (2010) *Awakening Joy*. New York: Bantam.
Bauby, Jean Dominic (1997) *The Diving Bell and the Butterfly*. London: Fourth Estate.
BBC News (2007) 'Blunkett Criticises Pond Officers' *BBC News*, 22 September.
Bennett, Christopher (2008) *The Apology Ritual*. Cambridge: Cambridge University Press.
Bennett, Jonathan (1974) 'The Conscience of Huckleberry Finn' in *Philosophy* 49, 123–34.
Bianchi, H. (1994) 'Abolition: Assensus and Sanctuary' in *A Reader on Punishment*. Antony Duff and David Garland (eds.), Oxford: Oxford University Press.
Bolan, K. (2010) 'Judge rules Jamie Bacon's rights violated by treatment in jail' *Vancouver Sun*, 10 June.
Bolt, Robert (1960) *A Man for All Seasons* (various edns).
Brandt R. B. (1989) 'Morality and its Critics' in *The American Philosophical Quarterly* 26: 2, 89–100.
Broad, C. D. (1973) 'Conscience and Conscientious Action' in *Conscience*. John Donnelly and Leonard Lyons (eds.), New York: Alba House.
Brooks, Thom (2004) 'A Defence of Jury Nullification' in *Res Publica* 10: 4, 401–23.
Brownlee, Kimberley (2004) 'Features of a Paradigm Case of Civil Disobedience' in *Res Publica* 10: 4, 337–51.
——(2007) 'The Communicative Aspects of Civil Disobedience and Lawful Punishment' in *Criminal Law and Philosophy* 1: 2, 179–92.

Brownlee, Kimberley (2008) 'Penalizing Public Disobedience' in *Ethics* 118: 4, 711–16.
—— (2009) 'Review of Gardner *Offences and Defences*' in *Ethics*, 119: 3, 561–6.
—— (2010a) 'Reasons and Ideals' in *Philosophical Studies* 151: 3, 433–44.
—— (2010b) 'Moral Aspirations and Ideals' in *Utilitas* 22: 3, 241–57.
—— (2010c) 'Retributive, Restorative, and Ritualistic Justice' in *Oxford Journal of Legal Studies* 30, 385–97.
—— (2010d) 'Responsibilities of Criminal Justice Officials' in *The Journal of Applied Philosophy* 27: 2, 123–39.
—— (2011) 'The Offender's Part in the Dialogue' in *Crime, Punishment, & Responsibility: The Jurisprudence of Antony Duff*. Rowan Cruft, Matthew Kramer, and Mark Reiff (eds.), Oxford: Oxford University Press.
—— (2012a) 'Conscientious Objection and Civil Disobedience' in *The Routledge Companion to the Philosophy of Law*. Andrei Marmor (ed.), London: Routledge.
—— (2012b) 'Social Deprivation and Criminal Justice' in *Canadian Perspectives on the Philosophy of Criminal Law*. François Tanguay-Renaud and James Stribopoulos (eds.), Oxford: Hart Publishing.
—— 'A Human Right against Social Deprivation' (in progress).
Brownlee, Kimberley and Stemplowska, Zofia (2010) 'Trapped in an Experience Machine with a Famous Violinist: Thought Experiments in Normative Theory' *MANCEPT Working Papers*.
Burke, Edmund (1774) 'Speech at the Conclusion of the Poll', (3 November 1774), *WS* 3, 69.
Bury, J. B. (1913) A *History of Freedom of Thought* (various edns).
Butler, Joseph (1983) *Fifteen Sermons Preached at the Rolls Chapel and a Dissertation upon the Nature of Virtue*. Stephen Darwall (ed.), Indianapolis: Hackett.
Cacioppo, John T. *Research Summary*. Faculty of Psychology, University of Chicago.
Cada, Chryss (2003) 'Three Nuns and a Test for Civil Disobedience' *The Boston Globe*, 27 May.
Calder, Gideon and Ceva, Emauela (eds.) (2010) *Diversity in Europe: Dilemmas of Differential Treatment in Theory and Practice*. London: Routledge.
Casella, J. and Ridgeway, J. (2010) 'No Evidence of National Reduction in Solitary Confinement' *Solitary Watch*, 15 June 2010.
Christie, N. (1981) *Limits to Pain*. London: Martin Robertson.
Chryssides, George (1999) 'Buddhism and Conscience' in *Conscience in World Religions*. Jayne Hoose (ed.), Notre Dame: University of Notre Dame Press.
Clarkson, C. M. V. (2004) 'Necessary Action: A New Defence' in *Criminal Law Review* February, 81–95.
Coady, C. A. J. (2008) *Messy Morality: The Challenge of Politics*. Oxford: Oxford University Press.
Cohen, G. A. (2006) 'Casting the First Stone: Who Can, and Who Can't, Condemn the Terrorists' in *Royal Institute of Philosophy Supplement* 81, 113–36.
Cranston, Maurice (1983) 'Are There any Human Rights?' in *Daedalus* 112: 4, 1–17.

Cruft, Rowan (2006) 'Why Aren't Duties Rights?' in *The Philosophical Quarterly* 56: 223, 175–92.
Dennis, Ian Howard (2009) 'On Necessity as a Defence to Crime: Possibilities, Problems and the Limits of Justification and Excuse' in *Criminal Law and Philosophy* 3, 29–49.
Duff, Antony (1986) *Trials and Punishments*. Cambridge: Cambridge University Press.
——(1998) 'Desert and Penance' in Andrew Ashworth and Andrew von Hirsch (eds.), *Principled Sentencing: Readings on Theory and Policy*. Oxford: Hart Publishing.
——(2000) 'In Defence of One Type of Retributivism: A Reply to Bagaric and Amarasekara' in *Melbourne University Law Review*, 24: 2, 411–26.
——(2001) *Punishment, Communication, and Community*. Oxford: Oxford University Press.
——(2003) 'Penance, Punishment, and the Limits of Community' in *Punishment and Society* 5, 295–312.
——(2010) 'Inaugural Address: Towards a Theory of Criminal Law?' in *Proceedings of the Aristotelian Society Supplementary Volume l*, xxxiv, 11.
——(2011) 'Reply' in *Crime, Punishment, & Responsibility: The Jurisprudence of Antony Duff*. Rowan Cruft, Matthew Kramer and Mark Reiff (eds.) Oxford: Oxford University Press.
Dworkin, Ronald (1977) *Taking Rights Seriously*. London: Duckworth.
Edmundson, William A. (2006) 'The Virtue of Law-Abidance' in *Philosophers' Imprint* 6: 4, 1–21.
Einstein, Albert (1950) *Out of my Later Years*. London: Thames and Hudson.
Eliot, George (2008 [1859]) *Adam Bede*. Oxford: Oxford University Press.
Elster, Jon (1983) *Sour Grapes*. Cambridge: Cambridge University Press.
Estlund, David (2007) 'On Following Orders in an Unjust War' in *The Journal of Political Philosophy* 15: 2, 213–34.
Feinberg, Joel (1992) 'In Defence of Moral Rights' in *Oxford Journal of Legal Studies* 12: 2, 149–69.
——(1994a) *Freedom and Fulfilment*. Princeton: Princeton University Press.
——(1994b) 'The Expressive Function of Punishment' in *A Reader on Punishment*. Antony Duff and David Garland (eds.), Oxford: Oxford University Press.
——(2003) *Problems at the Roots of Law*. Oxford: Oxford University Press.
Fletcher, George (1978) *Rethinking Criminal Law*. Boston: Little, Brown & Co.
Frey, Raymond (1980) *Interests and Rights: The Case Against Animals*. Oxford: Clarendon Press.
Galland, Nancy and Stander, Richard (2003) 'Bangor Judge, Too, Recognises Importance of Civil Disobedience' *Peace Talk*.
Gardner, John (1996) 'Justifications and Reasons' in *Harm and Culpability*. A. P. Simester and A. T. H. Smith (eds.), Oxford: Oxford University Press.

Gardner, John (2003) 'The Mark of Responsibility' in *Oxford Journal of Legal Studies* 23: 21, 157–71.

——(2004) 'The Wrongdoing that Gets Results' in *Philosophical Perspectives* 18, 53–88.

——(2007) *Offences and Defences*. Oxford: Oxford University Press.

Gardner, John and Macklem, Timothy (2002) 'Reasons' in *Oxford Handbook of Jurisprudence and Philosophy of Law*. Jules Coleman and Scott Shapiro (eds.), Oxford: Oxford University Press.

Gardner, Simon (2005) 'Direct action and the defence of necessity' *Criminal Law Review* May, 371–80.

Gawande, A. (2009) 'Hellhole: The United States holds tens of thousands of inmates in long-term solitary confinement. Is this torture?' *The New Yorker*, 30 March.

Gels, Sonya (2006) 'California puts Execution off after Doctors Refuse to Help', *The Washington Post*, 22 February.

George, Robert P. (1993) *Making Men Moral: Civil Liberties and Public Morality*. Oxford: Clarendon Press.

Gopnik, Adam (2010) 'The Man in the White Suit' *The New Yorker*, 29 November.

Green, Leslie (2002) 'Law and Obligations' in *The Oxford Handbook of Jurisprudence and Philosophy of Law*. Jules Coleman and Scott Shapiro (eds.), Oxford: Oxford University Press.

——(2003) 'Civil Disobedience and Academic Freedom' in *Osgoode Hall Law Journal* 41: (2–3), 381–405.

——(2007) 'The Duty to Govern' in *Legal Theory* 13, 165–85.

——(2010) 'Two Worries about Respect for Persons' in *Ethics* 120: 2, 212–31.

Greenawalt, Kent (1987) *Conflicts of Law and Morality*. Oxford: Clarendon Press.

Hanson, Rick and Mendius, Richard (2009) *Buddha's Brain: The Practical Neuroscience of Happiness, Love, and Wisdom*. Oakland: New Harbinger Publications.

Harcourt, Bernard E. (2008) 'Abolition in the U.S.A. by 2050: On Political Capital and Ordinary Acts of Resistance' in John M. Olin Program in Law and Economics Working Paper Series.

Hardimon, Michael O. (1994) 'Role Obligations' in *The Journal of Philosophy* 91: 7, 333–63.

Havel, Vaclav (1968) 'Letter to President Alexander Dubček', August 1968 in *Oxford Dictionary of Modern Quotations*. Knowles, Elizabeth (ed.) (3rd edn), Oxford: Oxford University Press.

Hickson, Michael (2010) 'Conscientious Refusals without Conscience: Why Not?' in *Philo* 13: 2, 167–84.

Hill, Thomas Jr (2002) *Human Welfare and Moral Worth, Kantian Perspectives*. Oxford: Oxford University Press.

Horder, Jeremy (2004) *Excusing Crime*. Oxford: Oxford University Press.

Hulsman, L. (1991) 'The Abolitionist Case: Alternative Crime Policies' in *Israel Law Review* 25, 681–709.

Husak, Douglas (2005) 'On the Supposed Priority of Justification to Excuse' in *Law and Philosophy* 24, 557–94.
Jackson, M. (2002) *Justice Behind the Walls*. Vancouver: Douglas & McIntyre.
Jones, Peter (1994) *Rights*. New York: Palgrave.
Kadish, Mortimer R. and Kadish, Sanford H. (1973) *Discretion to Disobey: A Study of Lawful Departures from Legal Rules*. Stanford: Stanford University Press.
Kamm, Frances (2007) *Intricate Ethics*. Oxford: Oxford University Press.
Kant, Immanuel (1889) *Critique of Practical Reason and Other Works on the Theory of Ethics*, trans. Thomas Kingsmill Abbott, 4th revised edn, London: Kongmans, Green and Co.
Kershaw, Sarah (2005) 'Governor Rejects Clemency for Inmate on Death Row' *The New York Times*, 13 December.
King, Martin Luther Jr (1963) 'Letter from Birmingham City Jail'. Reprinted in Bedau, Hugo (ed.), (1991), *Civil Disobedience in Focus*. London: Routledge.
Langston, Douglas (2001) *Conscience and Other Virtues*. University Park: Pennsylvania State University Press.
Lazar, Sara W. et al (2005) 'Meditation experience is associated with increased cortical thickness', in *Neuroreport* 28 November, 16(17), 1893–7.
Lefkowitz, David (2005) 'A Contractualist Defense of Democratic Authority' in *Ratio Juris* 18: 3, 346–64.
——(2007) 'On a Moral Right to Civil Disobedience' in *Ethics* 117: 2, 202–33.
Lewis, Paul and Prakash, Nidhi (2011) 'Ratcliffe coal protesters spared jail sentences' *The Guardian*, 5 January.
Lippke, R. (2004) 'Against Supermax' in *The Journal of Applied Philosophy* 21, 109–24.
——(2007) *Rethinking Imprisonment*. Oxford: Oxford University Press.
Lovell, Jarrett (2009) *Crimes of Dissent*. New York: New York University Press.
Luban, David (1988) *Lawyers and Justice: An Ethical Study*. Princeton: Princeton University Press.
Lutz, Antoine et al (2008) 'Regulation of the Neural Circuitry of Emotion by Compassion Meditation: Effects of Meditative Expertise' in *PLoS ONE* 3:3, e1897.
McLeod, Carolyn (2008) 'Referral in the Wake of Conscientious Objection to Abortion' in *Hypatia* 23: 4, 30–47.
McMahan, Jeff (2004) 'The Ethics of Killing in War' in *Ethics* 114, 693–733.
——(2009) *Killing in War*. Oxford: Oxford University Press.
MacIntyre, Alasdair (1981) *After Virtue*. Notre Dame: University of Notre Dame Press.
MacLeish, Archibald (1956) 'In Praise of Dissent' *The New York Times*, 16 December.
Margalit, Avishai (1996) *The Decent Society*. Cambridge: Harvard University Press.
Markovits, Daniel (2005) 'Democratic Disobedience' in *Yale Law Journal* 114, 1897–952.

Martí, José Luis (2011) 'Comment on Brownlee, "The Offender's Part in the Dialogue"', Workshop on Philosophy of Criminal Law, Pompeu Fabra University, Barcelona, 10 June.

Mason, Elinor (2011) 'Value Pluralism' in *The Stanford Encyclopedia of Philosophy* (Fall 2011 edn), Edward N. Zalta (ed.), <http://plato.stanford.edu/archives/fall2011/entries/value-pluralism/>.

Mill, John Stuart (1859) *On Liberty* (various edns).

Moraro, Piero (2007) 'Violent Civil Disobedience and Willingness to Accept Punishment' in *Essays in Philosophy*. 8: 2, Article 6.

Murphy, J. G. (1994) 'Marxism and Retribution' in *A Reader on Punishment*. Antony Duff and David Garland (eds.), Oxford: Oxford University Press.

Nathanson, Stephen (1985) 'Does it Matter if the Death Penalty is Arbitrarily Administered?' in *Philosophy and Public Affairs* 14: 2, 149–64.

Needleman, Jacob (2007) 'Why Can't We be Good?' Authors@Google Lecture Series, 30 April 2007.

Norton, Sara and DeWolfe, M. A. (eds.) (1913) *Letters of Charles Eliot Norton*. Boston: Houghton Mifflin.

O'Neill, Onora (1986) 'The Public Use of Reason' in *Political Theory* 14, 523–51.

——(2009) 'Ethics for Communication' in *European Journal of Philosophy* 17: 2, 167–80.

Pankhurst, Emmeline (1908) 'Speech from the Dock Police Court' in *Votes for Women* (29 October 1908) Reprinted in Bell, Susan G. and Offen, Karen M. (eds.) (1983) *Women, the Family, and Freedom: The Debate in Documents*. Vol II. 1880–950.

Pettit, Philip (1988) 'The Consequentialist Can Recognise Rights' in *The Philosophical Quarterly* 38: 150, 42–55.

Pettit, Philip and Brennan, Geoffrey (1986) 'Restrictive Consequentialism' in *Australasian Journal of Philosophy* 64:4, 438–55.

Pianalto, Matthew (2011) 'Moral Conviction' in *The Journal of Applied Philosophy* 28: 4, 381–95.

Postema, Gerald (1980) 'Moral Responsibility in Professional Ethics' in *NYU Law Review* 55, 63–90.

Potter, Will (2001) 'The New Backlash: From the Streets to the Courthouse, the New Activists Find Themselves under Attack' *Texas Observer*, 14 September 2001.

R v Bridges (1991) 62 C. C. C. (3d) 455 at 458 (B. C. C. A.).

Rawls, John (1971) *A Theory of Justice*. Cambridge: Harvard University Press.

Raz, Joseph (1979) *The Authority of Law: Essays on Law and Morality*. Oxford: Clarendon Press.

——(1986) *The Morality of Freedom*. Oxford: Oxford University Press.

——(1994) *Ethics in the Public Domain*. Oxford: Oxford University Press.

——(2001) *Value, Respect and Attachment*. Cambridge, Cambridge University Press.

——(2003a) 'Bound by their Conscience' *Haaret*, 31 December 2003.

——(2003b) *The Practice of Value*. Oxford: Oxford University Press.
——(2004) 'Incorporation by Law' in *Legal Theory* 10, 1–17.
——(2006) 'The Problem of Authority: Revisiting the Service Conception' in *Minnesota Law Review* 90, 1003–44.
Re A (Children) (Conjoined Twins: Medical Treatment) (No 1), [2001] Fam 147 (CA (Civ Div)).
Reader, Soran and Brock, Gillian (2004) 'Needs, Moral Demands, and Moral Theory' in *Utilitas* 16: 3, 251–66.
Reiff, Mark (2005) *Punishment, Compensation, and Law: A Theory of Enforceability*. Cambridge: Cambridge University Press.
The Report of the Commission on Safety and Abuse in America's Prisons (2006) <http://www.vera.org/project/commission-safety-and-abuse-americas-prisons>.
Russell, Bertrand (1998) *Autobiography*. London: Routledge.
Sartre, Jean Paul (1946) 'Existentialism is a Humanism' (various edns).
See, Lisa (2005) *Snow Flower and the Secret Fan*. London: Random House.
Sen, Amartya (2000) 'Consequential Evaluation and Practical Reason' in *The Journal of Philosophy* 97: 9, 447–502.
Shakespeare, William *Macbeth* (various edns).
——*Hamlet* (various edns).
——*Much Ado about Nothing* (various edns).
Sheppard, Stephen (2009) *I Do Solemnly Swear: The Moral Obligations of Legal Officials*. New York: Cambridge University Press.
Simmons, A. John (1996) 'External Justifications and Institutional Roles' in *The Journal of Philosophy* 93: 1, 28–36.
Skorupski, John (2006) *Why Read Mill Today?* London: Routledge.
——(2010) 'Conscience' in *The Routledge Companion to Ethics*. London: Routledge.
Smart, Brian (1991) 'Defining Civil Disobedience' in *Civil Disobedience in Focus*. Hugo A. Bedau (ed.), London: Routledge.
Smart, J. J. and Williams, Bernard (1973) *Utilitarianism: For and Against*. Cambridge: Cambridge University Press.
Smith, William (2012) 'Policing Civil Disobedience' *Political Studies*, doi: 10.1111/j.1467-9248.2011.00937.x.
Statman, Daniel (2008) 'On the Success Condition for Legitimate Self-Defense' in *Ethics*, 118, 659–86.
Süskind, Patrick (1985) *Parfum: A Story of a Murderer*. London: Penguin.
Tadros, Victor (2011) *The Ends of Harm*. Oxford: Oxford University Press.
Tasioulas, John (2003) 'Mercy' in *Proceedings of the Aristotelian Society* 103: 2, 101–32.
——(2006) 'Punishment and Repentance' in *Philosophy* 81, 279–322.
Thoreau, Henry David (1848) 'Civil Disobedience' in Hugo Bedau (ed.) (1991), *Civil Disobedience in Focus*. London: Routledge.
Twain, Mark (1884) *The Adventures of Huckleberry Finn* (various edns).
US v Cullen (1971) 454 F.2d 386, 392 (7th Cir.). Cited from *United States v Platte et al* (2005).

United States of America v Platte et al (2005) 401 F.3d 1176 (10th Cir.).
van Ness, Daniel (1993a) 'New Wine and Old Wineskins: Four Challenges to Restorative Justice' in *Criminal Law Forum* 4: 2, 251–76.
——(1993b) 'A Reply to Andrew Ashworth' in *Criminal Law Forum* 4: 2, 301–6;
Vidal, John (2008) 'Climb Every Chimney...' *The Guardian*, 12 September.
von Hirsch, Andrew (1998) 'Proportionate Sentences: A Desert Perspective' in *Principled Sentencing*. Andrew Ashworth and Andrew von Hirsch (eds.), Oxford: Hart Publishing.
Waldron, Jeremy (1981) 'A Right to do Wrong' in *Ethics* 92: 1, 21–39.
Walzer, Michael (1973) 'Political Action: The Problem of Dirty Hands' in *Philosophy and Public Affairs* 2: 2, 160–80.
Washington, J. M. (ed.) (1991) *Testament of Hope: The Essential Writings and Speeches of Martin Luther King Jr*. San Francisco: Harper Collins.
Wheeler Wilcox, Ella (1914) 'Protest' in *Poems of Problems*. W. B. Conkey.
Whitman, James Q. (2005) *Harsh Justice: Criminal Punishment and the Widening Divide between America and Europe*. New York: Oxford University Press.
Wicclair, Mark (2011) *Conscientious Objection in Health Care: An Ethical Analysis*. Cambridge: Cambridge University Press.
Wiesel, Elie (1986) 'Hope, Despair, and Memory: Nobel Lecture', 11 December 1986.
Williams, G. (1961) *Criminal Law: the General Part* (2nd edn) London: Stevens & Sons.
Williams, Lynne (2004) 'Restraining Dissent is Harmful' *Bangor Daily News*, 10 September.
Winch, Peter (1965) 'The Universalizability of Moral Judgements' in *The Monist* 49: 2, 196–214.
Woolf, Virginia (2008 [1929]) *A Room of One's Own*. Oxford: Oxford University Press.

Index

abortion 10, 20, 36–7, 41, 91, 101, 150, 156, 210
akrasia 168–9
Anderson, Terry 196 (n.31)
animals 6–7, 25–6, 127, 166, 170, 189, 191, 202, 204, 209–10, 239, 245
anti-war activism 4–5, 19, 20, 27, 36, 127, 158–9
Apartheid 45
Applbaum, Arthur 86 (n.2)
Aquinas, Thomas 52 (n.3)
Arendt, Hannah 209
Aristotle 52 (n.3), 75, 86 (n.4)
assisted suicide 24–7, 28
assistive disobedience 24–7, 28, 150
Aung San Suu Kyi 32, 51, 64, 71, 74, 77, 81, 85, 86
autonomy 8, 121, 137–9, 165–6, 167–8, 171–2, 193, 236, 239, 243–5

Bacon, James 196–7
Bauby, Jean-Dominique 139
Bennett, Christopher 224 (n.25)
Bennett, Jonathan 58 (n.14), 65 (n.21), 68 (n.26)
Bentham, Jeremy 124, 161
Blunkett, David 97
Bolt, Robert 15
Bonaventure 52 (n.3)
Brandt, R. B. 161
Broad, C. D. 57–8
Brock, Gillian 188–90
Burke, Edmund 85, 111
Bury, J. B. 135–6, 138
Butler, Joseph 55–8, 60

Cacioppo, John T. 196 (n.31)
Calder, Gideon 144 (n.49)

Ceva, Emanuela 144 (n.49)
civil disobedience 5–7, 104, 109–10, 141–8, 198–203; *see also* demands-of-conviction defence, necessity defence, moral right to civil disobedience, and punishment and civil disobedience
  and assistive disobedience 24–7
  as communicative 18–27
  direct and indirect 19, 150–1, 173, 199–200
  seriousness 155–9
  and violence 21–4, 198–9
Clarkson, C. M. V. 185
Coady, C. A. J. 71 (n.33), 72 (n.35), 73, 75, 76, 91 (n.14)
communicative principle of conscientiousness 1–2, 29–47, 107, 137, 145
  communication and dialogue 42–6, 140; *see also* dialogue
  consistency 30–4
  implications 46–7
  non-evasion 37–42
  universality 34–7
conscience 2, 10–12; *see also* moral right of conscience, and conscientious moral conviction distinguished from conscience
  clear conscience 70–1
  demands of conscience 62–6
  as evaluative 52
  as an ideal 72–9
  objective monistic conceptions 55–7
  and moral pluralism 62–6
  scope for error 66–70
  subjectivist conceptions 57–62

conscience (*cont.*)
  and virtue 79–83
conscientious moral conviction 1,
    5–10, 119, 160; *see also*
    demands-of-conviction defence
  and dialogue 9–10; *see also* dialogue
  distinguished from conscience 3–5,
    16–17, 47–50
  and legal excuse 8–9
  and moral rights 7–8; *see also* moral
    rights
conscientious objection 2, 4–6, 16, 27,
    46, 47–9, 142, 145, 171–2;
    see also personal disobedience
consent; *see* moral roles and
    voluntarism
criminal justice 102, 114, 116 (n.39);
    see also punishment
Cruft, Rowan 127 (n.17)

Dalai Lama 39, 76
demands-of-conviction defence 159,
    165, 167–72, 178, 193
  objections:
    democracy problem 174–8
    strategic action problem 172–4
Dempsey, Michelle Madden 59 (n.17),
    90 (n.11)
Dennis, Ian Howard 169, 181, 182,
    183, 184–92
dialogue 9, 20, 42–6, 217–27
dignity 2, 4, 7, 142, 147, 149–50,
    177–8; *see also* autonomy,
    humanism
discretion and expectation 88–92
Duff, Antony 29, 212–17, 223–34
Dworkin, Ronald 90 (n.11), 142

Edmundson, William 168 (n.26)
Einstein, Albert 51
Eliot, George 155
Elster, Jon 80
Estlund, David 89, 91
environment 127, 166, 175,
    179–80, 201–2
euthanasia; *see* assisted suicide
excuses 161–7

Feinberg, Joel 90, 97–8, 106, 123–4,
    126, 133 (n.33), 240, 243 (n.14)

formal positions 93–5
freedom of emotion 133
freedom of expression 133, 140–1
freedom of thought 128–139
Frey, Raymond 120–1, 124

Galland, Nancy 158–9, 251
Gandhi, Mahatma 23, 51, 74, 79, 81,
    85, 86
gap thesis 86–7, 95–7
Gardner, John 160–6, 236
Gardner, Simon 192 (n.26), 203–4
German Basic Law 124–5
George, Robert P. 121 (n.4)
Gilbert, Carol 127, 157
Greenawalt, Kent 98 (n.23), 156,
    158 (n.9)
Green, Leslie 45–6, 112 (n.37),
    142 (n.45), 225 (n.28)

Harcourt, Bernard E. 104 (n.29)
Hartz, Harris L. 157, 175
Havel, Vaclav 201
Hickson, Michael 17 (n.2)
Hill, Thomas Jr 56, 57, 59, 60, 66
von Hirsch, Andrew 212
Horder, Jeremy 5 (n.5), 145 (n.51), 147
    (n.56), 167, 171–2, 174 (n.36),
    177–8
Hudson, Jackie Marie 127, 157
humanism, principle of 7, 120, 145–6,
    171–2, 193
Hunter, Allen 158–9, 251

ideals 129–30
  aspirationality 74–5
  comprehensiveness 73–5
  constitutive cultivation 75–6
  present unrealizability 76–9
  value 79

Jones, Peter 241 (n.7), 248 (n.23)
jury nullification 88, 106, 124–5
justification 161–7

Kamm, Frances 25
Kant, Immanuel 10 (n.9), 55–7, 58, 60,
    161, 205–6, 244, 246–7
King, Martin Luther Jr 19, 23 (n.16),
    74, 179, 194

Langston, Douglas 52 (n.3), 56
last resort 44–5, 141, 200
legal rights; *see* moral rights and legal rights
Lefkowitz, David 110 (n.34), 143–4, 240–8
Lewis, Megan 209–10, 239, 245
liberal democracy 194–7; *see also* demands-of-conviction defence democracy problem
liberty rights; *see* moral rights
Locke, John 52 (n.3)

McEachern, Allan 156
MacIntyre, Alastair 75 (n.41)
Macklem, Timothy 163
MacLeish, Archibald 129 (n.27)
McLeod, Carolyn 37 (n.34)
McMahan, Jeff 89 (n.9), 113–14, 182
Mandela, Nelson 32, 64, 71, 77
Margalit, Avishai 34 (n.30)
Markovits, Daniel 110, 176 (n.38)
Martí, José Luis, 219
Mason, Elinor 60–1 (n.18)
Mill, John Stuart 7, 119–20, 129, 136–7, 138, 194–5
minimum moral burdens principle 11, 100–3, 114, 116
modesty of law thesis 180, 192
moral rights:
  to civil disobedience 123, 240–53
    as defeasible 250–1
    restorative approach 251–3
  of conscience 126–8
  of conscientious action 141–8
  as duty-based rights 126–8
  to inner control and free thought 128–39
  and free expression 135–9
  limitations of the right 130–5
  nature of the right 128–30
  and legal rights 120–6, 203–4
  as liberty rights 241–3
moral roles 92–3
  moral roles thesis 87, 96, 97–100; *see also* minimum moral burdens principle
  burdens of judgement 110–11
  competence and epistemic limitations 107–9

democratic process 109–10
valuable institutions 112–13
value pluralism 114–17
voluntarism 111–12
moral pluralism 60–72, 115, 184–92, 192–7; *see also* moral roles and value pluralism, necessity defence and pluralism, and punishment and pluralism
coordination principle 117
deliberative democratic principle 116
Moraro, Piero 23 (n.17)

Nathanson, Stephen 166 (n.23), 201 (n.43)
necessity defence 179
  and the competition of values 160
  as lesser of two evils 181–2
  as moral involuntariness 182–3
  and pluralism 184–92, 192–7
  and proportionality 197–203
  avoidance of punishment 204–5
  slippery slope 205–6
Needleman, Jacob 219
needs 188–92, 198
  as contingent 188
  as non-contingent and basic 188–91
non-conformity 104–9
  and dissociation 104–5
  and disruption 104–5
  and education 104–5
  and self-expression 104–5
Norton, Charles Eliot 194 (n.28)

O'Neill, Onora 140 (n.43), 222

Pankhurst, Emmeline 209
Parks, Rosa 10, 18–19, 74, 128, 173
parsimony 186–7, *see also* proportionality
personal disobedience 149–51
  evasive and non-evasive 28–9
  as non-communicative 27–9
  and legal excuse 170–4
Pettit, Philip 80
Pianalto, Matthew 42 (n.40)
Platte, Ardeth 127, 157
Plato 52 (n.3)
Postema, Gerald 69 (n.28), 108
proportionality 186, 197
psychological integrity 168–9

punishment:
  capital punishment 100, 114–15
  and civil disobedience 240–53
  communicative theory 9–10, 212–37
    the scripting problem 215–17
    the generic-script problem 222–7
    the status change problem 227–34
  deterrence theory 210–12
  and pluralism 234–5
  retributive theory 210–12
  symbolic 248–50

Quong, Jonathan 187 (n.17), 200 (n.40)

radical protest 20, 24, 26, 44–5, 235, 245–6
Rawls, John 6 (n.5; n.7), 18 (n.7), 21, 23–4, 58–9, 141, 146 (n.55), 158 (n.9), 200, 244 (n.16)
Raz, Joseph 5 (n.5), 6 (n.6; n.7), 19 (n.8), 22, 23 (n.15), 43 (n.41), 47–9, 63, 64, 72 (n.36), 96 (n.18), 98, 100 (n.25), 120 (n.2), 121–3, 127 (n.18), 141–3, 145, 146 (n.54), 171–2, 199, 239 (n.2)
Reader, Soran 188–90
Reiff, Mark 122 (n.8), 155 (n.3)
responsibilities; *see also* moral roles
  priority of special responsibility principle 11, 87, 98–100
rights; *see* moral rights
Rodin, David 182
rule of law 96

same-sex partnership 9, 36–7, 101, 149–50
sexuality 45–6
See, Lisa 93 (n.15)
Sen, Amartya 70
Shakespeare, William 4, 31 (n.25)

Sheppard, Stephen 86 (n.2)
Skorupski, John 52 (n.3), 129
Smith, William 155 (n.2), 233 (n.41)
Socrates 38, 74, 136
Stander, Richard 158–9, 251
Stemplowska, Zofia 78 (n.45)

Tadros, Victor 210–11
Taite, Ralph 209–10, 245
Tasioulas, John 34 (n.30), 112 (n.36), 186 (n.16), 212 (n.6; n.9), 213, 217 (n.17), 234–5, 248 (n.22), 249–50
Teare, Jonathan 179 (n.3), 251
terrorism; *see* radical protest
Thoreau, Henry David 98 (n.21)
Trudeau, Pierre 125
Twain, Mark 68 (n.27)

Universal Declaration of Human Rights 4

violence 21–4, 198–9
  violent civil disobedience; *see* civil disobedience
virtue 79–83
  Virtuous Person 80–2
voluntarism 111

war 4, 70, 89, 91, 101–2, 113–14, 127, 131–2, 145–6, 175, 196 (n.31), 201
weakness of will; *see* akrasia
Wicclair, Mark 6 (n.8)
Wiesel, Elie 200
Wilcox, Ella Wheeler 67
Williams, Bernard 70
Williams, Stanley 'Tookie' 33–4
Woolf, Virginia 130 (n.28)
Wordsworth, William 138
wrongdoing 161–7